A Handlist of Rhetorical Terms

A Handlist of Rhetorical Terms

SECOND EDITION

Richard A. Lanham

UNIVERSITY OF CALIFORNIA PRESS
Berkeley / Los Angeles / Oxford

University of California Press
Berkeley and Los Angeles, California

University of California Press
Oxford, England

Library of Congress Cataloging-in-Publication Data

Lanham, Richard A.
    A handlist of rhetorical terms : a guide for students of English
literature/Richard A. Lanham.
        p.   cm.
    Includes bibliographical references.
    ISBN 0-520-07668-0 (alk. paper) 0-520-07669-9 (pbk: alk. paper)
    1. Figures of speech.   2. English language—Rhetoric.   I. Title.
PE1445.A2L3 1991
428.1—dc20   91-27410
                                                                     CIP

Printed in the United States of America

    3   4   5   6   7   8   9

The paper used in this publication meets the minimum requirements of American National Standard for Information Sciences—Permanence of Paper for Printed Library Materials, ANSI Z39.48-1984 ∞

Omnibus scriptores sua nomina dederunt,
sed varia et ut cuique fingenti placuit.

–Quintilian

*(Writers have given special names to all the figures,
but variously and as it pleased them.)*

Contents

Preface to the Second Edition

In the two decades of its life, this handlist has found both a more numerous audience than I had anticipated and a more varied one. It has been used not only by students of English literature but of other literatures as well, and for rhetorical and stylistic inquiry of all sorts. It has also been found useful by scholars working in strands afar remote from literature — art history and anthropology, economics and philosophy. This pattern of use has been occasioned, no doubt, more by the changing role of rhetoric in our cultural conversation than by the book itself. I have, however, in the second edition, striven to preserve the basic configuration of the book — an inexpensive, readily available, short and nonprescriptive beginner's guide to a perplexing terminology — which this varied readership has found useful. The scope, method, and limitations which I explained in the original preface remain unchanged.

I have, however, tried to correct two main shortcomings that were repeatedly brought to my attention. First, the typographical design of the first edition left much to be desired. Second, more, and more modern, examples would be welcome. The book has been completely redesigned to address the first deficiency, and new examples supplied to help cure the second. I have made numerous small corrections, dropped a few terms, added a few, done some rearranging, and revised the pronunciation guide, especially its syllabification, where needed. I have also fussed a good deal about nonstrategic issues such as the relation of *Anapodoton* to *Anantapodoton*, but such fussing seems to come with the territory of a book like this. Readers over the last twenty years have asked for more longer, analytical entries for key terms, and I have complied by adding a dozen or so amplifications. I have also sought a toehold in nomenclatural immortality by inventing a term of my own: **Skotison.**

When the *Handlist* first appeared, the only thing like it was Warren Taylor's *Tudor Figures of Rhetoric*. Since then, the field has been much enriched. Lee A. Sonnino's excellent *Handbook to Sixteenth-Century Rhetoric* provides many useful cross-listings. Arthur Quinn has published a lively popular guide, *Figures of Speech: 60 Ways to Turn a Phrase*. Willard R. Espy has produced a very clever selective adaptation of Peacham's *Garden of Eloquence*. Dupriez's quirky and delightful *Gradus: Les procédés littéraires* has become available and an English translation is announced for 1991. Gérard Genette has edited a new edition of Pierre Fontanier's *Les Figures du discours*. The Enlarged Edition of the *Princeton Encyclopedia of Poetry and Poetics* has appeared. And of course numerous detailed studies of rhetorical figuration have been done, following the path created by Sister Miriam Joseph's landmark *Shakespeare's Use of the Arts of Language*. My favorite is William C. Carroll's sparkling *The Great Feast of Language in "Love's Labour's Lost."* I have used them all in the spirit laid down in the preface to John Alday's 1566–67 translation of Pierre de la Primaudaye's *L'Academie Francoise*: "I have left no Author, sacred or profane, Greek, Latine, or in our vulgar tongue, but I have bereft him of a leg or a wing, for the sounder decking and furniture of my work."

I had envisaged this preface as a long and reflective one, surveying the astonishing changes in rhetoric's place in our current cultural conversation over the last twenty years. I speedily found out, though, the truth of Father Ong's remark that the history of rhetoric's revival is the history of modern thought. My subject kept running away with me. An attempted survey of how rhetorical thinking and terminology had penetrated other fields of inquiry grew into an article ("Twenty Years After: Digital Decorum and Bistable Allusions") much too long for this preface. An attempt to trace a central rhetorical concept — Quintilian's repeated assertion that the perfect orator must encompass moral as well as oratorical perfection — again grew into a long article ("The 'Q' Question"). And an effort to synchronize social and technological issues with developments in rhetorical and literary theory ("The Extraordinary Convergence: Democracy, Technology, Theory, and the University Curriculum") also outgrew decorous bounds. To have included this material would have distended the *Handlist* out of its natural shape. Here, I can only point the reader toward these efforts to manage an unmanageable subject, and to the works and events they discuss. (See *Works Cited* for full citations.)

One development in the last twenty years, however, has created so new an expressive medium for reference works like this one that it cannot be relegated to outside discussion. Electronic text, the stylistic world created by the personal digital computer, was completely unknown when the first edition appeared. Now it has transformed our logological landscape. Hypertextual presentation, especially, makes possible a kind and level of internal cross-reference which seems designed for a work such as this *Handlist*. It also makes possible animations, voiced pronunciations, and a more genial welcome for the beginning student. With these changes in mind, I have prepared a *Hypercard Handlist*, for use on Macintosh computers; information about it will be available from the University of California Press.

I have many thanks to record for help in preparing this second edition. Above all, to my wife, Carol, now a professional editor as well as a medieval Latinist interested in rhetoric. Without her unceasing attention, relentless editing, and superb classical scholarship, the second edition would have been a much diminished thing. Without her love and support, it would not have gotten done at all.

I must also register thanks to the many readers of the first edition who have made suggestions for the second. To the many other fellow-laborers in the scholarly vineyard of rhetorical terminology whose works I have cited. To the UCLA Faculty Research Committee and the UCLA Office of Instructional Development for financial support. To the John Simon Guggenheim Memorial Foundation, for support of a related project which permitted some moonlighting on this one. To Lisa Spangenberg, who supplied research assistance for the book and who did most of the original programming for the *Hypercard Handlist*. And to the UCLA students in English 132 (Spring 1990), who helped redesign the book (Jacquie Abboud, Josh Davidson, Elizabeth Proctor, and Doug Yoshida). If he were alive to receive my thanks, I would also pass them on to the great orator of our time, Winston Churchill, to whom I have so frequently turned for modern examples, and whose books have given me a lifetime of pleasure and inspiration.

To all, again, *gratias ago.*

Los Angeles, November, 1990

Preface to the First Edition

This is not an original rhetorical treatise. It is simply an attempt to put together in one convenient, accessible, inexpensive place the rhetorical terms that students of English literature, especially of the earlier periods, are likely to come across in their reading or to find useful in their writing. The terms are for the most part classical (though I have included Puttenham's Englished ones); they have been presented in a way aimed at the beginning student as well as the learned. The alphabetical list is designed for the reader who encounters an unfamiliar term, or one used in an unusual way, and needs a definition of it. The descriptive lists are designed for one who, having observed a particular verbal pattern in a text and helpless with an alphabetical list, seeks the proper name for it. Thus the alphabetical list tries to provide a manageable dictionary; the descriptive lists, something more like a thesaurus or synoptic grouping. I hope students of the classics may find this list useful, but it was not designed for them and so will not tell them, for example, whether *antimetabole* meant to Cicero precisely what it did to Rutilius Lupus. Neither does it attempt to decide which of several conflicting meanings for a term is to be preferred. There is a strong need for a careful survey of rhetorical terms, from the early Greeks through John Smith's *The Mysterie of Rhetorique Unvail'd*, with full-length articles on central, disputed forms and how their meanings change. But this is not it. In the face of continually surprising differences of opinion about what sometimes basic terms mean, I have merely listed the main differences. This should help. So should the reasonable attempt at cross-referencing. The final criterion for the *Handlist* as a whole has been ease of use, not any prescriptive system the compiler happens to favor. No attempt has been made to single out terms that any one rhetorical or critical body of opinion might favor, or think important. Such invidious distinctions, probably ill-advised, in practice become simply impossible: only the individual scholar can weight a term as he wishes.

In the best of all possible worlds, a list like this would canvass the whole of rhetorical theory. What I have done is use as a base the terms of the Renaissance theorists and add to them those terms that seem to me useful or common from Aristotle's *Rhetoric*, Demetrius' *On Style*, Quintilian, the various works by Cicero and the pseudo-Ciceronian *Rhetorica ad Herennium*, and Halm's *Rhetores Latini Minores* (which includes Bede's brief *Liber de Schematibus et Tropis*). I have also included all the terms in Susenbrotus' *Epitome Troporum ac Schematum* and Smith's *The Mysterie of Rhetorique Unvail'd*. The major modern secondary studies, from a glossary's point of view, are those by Sister Miriam Joseph, Warren Taylor, and Veré Rubel (see Works Cited), and I have used them continually, particularly for examples. I have also taken a few examples from Bartlett's *Familiar Quotations*. The best modern study of Greek rhetoric and rhetoricians is Kennedy's; his discussions, especially of Aristotle, have been invaluable. I know of no study of strictly Latin rhetoric to equal it. The Loeb Library *Rhetorica ad Herennium* has a useful chart-outline of figures in its introduction and a good index; Halm's index is very useful, as is Sister Miriam Joseph's (Halm's index is not fully cross-referenced). There is a convenient Index of Words at the end of the fourth volume of the Loeb Quintilian. The large Liddell and Scott *Lexicon*, and Lewis and Short's *A Latin Dictionary*, are essential, of course, especially for the less common terms. For logical terms I have mainly consulted Copi's *Introduction to Logic*. All references are to works listed in Works Cited. I have modernized spellings in the examples where appropriate, and identified them sufficiently to guide the occasional reader who will wish to seek out the context.

A work of this kind would perhaps most naturally fall into two categories, figures and other terms, and the reader deserves an explanation as to why it has not been followed here. It simply proved too difficult to decide, except on a prescriptive basis, what was a figure and what was not. (*See* TROPE.)

I have adopted the indications of syllable-stress found in *Webster's Third International* when it lists a term. For Latin terms not so listed as being in the language, I have generally followed the original stress. In a few instances, however, I have indicated a stress taken from an analogous word that *has* entered the language (e.g., "ge o GRAPH i a" rather than "ge o graph I a"). For stress of Greek terms, I have followed the Latin penultimate rule. An effort to prescribe pronunciation further than to indicate stress was given up as unnecessary and artificial.

I have not included all the possible variant spellings of terms, especially of Greek terms, as there are impossibly many. Thus *v* sometimes comes into English as "y", sometimes as "u"; the rough breathing is sometimes indicated by an "h" and sometimes not; Greek terminal "os" is sometimes Englished as "os", sometimes "us". Again, I have not tried to systematize an inconsistent usage.

The only guide I have followed in omitting terms has been my common sense, and its fallibility has been adequately demonstrated by the process. I have omitted quasi-rhetorical terms to be found in any handbook of literary terms, unless there was a special reason to include them. I have also omitted terms whose meanings are obvious and Latin equivalents for English terms (and vice versa): for example, *accentus* and accent. I have included a few common terms from logic for convenience. Synonyms are listed following the terms. I have omitted an etymology when it duplicates the definition. Since I have not included all the terms I have come across, it seems likely that I have not come across all the terms I might have wanted to include. Many of the terms listed are near-synonyms and many have broad or disputed meanings. This should not deter anyone from using them with assurance; it certainly has not in the past.

Permission has been obtained for the reproduction of substantial quotations, as follows: Methuen & Co., Ltd. and Peter Smith for the material from J. W. Atkins' *English Literary Criticism: The Medieval Phase* which appears on pages 130–132; and W. W. Norton & Co., Inc. for the quotations and clock diagram from Graham Hough's *A Preface to the "Faerie Queene"* which appear on pages 4–5.

The efficient cause of the Handlist is evenly divided between a research grant from the University of California, Los Angeles, and the student who worked under it, Michael A. Anderegg. The earliest stimulus for such a list came to me from the teachings of the late Helge Kökeritz, the most recent, from the classical studies of my wife. *Gratias ago.*

R. A. L.

Los Angeles, California

1 / *Alphabetical List of Terms*

Abbaser. Puttenham's term for **Tapinosis**.

Ablatio (ab LA ti o; L. "taking away") — **Aphaeresis**.

Abode. Puttenham's term for **Commoratio**.

Abominatio (a bo mi NA ti o; L. "deserving imprecation or abhorrence") — **Bdelygma**.

Abscissio (ab SCIS si o; L. "breaking off"); alt. sp. **Absissio** — **Apocope**.

Abuse. Puttenham's term for **Catachresis**.

Abusio (a BU si o; L. "harsh use of tropes") — **Catachresis**.

Acclamatio (ac cla MA ti o; L. "calling to, exclamation, shout") — **Epiphonema**.

Accumulatio (ac cu mu LA ti o; L. "heaping up") — **Synathroesmus**. Heaping up praise or accusation to emphasize or summarize points or inferences already made:

> He [the defendant] is the betrayer of his own self-respect, and the waylayer of the self-respect of others; covetous, intemperate, irascible, arrogant; disloyal to his parents, ungrateful to his friends. . . .
> (*Rhetorica ad Herennium*, I.xl.52)

See also **Congeries**.

Accusatio (ac cu SA ti o; L. "complaint, accusation, indictment") — **Categoria**.

Accusatio concertativa (ac cu SA ti o   con cer ta TI va; L. "recrimination, countercharge") — **Anticategoria**.

1

Actio (AC ti o). The Latin term for **Delivery**, the last of the five traditional parts of rhetoric. See chapter 2 at **Rhetoric: The five parts**.

Acyrologia (a cy ro LO gi a; G. "incorrect in phraseology") — **Improprietas; Uncouthe.**
   Use of an inexact or illogical word; for Quintilian, impropriety. "O villain! thou wilt be condemn'd into everlasting redemption for this" (*Much Ado about Nothing*, IV, ii). *The Goon Show* was fond of joking with this figure: "Do you think he is going to capitulate?" "I don't know — but stand back in case he does."
See also **Malapropism.**

Adage (L. "proverb"); alt. sp. **Adagium — Proverb.**

Addubitation (L. "doubting") — **Aporia.**

Adhortatio (ad hor TA ti o; L. "exhortation, encouragement") — **Protrope.**

Adianoeta (a di a no E ta; G. "unintelligible").
   An expression that has an obvious meaning and an unsuspected secret one beneath. So one says to a good friend who is also a poor novelist: "I will lose no time in reading your new book." Or, as the Foundation says to the unsuccessful applicant: "For your work, we have nothing but praise."

Adinventio (ad in VEN ti o; L. "invention") — **Pareuresis.**

Adjudicatio (ad ju di CA ti o; L. "judgment") — **Epicrisis.**

Adjunctio (ad JUNC ti o; L. "joining to").
   The use of one verb to express two similar ideas at the beginning or end of a clause.

> Beginning: "*Fades* physical beauty with disease or age," *or*
> Ending: "Either with disease or age physical beauty *fades.*"
> (Rhetorica ad Herennium, IV.xxvii.38)

See also **Zeugma.**

Admiratio (ad mi RA ti o) — **Thaumasmus.**

Admittance. Puttenham's term for **Paromologia.**

Admonitio (ad mo NI ti o; L. "reminding, recalling to mind, suggestion") — **Paraenesis.**

Adnexio (ad NEX i o; L. "binding to") — **Zeugma**.

Adnominatio (ad no mi NA ti o; L. "two words of different meaning but similar sound brought together"); alt. sp. **Agnominatio**.
1. **Polyptoton**.
2. **Paronomasia**. (A distinction sometimes has been made, however, between adnominatio as mainly a play on sounds of words and paronomasia as a play on sense of words.)
This description of the young James Watson would seem to illustrate adnominatio as both polyptoton, paronomasia, and **Antanaclasis**: a "midwestern American youth in Europe back then before youth fares, growing his hair longer long before long hair" (*The Eighth Day of Creation*).

Adtenuata (ad te nu A ta; L. "weakened, reduced").
The third, or simple, type of **Style**. See **Style: The three types** in chapter 2.

Adynata (a DY na ta) — **Adynaton; Impossibilia**.
A stringing together of impossibilities. Sometimes, a confession that words fail us: "Not if I had a hundred mouths, each with an eloquent tongue, could I do justice to my feelings for you."

Aenigma — **Enigma**.

Aenos (AE nos; G. "tale, story [esp. with a moral], fable").
A riddling **Fable**, often an animal fable, or the quoting of a wise saying from such. Northrop Frye instances the parables of Jesus as an example.

Aeschrologia — **Aischrologia**.

Aetiologia (ae ti o LO gi a; G. "giving a cause"); alt. sp. **Etiologia, Etiology** — **Enthymeme; Reason Rend; Redditio causae; Tell Cause**.
Giving a cause or reason; enthymeme (abridged **Syllogism**), since by giving first a cause and then a result, an inverted abbreviated syllogism is sometimes created, as in Hamlet on the players: "Let them be well us'd; for they are the abstract and brief chronicles of the time" (II, ii).

Affirming the Consequent (Fallacy of).
To affirm the second part (consequent) of a hypothetical proposition rather than the first:

> If John ran a four-minute mile he is a fast miler.
> John is a fast miler.
> Therefore, John has run a four-minute mile.

Opposite of **Denying the Antecedent**.

Aganactesis (a ga nac TE sis; G. "vexation") — **Indignatio**.

Aggressio (ag GRES si o; L. "going forward"; rhet. "a rhetorical syllogism") — **Epicheireme**. *See* **Enthymeme**.

Agnominatio — **Adnominatio**.

Aischrologia (ai schro LO gi a; G. "foul language, abuse"); alt. sp. **Aeschrologia** — **Cacemphaton**.

Allegory (G. "speaking otherwise than one seems to speak") — **False Semblant; Inversio; Permutatio**.

1. Extending a metaphor through an entire speech or passage; the rhetorical meaning is narrower than the literary one, though congruent with it. The allegory is sometimes called "pure" when every main term in the passage has a double significance, "mixed" when one or more terms do not. Thus St. Augustine might elaborate on the saints as the Teeth of the Church.

2. One of four levels or senses of interpretation common in medieval and Renaissance exegesis, and thus a method of reading and of listening: (a) literal; (b) allegorical; (c) moral or tropological; (d) anagogical or spiritual. As the medieval catchverse has it:

> Littera gesta docet, quid credas, allegoria,
> Moralia, quid agas, quo tendas, anagogia.

> ("The letter teaches the deed, the allegory what you believe, the moral what you should do, the anagogue what you strive for.")
> (Gellrich, *The Idea of the Book*, p. 73)

Allegorizing of this sort had begun with Greek commentary on Homer and by the Middle Ages was common in reading Virgil as well. With such a method, more often than not one could find what one sought, whatever the text, and thus interpretation became radically interactive, requiring the self-conscious collaboration of the audience. Indeed, as it worked out in practice, it must have been similar to an aleatory composition in music, where the performer establishes certain rules which allow a collaboration with chance.

Further discussion. One of these two definitions ought to satisfy most rhetorical uses of the term. As used in literary criticism, however, the term is so complex as to lie well outside the scope of such a listing as this. For a hint of how the term moves over into rhetorical analysis of literature, perhaps brief quotations from two authorities may be of some help. Of the range of literature that can be called allegorical, Angus Fletcher writes:

> An allegorical mode of expression characterizes a quite extraordinary variety of literary kinds: chivalric or picaresque romances and their

modern equivalent, the 'western,' utopian political satires, quasi-philosophical anatomies, personal attacks in epigrammatic form, pastorals of all sorts, apocalyptic visions, encyclopedic epics . . . , naturalistic muck-raking novels whose aim is to propagandize social change, imaginary voyages . . . , detective stories . . . , fairy tales . . . , debate poems . . . , complaints like Alain de Lille's *De Planctu Naturae* and Allen Ginsberg's "Howl". . . .

(Allegory: The Theory of a Symbolic Mode, pp. 3–4)

The problem here would seem to be a conception of allegory so wide as to equal all "meaning" in literature. (Northrop Frye has made the analogous point [*Anatomy of Criticism*, pp. 89ff.] that all commentary on literature is allegorical, changing one kind of meaning into another.) Among the descriptions of the range of *meaning* the term "allegory" covers (rather than the range of *works* to which it can apply), Graham Hough's is perhaps the clearest. In an analysis that builds on Frye's in the *Anatomy*, he uses the clock diagram that appears below.

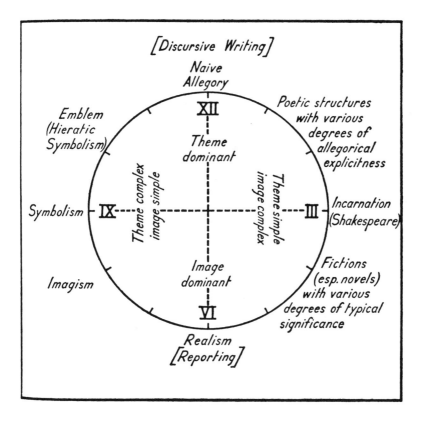

He explains it this way:

> At twelve o'clock we have naive allegory. . . . In naive allegory theme is completely dominant, image merely a rhetorical convenience with no life of its own. . . . It is properly described in the terms which anti-allegorical critics use of allegory in general — a picture-writing to transcribe preconceived ideas.
>
> At three o'clock we have the kind of literature best represented by the work of Shakespeare, in which theme and image are completely fused and the relation between them is only implicit, never open or enforced. We have not yet found a name for this. . . . I shall call it incarnation. . . .
>
> At six o'clock, opposed to naive allegory, we find what I have called realism. Here image is predominant and theme at a minimum. That literature which presents itself as the direct mimesis of common experience comes here — realist and quasi-documentary fiction, descriptive writing and so forth.
>
> At nine o'clock we find symbolism, like incarnation a form in which theme and image have equal weight, but opposed to incarnation because the relation between the two elements is different. In symbolism there is none of the harmonious wholeness of incarnational literature. Theme and image are equally present, they assert their unity, but the unity is never achieved, or if it is, it is only a unity of tension.
>
> . . . with symbolism we enter the last quarter and are already well on our way back to naive allegory again.
>
> But as before there is an intermediate stage. Half-way between symbolism and naive allegory we have what I will call emblem or hieratic symbolism. It exists largely outside literature — its special field is iconography and religious imagery. There is a tendency for symbolism to become fixed; the image shrinks and becomes stereotyped, and theme expands. . . . And so by a commodious vicus of recirculation we come back to our starting point.
>
> (*A Preface to "The Faerie Queene,"* pp. 106ff.)

The rhetorical power of allegory comes, finally, from our acceptance of behavior as itself a kind of referential thinking, a way of making sense of the world alternate to conceptual analysis. To allegorize, to fabulate, introduces a new kind of proof. The Cartesian world has always found such "reasoning" to be derivative ornament only, but it may be that a world conditioned by behavioral biology will understand better this kind of thought.

Alleotheta (al le o THE ta).

Substitution of one case, gender, number, tense, or mood for another. **Anthimeria, Antiptosis**, and **Enallage** are sometimes subdivisions of this term, sometimes synonyms; examples are listed under them. See main entry at **Enallage**.

Alliteration — **Homoeoprophoron**.

Originally, recurrence of an initial consonant sound (and so a type of **Consonance**), but now sometimes used of vowel sounds as well (where it overlaps with **Assonance**):

> Warm-laid grave of a womb-life grey;
> Manger, maiden's knee . . . .

(G. M. Hopkins)

Recurrence of both kinds of alliteration at once (*ark, art, arm*) yields what is sometimes called "front rhyme":

> Yea, to such freshness, fairness, fulness,
>   fineness, freeness
> Yea, to such surging, swaying, sighing,
>   swelling, shrinking . . .

(Hardy)

Alliteration has, for some reason, made a comeback in American political rhetoric, from Spiro Agnew to Jesse Jackson's recent: "My style is public negotiations for parity, rather than private negotiations for position." "Alliteration and assonance," Morse Peckham comments, "are really identical; both are concerned with overdetermination of sound sequence. The judgment as to whether or not alliteration and assonance actually appear in a particular passage is frequently imprecise. Because the phonic character of any language is already preselected and limited, the mere use of the language is bound to produce what appears to be planned overdetermination *if* one is looking for it." Both serve, "if nothing else, to intensify any attitude being signified" (*Man's Rage for Chaos*, pp. 141–142). Alliteration is an early modern term; more common before was **Paroemion**.

Alloiosis (al loi O sis; G. "difference, alteration").

Pointing out "the differences between men, things, and deeds" (Quintilian, IX.iii.92) by breaking down a subject into alternatives: In youth we seek either glory or money. Rutilius, whom Quintilian cites, gives the following example: "Living in a just state, where justice prospers under law, is not the same thing as being subject to tyrannical power, where a single man's whim holds sway" (Halm, p. 13). If used on a narrow scale, this becomes **Antithesis**. On a large scale, Quintilian continues, it is no figure. It may also mean **Hypallage (2)**, that is, **Metonymy** (VIII.vi.23).

Amara irrisio (a MA ra   ir RI si o; L. "bitter laughing at") — **Sarcasmus**.

Ambage. Puttenham's term for **Periphrasis**.

Ambiguous. Puttenham's term for **Amphibologia**.

Ambitus (AM bi tus) — **Period**.

Amphibologia (am phi bo LO gi a; G. "ambiguity"); alt. sp. **Amphibolia** — **Ambiguous**.

Ambiguity, either intended or inadvertent. An ambivalence of grammatical structure, usually by mispunctuation. Sister Miriam Joseph cites this example:

> *Cassio*. Dost thou hear, my honest friend?
> *Clown*. No, I hear not your honest friend. I hear you.
>
> *(Othello*, III, i)

When inadvertent, the figure produces misconception, as in the following example: "In accordance with instructions, I have given birth to twins in the enclosed envelope" instead of "In accordance with instructions in the enclosed envelope, I notify you. . . ." Or, "The announcer called the players names" vs. "The announcer called the players' names."

One kind is the ambiguous **Sententia**. During his Watergate testimony, John Dean told of an interview with John Mitchell. Mitchell reminded Dean, in a telling **Chiasmus**, that "When the going gets tough, the tough get going!" Dean read it as an exhortation not to defend the Nixon administration but, as Mitchell himself was doing, to save his own hide.

Quintilian uses *amphibolia* (III.vi.46) to mean "ambiguity," and tells us (VII.ix.1) that its species are innumerable; among them, presumably, are **Pun** and **Irony**. The term was often used in connection with **Status** theory, and could be, of course, either positive figure or negative vice.

Amphidiorthosis (am phi di or THO sis; G. "guarding oneself both before and after").

To hedge a charge made in anger by qualifying it either before the charge has been made or (sometimes repeating the charge in other words) after.

Amplificatio (am pli fi CA ti o; L. "enlargement").

Rhetorical device used to expand a simple statement. Quintilian (VIII.iv.3) subdivides amplificatio into *incrementum, comparatio, ratiocinatio*, and *congeries*. Hoskyns isolated five means of amplification (comparison, division, accumulation, intimation, progression) and the following figures that amplify: **Accumulatio; Correctio; Divisio; Exclamatio; Hyperbole; Interrogatio; Paralepsis; Sententia; Synoeciosis**. Another theorist lists seventeen figures, a third sixty-four; logically, any figure except those specifically aimed at brevity should fit.

Amplification, as Havelock, Ong, and others have pointed out, is a natural virtue in an oral culture, providing both redundancy of information, ceremonial amplitude, and scope for a memorable syntax and diction. In a literate culture, it moves from **Copia** to copy, and is more likely to seem, as Poo Bah has it in *The Mikado*, "mere corroborative detail intended to give verisimilitude to an otherwise bald and unconvincing narrative." It is usually thought to be suitable for the grand style rather than ordinary discourse, but five minutes worth of ordinary discourse puts this distinction to rout. As a formal rhetorical technique, amplification collaborates with chance, introducing a seeming synonymy by dividing and particularizing an assertion, creating thereby an expanded set of words for which, in turn, the audience can invent an expanded sense of reality. If the new reality is convincing, the amplification evaporates, becomes literal description once again when measured against the new reality. When theorists (Quintilian or Peacham, for example) argue that amplification can either elevate or diminish a subject, the success in creating a new reality would seem to make the difference between the two.

Pope gives, in his comic formulary rhetoric *Peri Bathous*, a characteristic example of what amplificatio looks like to the literate imagination:

> In *The Book of Job* are these words, "Hast thou commanded the morning, and caused the dayspring to know his place?" How is this extended by the most celebrated Amplifier of our age?
>
>> Canst thou set forth th' etherial *mines* on high,
>> Which the refulgent *ore* of light supply?
>> Is the celestial *furnace* to thee known,
>> In which I *melt* the golden metal down?
>> Treasures, from whence I deal out light as fast,
>> As all my stars and lavish suns can waste.
>>
>> (Blackmore, *Job*)

See also **Auxesis; Indignatio.**

Anabasis (a NA ba sis; G. "going up from") — **Climax.**

Anacephalaeosis (an a ce pha LAE o sis; G. "summary") — **Dinumeratio (2).**

See also **Anamnesis.**

Anachinosis — **Anacoenosis.**

Anaclasis (a NA cla sis; G. "bending back") — **Antanaclasis.**

Anacoenosis (an a coe NO sis; G. "communication") — **Anachinosis; Epitrope; Impartener.**

Asking the opinion of one's readers or hearers. Smith (*Mysterie of Rhetorique*) adds that this figure is elegantly used with such as are (1) dead, (2) the judge, (3) absent, (4) inanimate. An example of this last:

> Then ev'n of fellowship, o Moone, tell me
> Is constant *Love* deem'd there but want of wit?
> Are Beauties there as proud as here they be?
> Do they above love to be lov'd, and yet
> Those Lovers scorne whom that *Love* doth possesse?
> Do they call *Vertue* there ungratefulnesse?
>
> (Sidney, *Astrophil and Stella*, 31)

See also **Apostrophe.**

Anacoluthon (an a co LU thon; G. "inconsistent, anomalous").

1. Ending a sentence with a different grammatical structure from that with which it began. Both a vice and a device to demonstrate emotion and, Dupriez reminds us, an affair of conversation rather than written utterance. As Satan is described in *Paradise Lost*: "If thou beest he — But, O, how fall'n! how changed!" Bergin Evans, in *A Dictionary of Contemporary American Usage*, gives an example from Luke 5:14 which is an anacoluthon in the King James Version but revised into correctness in the Revised Standard Version:

> KJ: And he charged him to tell no man; but go, and shew thyself to the priest.
> RSV: And he charged him to tell no one; but "go and show yourself to the priest."

2. **Anantapodoton.**

Anadiplosis (an a di PLO sis; G. "repetition, duplication") — **Duplicatio; Palilogia; Redouble; Reduplicatio.**

Repetition of the last word of one line or clause to begin the next. As in this example, anadiplosis often also creates **Climax:**

> For your brother and my sister no sooner met but they looked; no sooner looked but they loved; no sooner loved but they sighed; no sooner sighed but they asked one another the reason; no sooner knew the reason but they sought the remedy; and in these degrees have they made a pair of stairs to marriage.
>
> (*As You Like It*, V, ii)

See also **Conduplicatio.**

Anagogical Level. *See* **Allegory.**

Analogy (G. "equality of ratios, proportion") — **Proportio.**
Reasoning or arguing from parallel cases.

See also **Simile.**

Anamnesis (an a MNE sis; G. "remembrance") — **Recordatio**.
Recalling ideas, events, or persons of the past:

> When I, good friends, was called to the bar,
>   I'd an appetite fresh and hearty,
> But I was, as many young barristers are,
>   An impecunious party . . .
> In Westminster Hall I danced a dance,
>   Like a semi-despondent fury;
> For I thought I should never hit on a chance
>   Of addressing a British Jury.
>   (Gilbert and Sullivan, *Trial by Jury*)

See also **Dinumeratio (2)**.

Anangeon — **Dicaeologia**.

Anantapodoton (a nan ta PO do ton; G. "without apodosis; hypothetical proposition wanting the consequent clause"); alt. sp. **Anapodoton**.
A kind of **Ellipsis** in which the second member of a correlative expression is left unstated. "If you eat the bear, you have become a man; if the bear eats you, well then. . . . "

See also **Anacoluthon**.

Anaphora (a NA pho ra; G. "carrying back") — **Epanaphora; Epembasis; Iteratio; Relatio; Repetitio; Report**.
Repetition of the same word at the beginning of successive clauses or verses:

>   Show men dutiful?
> Why, so didst thou. Seem they grave and learned?
> Why, so didst thou. Come they of noble family?
> Why, so didst thou. Seem they religious?
> Why, so didst thou.
>   (*Henry V*, II, ii)

> You know, my friends, *there comes a time* when people get tired of being trampled over by the iron feet of oppression. . . . *There comes a time*, my friends, when people get tired of being thrown across the abyss of humiliation where they experience the bleakness of nagging despair. . . . *There comes a time* when people get tired of being pushed out of the glittering sunlight of life's July, and left standing amidst the piercing chill of an Alpine November.
>   (Martin Luther King, quoted in Taylor Branch, *Parting the Waters: America in the King Years 1954–63*; emphasis mine)

(See also the example from *Man and Superman* under **Syncrisis**.)

Anapodoton — **Anantapodoton**.

Anastrophe (a NA stro phe; G. "turning back") — **Perversio; Reversio**.

1. Kind of **Hyperbaton**: unusual arrangement of words or clauses within a sentence, often for metrical convenience or poetic effect:

> Yet I'll not shed her blood,
> Nor scar that whiter skin of hers than snow.
>
> (*Othello*, V, ii)

Quintilian would confine anastrophe to a transposition of two words only, a pattern Puttenham mocks with "In my years lusty, many a deed doughty did I."

2. **Anadiplosis**.

See also **Hysteron proteron**.

Anatomy (G. "cutting up, dissection").

The analysis of an issue into its constituent parts, for ease of discussion or clarity of exegesis. The term is not a traditional one, but it has been increasingly used as a generic term for a technique that includes a number of the traditional dividing and particularizing figures.

Anemographia (a ne mo GRA phi a).

Description of the wind. A type of **Enargia**.

Anoiconometon (a noi co no ME ton; G. "not set in order").

". . . when there is no good disposition of the words, but all are confused up and down and set without order" (Sherry). Want of proper arrangement.

> It was a perfect title. . . . "In considering this strangely neglected topic," it began. This what neglected topic? This strangely what topic? This strangely neglected what?
>
> (Kingsley Amis, *Lucky Jim*)

Antanaclasis (an ta NA cla sis; G. "reflection, bending back") — **Anaclasis; Pun; Rebounde; Reciprocatio; Refractio; Transplacement**.

1. One word used in two contrasting, usually comic, senses. The classical term closest to a plain English pun. Thus a men's clothing store advertises "Law suits our speciality," with some three-piece suits illustrated.

2. Homonymic pun, as when Lady Diana Cooper, in one of her famous misspellings, sent someone a recipe for "Souls in Sauce."

3. Punning **Ploce**: "the goods of life rather than the good life" (Lewis Mumford).

See also **Paronomasia**.

Antanagoge (an ta na GO ge; G. "leading or bringing up against, instead") — **Compensatio; Recompencer**.
Ameliorating a fault or difficulty implicitly admitted by balancing an unfavorable aspect with a favorable one: "A mighty maze but not without a plan."

Antapodosis (an ta PO do sis; G. "giving back in return") — **Redditio contraria**. A simile in which the objects compared correspond in several respects:

> As they say that those, among the Greek musicians, who cannot become players on the lyre, may become players on the flute, so we see that those who cannot become orators betake themselves to the study of law.
> (Cicero, *Pro Murena*)

> The Passion is all that man can know of God: his conflicts, duly faced, are all that he can know of himself. The last judgment is the always present self-judgment.
> (Erickson, *Young Man Luther*, p. 213)

Antenantiosis (an te nan ti O sis; G. "positive statement made in a negative form") — **Litotes**.

Ante occupatio (an te oc cu PA ti o) — **Prolepsis (1)**.

Anthimeria (an thi MER i a; G. "one part for another").
Functional shift, using one part of speech for another: "His complexion is perfect gallows"(*The Tempest*, I, i); "Lord Angelo dukes it well" (*Measure for Measure*, III, ii). See main entry under **Enallage**.

Anthypallage (an thy PAL la ge; G. "substitution").
Change of grammatical case for emphasis. Demetrius cites *Odyssey* 12.73, where Homer adds some vowel music by case-change, as an instance of how the high style is created (*On Style*, 60). This is one of those figures which really make sense only in an inflected language like Latin or Greek. See main entry under **Enallage**.

Anthypophora (an thy PO pho ra; G. "reply") — **Hypophora; Responce**.

Anticategoria (an ti ca te GO ri a; G. "countercharge") — **Accusatio concertativa**.
Mutual accusation or recrimination. So in the famous interchange between Lady Astor and Winston Churchill: "Sir, if you were my

husband I would give you poison." "Madame, if you were my wife, I would drink it."

Anticiceronianism.

The revolt against a slavish imitation of Cicero's periodic prose style. Morris Croll ("Attic Prose: Lipsius, Montaigne, Bacon," in *Style, Rhetoric, and Rhythm*, pp. 167ff.) saw three basic anti-Ciceronian tendencies:

(1) the curt Senecan style (Lipsius)
(2) the loose Senecan style (Montaigne)
(3) the obscure (Bacon)

See also **Ciceronian Style; Period; Senecan Style**.

Anticipatio (an ti ci PA ti o; L. "anticipation") — Prolepsis (1).

Anticlimax — Catacosmesis.

Antilogy (an TI lo gy; G. "controversy").

Two or more opposed speeches on the same topic. See **Dissoi logoi**.

Antimetabole (an ti me TA bo le; G. "turning about") — Commutatio; Counterchange; Permutatio.

In English, inverting the order of repeated words (ABBA) to sharpen their sense or to contrast the ideas they convey, or both. "I pretty, and my saying apt? Or I apt, and my saying pretty?" (*Love's Labor's Lost*, I, ii). Latin use of the term was slightly different from the English and not precisely synonymous with **Chiasmus**. Quintilian, for example, defines it:

> Antithesis may also be effected by employing that *figure*, known as [antimetabole], by which words are repeated in different cases, tenses, moods, etc., as for instance when we say, *non ut edam, vivo, sed ut vivam, edo* [I do not live to eat, but eat to live] (IX.iii.85).

Chiasmus and commutatio sometimes imply a more precise balance and reversal, antimetabole a looser, but they are virtual synonyms.

Antinomasia — Antonomasia.

Antinomy (an TI no my; G. "opposition of law; ambiguity in law").

A comparison of one law to another, or of one part of a law to another.

Antiphora (an TI pho ra; G. "contrary motion") — Hypophora.

Antiphrasis (an TI phra sis; G. "expression by the opposite") — Broad Floute.

Irony of one word, calling a "dwarf" a "giant," a worst "enemy" in a debate "my learned friend."

Antiptosis (an ti PTO sis; G. "exchange of case") — **Casus pro casu.**
Substituting one case for another; a type of **Enallage**. Peacham's example shows how strained one can become when applying Latin grammatical categories to English: "I give you this gift with hearty good will, *for* I give this gift to you with hearty good will — the accusative for the dative; he is condemned for murder *for* he is condemned of murther — the dative or accusative for the genitive." A computer virus Cookie Monster's non-negotiable demand, "Me want cookie!," shows that the figure still lives. See main entry under **Enallage**.

Antirrhesis (an tir RHE sis; G. "refutation, counterstatement").
Rejecting an argument because of its insignificance, error, or wickedness. Churchill was great at this: "I have been mocked and censured as a scare-monger and even as a war-monger, by those whose complacency and inertia have brought us all nearer to war and war nearer to us all." "Appeasement from weakness and fear is alike futile and fatal." And, commenting on the neutral European states temporizing under the gaze of Hitler, "Each one hopes that if he feeds the crocodile enough, the crocodile will eat him last."

Antisagoge (an ti sa GO ge; G. "compensatory antithesis") — **Compensatio.**
1. Assuring a reward to those who possess a virtue, or a punishment to those who hold it in contempt. Leontes, in *The Winter's Tale* (I, ii), says:

Do't, and thou hast the one half of my heart;
Do't not, thou splitt'st thine own.

2. Stating first one side of a proposition, then the other, with equal vigor:

Love seeketh not itself to please,
Nor for itself hath any care,
But for another gives its ease,
And builds a Heaven in Hell's despair.

Love seeketh only Self to please,
To bind another to its delight,
Joys in another's loss of ease,
And builds a Hell in Heaven's despite.
(Blake, "The Clod and the Pebble")

Antistasis (an TI sta sis; G. "opposition, counterplea") — **Contentio; Refractio.**

15

Repetition of a word in a different or contrary sense, as when Richard II reflects on the decline of both fortune and appearance in prison: "I wasted time and now doth time waste me" (*Richard II*, V, v).

Antisthecon — **Antistoecon.**

Antistoecon (an ti STO e con; G. [of letters] "corresponding"); alt. sp. **Antisthecon** — **Metathesis; Transposition.**

A type of **Metaplasm**: substituting one letter or sound for another within a word: "strond" for "strand."

Antistrephon (an TI stre phon; G. "turning to the opposite side").

An argument that turns one's opponent's arguments or proofs to one's own purpose:

> He says when tipsy, he would thrash and kick her,
>   Let's make him tipsy, gentlemen, and try!
> > > (Gilbert and Sullivan, *Trial by Jury*)

Antistrophe (an TI stro phe; G. "turning about").

1. **Conversio; Conversum; Counterturne; Epiphora; Epistrophe.** Repetition of a closing word or words at the end of several (usually successive) clauses, sentences, or verses. Peacham cites 1 Corinthians 13:1: "When I was a child, I spake as a child; I understood as a child; I thought as a child: but when I became a man, I put away childish things."

2. The repetition of a word or phrase in a second context in the same position it held in an earlier and similar context. Puttenham:

> . . . anon with great disdain
> She shuns my love, and after by a train
> She seeks my love, and saith she loves me most,
> But seeing her love, so lightly won and lost, etc.

Perhaps because so many rhetorical figures involve a "counter-turning" of some sort, this term has attracted a cluster of different meanings in addition to the above. It has been made synonym to **Anaphora, Conduplicatio, Paronomasia,** and other terms. And **Epiphora** and **Epistrophe** are full synonyms of equal authority. *Caveat scriptor.*

Antithesis (an TI the sis; G. "opposition") — **Antitheton; Contentio; Contraposition; Oppositio.**

Conjoining contrasting ideas, as in Sidney's *Arcadia*:

> . . . neither the one hurt her, nor the other help her; just without partiality, mighty without contradiction, liberal without losing, wise without curiosity. . . .

Or Pope's description of *Sporus*:

> Whether in florid impotence he speaks,
> And, as the prompter breathes, the puppet squeaks;
> Or at the ear of *Eve*, familiar Toad,
> Half froth, half venom, spits himself abroad, . . .
> His wit all seesaw, between *that* and *this*,
> Now high, now low, now master up, now miss,
> And he himself one vile Antithesis.
>
> (Epistle to Dr. Arbuthnot, 317–325)

See also **Alloiosis; Syncrisis.**

Antitheton (an TI the ton; G. "opposed") — **Antithesis; Quarreller.**

Antonomasia (an to no MA si a; G. "use of an epithet or patronymic, instead of a proper name, or the reverse"); alt. sp. **Antinomasia — Nominatio; Pronominatio; Surnamer.**

Descriptive phrase for proper name, as when Churchill crossed out a cabinet minister's name and inserted "Some funkstick in the Air Ministry." Or, proper name for quality associated with it: "Perfect! Pollyana marries Milquetoast!" Quintilian points out the similarity to **Synecdoche.**

Apaetesis (a pae TE sis; G. "demanding back").
A matter put aside in anger is resumed later.

Aphaeresis (a PHAE re sis; G. "taking away") — **Ablatio.**
Omitting a syllable from the beginning of a word: "Rally 'round the flag, boys." The converse (omission of final vowel or syllable) is **Apocope.**

Aphelia (a PHE li a; G. "plainness").
Plainness of writing or speech. Churchill pleads for it in a WWII directive to his staff: "Let us not shrink from using the short expressive phrase, even if it is controversial."

Aphorismus (a pho RIS mus; G. "distinction, definition").
1. **Proverb.**
2. A point is made or a description amplified by questioning the force or applicability of a word or an aphorism: "What laws be these, if at least wise they may be termed laws, which bear in them so vile customs, and not rather firebrands of the city, and the plague of the whole commonweal" (Day). In this sense, it would seem to be **Correctio (1).**

Apocarteresis (a po car te RE sis) — **Tolerantia.**

Giving up one hope and turning to another: No man can help me; I'll pray. Peacham uses the term, having borrowed it, presumably, from Quintilian, VIII.v.23, where the word is used, in Greek, in its usual meaning, "suicide by fasting," i.e. giving up all hope. Quintilian's context does not altogether support Peacham's redefinition.

Apocope (a PO co pe; G. "cutting off") — **Abscissio**.
Omitting the last syllable or letter of a word: "Oft in the stilly morn."

Apocrisis (a PO cri sis; G. "answer") — **Hypophora**.

Apodeixis — **Apodixis**.

Apodioxis (a po di OX is; G. "driving away") — **Rejectio**.
Rejecting an argument indignantly as impertinent or absurdly false.

> But he turned, and said unto Peter, Get thee behind me, Satan: thou art an offence unto me: for thou savourest not the things that be of God, but those that be of men.
>
> (Matt. 16:23)

See also **Antirrhesis; Diasyrmus**.

Apodixis (a po DIX is; G. "demonstration, proof"); alt. sp. **Apodeixis**.
1. **Experientia**. Confirming a statement by reference to generally accepted principles or experience: "Be not deceived; God is not mocked: for whatsoever a man soweth, that shall he also reap" (Gal. 6:7).
2. An incomplete **Epicheireme**; the proof of an epicheireme. Quintilian summarizes classical agreement, or disagreement, with the definition: "a method of proving what is not certain by means of what is certain" (V.x.8). He does not give an example, however. He does remark that "some think that an *apodeixis* is a portion of an *epicheireme*, namely the part containing the proof." This would seem to agree with Aristotle:

> The enthymeme must consist of few propositions, fewer often than those which make up the normal syllogism. For if any of these propositions is a familiar fact, there is no need even to mention it; the hearer adds it himself. Thus, to show that Dorieus has been victor in a contest for which the prize is a crown, it is enough to say "For he has been victor in the Olympic games," without adding "And in the Olympic games the prize is a crown," a fact which everybody knows.
>
> (*Rhetoric*, I, 1357a)

Apologue (AP o logue; G. "account, story, fable") — **Fable**.

Apomnemonysis (a po mne mo NY sis; G. "recounting, summarizing") — **Commemoratio.**

The quotation of an approved authority from memory. So Falstaff, impersonating the King, to Prince Hal:

> There is a thing, Harry, which thou hast often heard of, and it is known to many in our land by the name of pitch. This pitch, as ancient writers do report, doth defile; so doth the company thou keepest.
>
> *(1 Henry IV*, II, iv)

So the Archbishop of Canterbury lecturing Prince Hal, now become Henry V, about the Salic Law:

> For in the Book of Numbers is it writ:
> When the man dies, let the inheritance
> Descend unto the daughter.
>
> *(Henry V*, I, ii)

Apophasis (a PO pha sis; G. "denial").

1. **Negatio.** Pretending to deny what is really affirmed. A type of **Irony** or **Occultatio.**

2. **Expeditio.**

Apoplanesis (a po pla NE sis; G. "digression") — **Heterogenium.**

Evading the issue by digressing; irrelevant answer to distract attention from a difficult point: "I ask you of cheese, you answer me of chalk" (Fenner). Or:

> *Justice.* Sir John, I sent for you before your expedition to Shrewsbury.
> *Falstaff.* An 't please your lordship, I hear his Majesty is return'd with some discomfort from Wales.
> *Justice.* I talk not of his Majesty: you would not come when I sent for you.
> *Falstaff.* And I hear, moreover, his Highness is fall'n into this same whoreson apoplexy.
>
> *(2 Henry IV*, I, ii)

Aporia (a po RI a; G. "difficulty, being at a loss") — **Addubitation; Diaporesis; Doubtfull; Dubitatio.**

True or feigned doubt or deliberation about an issue. True:

> *York.* God for his mercy! what a tide of woes
> Comes rushing on this woeful land at once!
> I know not what to do. . . .
> If I know how or which way to order these affairs,
> Thus disorderly thrust into my hands,
> Never believe me.
>
> *(Richard II*, II, ii)

Feigned:

Say what strange Motive, Goddess! could compel
A well-bred Lord t'assault a gentle Belle! . . .
In tasks so bold, can little men engage,
And in soft bosoms dwells such mighty Rage?

(*Rape of the Lock*)

Aposiopesis (a po si o PE sis; G. "becoming silent") — **Interpellatio; Interruption; Obticentia; Praecisio; Reticentia; Silence.**
Stopping suddenly in midcourse, leaving a statement unfinished; sometimes from genuine passion, sometimes for effect. Hotspur's dying breath provides an authentic instance of inability to continue:

Hotspur.   O, I could prophesy,
But that the earthy and cold hand of death
Lies on my tongue. No, Percy, thou art dust,
And food for —
Prince. For worms, brave Percy.

(*1 Henry IV*, V, iv)

Pope comments in the *Peri Bathous*: "An excellent figure for the Ignorant, as, 'What shall I say?' when one has nothing to say: or 'I can no more,' when one really can no more."

Apostrophe (G. "turning away") — **Aversio; Turne Tale.**
Breaking off a discourse to address some person or personified thing either present or absent.

Soul of the age!
The applause! delight! the wonder of our stage!
My Shakespeare rise.

(Ben Jonson)

See also **Ecphonesis.**

Apothegm (AP o thegm; G. "terse saying") — **Proverb.**

Appositio (ap po SI ti o; L. "a setting before").
1. Apposition; two juxtaposed nouns, the second elaborating the first: *Henry, King* of England. *See also* **Epexegesis.**
2. **Prothesis (1).**

Appositum (ap PO si tum) — **Epitheton.**

Ara (A ra; G. "prayer, vow, curse") — **Execratio; Imprecatio.**
Curse or imprecation, especially at length.

Let his days be few;
And let another take his office.
Let his children be fatherless,
And his wife a widow.

Let his children be vagabonds, and beg:
And let them seek their bread out of their desolate places.

(Psalm 109:8–10)

Argument. *See* **Proof; Topics.**

Argumentum ad baculum (ar gu MEN tum ad BA cu lum; L. "scepter, staff").

An appeal to force (literally, "to the staff, or club") to settle the question.

See also **Fallacy.**

Argumentum ad hominem (HO mi nem; L. "man").

1. Abuse of your opponent's character.
2. Basing your argument on what you know of your opponent's character.

Churchill's reputed description of Atlee may exemplify both: "He was a modest man, with much to be modest about."

See also **Fallacy.**

Argumentum ad ignorantiam (ig no RAN ti am).

A proposition is true if it has not been proved false.

See also **Fallacy.**

Argumentum ad misericordiam (mi se ri COR di am).

Appeal to the mercy of the hearers.

> The quality of mercy is not strained;
> It droppeth as the gentle rain from heaven
> Upon the place beneath. . . .
>
> *(The Merchant of Venice, IV, i)*

See also **Fallacy.**

Argumentum ad populum (PO pu lum).

An appeal to the crowd.

> Friends, Romans, countrymen, lend me your ears;
> I come to bury Caesar not to praise him. . . .
>
> *(Antony and Cleopatra, III, ii)*

See also **Fallacy.**

Argumentum ad verecundiam (ve re CUN di am; L. "shame, fear of wrongdoing").

An appeal to reverence for authority, to accepted traditional values.

See also **Fallacy.**

Argumentum ex concessis (con CES sis; L. "[points] granted, conceded").

Reasoning that the conclusion of an argument is sound, on the basis of the truth of the premises of one's opponent. He may have exaggerated the soundness of his premise for his purposes; you use the exaggeration for yours.

See also **Fallacy**.

Arrangement — Dispositio; Taxis.

The second of the five traditional parts of rhetoric, that having to do with the ordering of arguments. See chapter 2 at **Rhetoric: the five parts** and **Arrangement: The parts of an oration**.

Ars dictaminis (dic TA mi nis; L. "art of expressing in language, composing") — **Dictamen**.

Dictare can mean simply "to dictate to," and dictamen sometimes refers to just this. More largely, ars dictaminis referred to the art of letter-writing in the Middle Ages. Such letter-writing was a public, formal, and highly rhetorical activity. "In view of the way in which letters were written and sent, and also of the standards of literacy in the Middle Ages, it is doubtful whether there were any private letters in the modern sense of the term" (Constable, *Letters and Letter-Collections*, p. 11). The training for and practice of ars dictaminis gradually came to usurp much of the doctrine formerly grouped under ars rhetorica. Erich Auerbach has described it as the flowering of medieval Latin stylistic mannerism, with its principal stylistic elements being "rhythmical movement of clauses, rhymed prose, sound patterns and figures of speech, unusual vocabulary, complex and pompous sentence structure" (*Literary Language and Its Public*, p. 273). The art of letter-writing sometimes overlapped with the ars notariae, that branch of medieval rhetorical theory which laid down the rules for the composition of legal, or formal state, documents.

It might perhaps be argued that the role played in the classical period by the formal speech or **Declamation**, as the central pattern for educated utterance, was taken over in the Middle Ages by the formal letter, and that this yielded to the essay in the Renaissance, only to be giving way, today, to a new form of electronic on-line exchange which is part speech, part conversation, part essay, and part letter.

Ars praedicandi (prae di CAN di).

The part of medieval rhetorical theory concerned with eloquence in preaching. The response of the Christian Middle Ages to pagan rhetoric, in spite of Augustine's discussion of Ciceronian rhetoric in book 4 of *On Christian Doctrine*, was bound to be vexed and equivocal, and it was only in the thirteenth century that manuals of preaching rhetoric appeared. (For a discussion of them and their background, see "The Art of Preaching" in J. J. Murphy, *Rhetoric in the Middle Ages*.)

Articulus (ar TI cu lus; L. "a [small] part, division"); alt. sp. **Articulo — Asyndeton**.
Sonnino discriminates between this term meaning **Asyndeton** and meaning **Brachylogia**, but it is hard to see any real difference between them.

Artificial Proofs.
We think of "proof" as meaning "evidence," and the investigation and testing of this evidence as the central part of any persuasive case, especially in the courts. Classical rhetorical training did not conceive the problem thus. Aristotle argues in the *Rhetoric*, for example, that witnesses and contracts (along with testimony gained from torture!) do not fall within the purview of rhetoric. These **Inartificial Proofs** were thought to be given to the orator, and so no training was provided in how to develop them. The true test of the orator was his skill in devising *artificial* proofs, those developed by the principles of rhetoric itself. Artificial proofs amount to what we would call the interpretation an orator puts on the "inartificial" proofs or evidence. Thus we would not, properly speaking, consider artificial proofs as "proofs" at all. Both kinds of proof were of course present in every case, but we emphasize the evidence as primary, the interpretation as following from it. It might not be too inaccurate to think that the classical world tended to reverse this relationship.
See also **Proof**.

Ascensus (as CEN sus; L. "ascent, climb") — **Climax**.

Aschematiston (a sche ma TIS ton; G. "without form; not employing figures of speech") — **Male figuratum**.
1. Absence of ornamental or figured language. Quintilian reckoned this no small vice (*quod vitium non inter minima est*, IX.i.13 [this phrase is omitted from the Loeb Library translation]), whereas we are more likely to see it as a healthy sign of the plain style. Churchill offers an example of aschematiston from a doughty sea dog, set off by the contrast of his own more figured prose:

> The *Indefatigable* had disappeared beneath the waves. The *Queen Mary* had towered up to heaven in a pillar of fire. The *Lion* was in flames.

23

A tremendous salvo struck upon or about her following ship, the *Princess Royal*, which vanished in a cloud of spray and smoke. A signalman sprang on to the *Lion*'s bridge with the words: "*Princess Royal* has blown up, sir." On this the Vice-Admiral said to his Flag Captain, "Chatfield, there seems to be something wrong with our ———— ships to-day."

(*The World Crisis*, 3.129)

2. Unskillful use of figures.

(This figure occasions the only humorous aside in Sister Miriam Joseph's mammoth survey of *Shakespeare's Use of the Arts of Language*: "This vice has not been observed in Shakespeare's work" [p. 304, n. 12].)

Asianism.

". . . a kynde of endighting used of the Asians, full of figures, and wordes, lackyng matter" (Sherry). A highly ornamented style common when the multiethnic populations of Asia wrote in Greek without the restraints traditional in earlier stylistic decorum. Cicero (*Brutus*, 325) distinguishes two types of Asianism, one "sententious and studied," the other notable for "swiftness and impetuosity"; in practice, modern scholars may have difficulty distinguishing the two. Let me try, though, borrowing examples from Pope's *Peri Bathous*:

Plain style: "Snuff the Candle."
Sententious Asianism:
   "Yon Luminary amputation needs,
   Thus shall you save its half-extinguished life."
Plain style: "Light the Fire."
Impetuous Asianism:
   "Bring forth some remnant of *Promethean* theft,
   Quick to expand th' inclement air congealed
   By *Boreas*' rude breath."

See also **Atticism; Bomphiologia; Euphuism; Macrologia; Poicilogia; Rhodian Style.**

Asphalia (as pha LI a; G. "security, certainty, bond") — Certitudo; Securitas.

Offering oneself as surety for a bond. So Miranda pleads with her father to make friends with Ferdinand: "Sir, have pity. I'll be his surety" (*The Tempest*, I, ii).

Assonance.

Identity or similarity in sound between internal vowels in neighboring words. Thus Churchill remarked on a "tiny, timid, tentative, tardy" increase in air strength in Britain's rearmament before World War II.

See also **Alliteration; Paronomasia**.

Asteismus (as te IS mus; G. "wit") — **Civill Jest; Merry Scoffe; Urbanitas**.

Facetious or mocking answer that plays on a word, as in this exchange from *The Goon Show*: "Did you put the cat out?" "No, it wasn't on fire." Or as in this anecdote about Isabella Stewart Gardner: "At last in exasperation, when asked to subscribe to the Charitable Eye and Ear Infirmary, she replied that she did not know there was a charitable eye or ear in Boston" (Walker, *Self-Portrait with Donors*, p. 73). Or in Fritz Kreisler's famous reply when someone asked him the way to Carnegie Hall. "Practice," he replied.

Asteismus comes from the Greek word for "city," as *urbanitas* does from the Latin, and both reflect the quick wit attributed to the city-dweller. Quintilian comments: "First, there is *urbanitas*, which I see as language with a city flavor to its words, accent, and idiom" (VI. iii.17).

See also **Pun**.

Astrothesia (as tro THE si a; G. "group of stars; constellation").

The description of a star, as in the song "My Evenin' Star," or in Sir Philip Sidney's sonnet sequence *Astrophil and Stella*, where the mistress is his star (Latin *stella*) while he is her star-lover (Greek *aster-philos*). Sidney's whole sonnet-sequence can be seen as variations on this figure. It would be too raffish, though, to extend it to cover movie stars, as in Dorothy Parker's comment on Katherine Hepburn: "She runs the gamut of emotions from A to B."

Asyndeton (a SYN de ton; G. "unconnected") — **Articulus; Brachylogia (1); Dialyton; Dissolutio; Loose Language**. Omission of conjunctions between words, phrases, or clauses.

> Faynt, wearie, sore, emboyled, grieved, brent
> With heat, toyle, wounds, armes, smart, and inward fire.
> > (Spenser, *Faerie Queene*, I, xi, 28)
> All is over. Silent, mournful, abandoned, broken, Czechoslovakia recedes into the darkness.
> > (Churchill on the Munich Agreement, 1938)

Opposite of **Polysyndeton**.

Atticism. The mid-first-century B.C. reaction against **Asianism** called itself "Atticism" because it went back for a model to the Attic orators of the classical period. The word, applied to the styles of other literatures, has generally meant a style that is the opposite of the ornamental, one brief, witty, sometimes epigrammatic. (For further clarification, see Croll, *Style, Rhetoric, and Rhythm*.)

See also **Rhodian Style.**

Attribution. Puttenham's second term for **Epitheton.**

Augendi causa (au GEN di CAU sa; L. "for the purpose of increasing").
Raising the voice for emphasis.

Auxesis (aux E sis; G. "increase, amplification").
1. Use of a heightened word in place of an ordinary one: calling a corporation president a "titan of industry." Opposite of **Meiosis.**
2. **Avancer; Incrementum.** Words or clauses placed in climactic order: "Give up money, give up fame, give up science, give up the earth itself and all it contains, rather than do an immoral act" (Jefferson).
3. **Dirimens copulatio; Progressio.** Building a point around a series of comparisons.
4. A general term for **Amplificatio** or one of the subdivisions thereof.

Further discussion. The order of definitions above represents a somewhat arbitrary ranking of the meanings this term has accrued down through the ages. Chronicling the learned disagreement my ordering attempts to rationalize may do more harm than good, but it will at least illustrate how easily a simple Greek word becomes a vexed rhetorical term.

First, the basic sense of the word. In the course of discussing speeches of praise in the *Rhetoric*, and how to make your man seem more important by comparing him with other great men, Aristotle says, "It is only natural that methods of 'heightening the effect' (ἡ αὔξησις) should be attached particularly to speeches of praise" (I, 1368a22). He continues: "And, in general, of the lines of argument which are common to all speeches, this 'heightening of effect' is most suitable for declamations, where we take our hero's actions as admitted facts" (1368a27). And, in the course of discussing *asyndeton*, A. says that omitting the conjunctions "makes everything more important" (ἔχει οὖν αὔξησιν, 1413b34).

One way to make something more important is to call it by a fancier name. Erasmus, in the *De copia*, thus remarks: "We can also use auxesis, that is, increase, when we use a more violent word in place of the normal one in order to heighten what we are saying; for example, to say 'slain' for 'killed,' or 'highway robber' for 'dishonest' " (vol. 24, p. 343). This makes auxesis of a single word into the opposite of meiosis, and other theorists, Peacham for example, use it thus ("when we use a greater word for a lesse, or when the word is greater than the thing is in deede"). This sense seems closest to Aristotle's original but general use of the term.

Another way to make something more important is to put it into a climactic series, and this has come to be another meaning of auxesis. Auxesis is usually *not* listed by theorists as synonymous with the **Climax/Anadiplosis** cluster of terms, but the difference between auxesis, in its main sense of augmentation, and climax is a pretty fine one. Sonnino, for example, makes Quintilian's term *incrementum* (VIII.iv.3) a synonym for auxesis. But Quintilian exemplifies incrementum by a quotation from Cicero which seems a straightforward climax. And Erasmus's discussion of incrementum in the *De copia* quotes Quintilian quoting Cicero using the same example (vol. 24, p. 592). The difference between the auxesis and climax clusters seems to be that in the climax cluster, the climactic series is realized through *linked pairs of terms*. One might therefore say that the auxesis cluster is a figure of amplification and the climax cluster a scheme of arrangement. Observing this distinction, however, we can call a climactic series a climax only when the terms are linked (see example at **Climax**).

Now the third meaning, building a series of progressive comparisons. Wilson uses the term *progressio* for a pattern in which "contrary sentences . . . answer one another." He gives this example: "If we would rebuke a naughty boy, we might with commending a good boy, say thus. 'What a boy art thou in comparison of this fellow here. Thou sleeps; he wakes. Thou plays; he studies. Thou art ever abroad; he is ever at home. Thou never waits; he still doth his attendance' " (p. 401). This seems an idiosyncratic definition, closer to **Antitheton** or **Syncrisis** than anything else (see, for example, Quintilian, IX.iii.32; Rufinianus 37 [Halm, p. 47]). But an excellent modern theorist, Sonnino, equates progressio as defined by Wilson (contrary sentences which answer one another) with auxesis and incrementum.

How do we connect the two different meanings, a climactic series and a series of antithetical comparisons, and yet discriminate between them? The closest to an explanation I have found occurs at the end of Hoskyns' discussion of progressio (for him, a fifth category of amplificatio): ". . . may not a matter be as well amplified in this form, by examining the comparison in every particular circumstance, that the whole may seem the greater?" (p. 142). Hoskyns then gives an example which fits the puzzling figure **Dirimens copulatio**, a series of minus/plus, not-only-but-also comparisons. (Peacham is the only authority I have consulted for this term; Sonnino gives also Trapezuntius [George of Trebizond], whose *Rhetoricorum libri quinque* appeared in a London edition in 1547.) So, we might conceive the progressio/dirimens copulatio cluster to be a subset of auxesis: a technique of amplification which develops a matter through a climactic series, each stage of the series being further subdivided into a series of favorable/unfavorable comparisons. Otherwise, progressio is simply **Auxesis (1)**.

Quintilian's discussion of incrementum in VIII.iv.3–9 is part of a discussion of amplificatio; incrementum is one of four kinds, along with **Comparatio, Ratiocinatio**, and **Congeries**. Following this, some theorists have used auxesis either as a simple synonym for amplificatio of all sorts or as a synonym for incrementum alone. It seems a little confusing — though hardly unprecedented — to use a term to mean both a general category and a subdivision thereof.

In a simpler, gentler world, might we get by with two terms, one for a climactic series (auxesis? gradatio? climax?) and one for progressing through a series of comparisons, progressio (leaving dirimens copulatio to flourish, perhaps, *in sensu obsceno*)?

Avancer. Puttenham's term for **Auxesis (2)**.

Aversio (a VER si o; L. "turning away") — **Apostrophe**.

Barbarismus (bar ba RIS mus; G. "foreign mode of speech") — **Barbarolexis; Forrein Speech**.
 1. Mispronunciation through ignorance:

> Is it that fery person for all the 'orld, as just as you will desire. And seven hundred pounds of moneys, and gold and silver, is her grandsire, upon his death's-bed — Got deliver to a joyful resurrections — give, when she is able to overtake seventeen years old.
>
> > (*The Merry Wives of Windsor*, I, i)

 2. **Metaplasm**. Wrenched accent to fit meter or rhyme:

> But — Oh! ye lords of ladies intellectual,
> Inform us truly, have they not hen-peck'd you all?
>
> > (Byron, *Don Juan*, I, xxii)

Further discussion. Originally the errors of grammar, pronunciation, and usage committed by *barbaroi*, foreigners, when they spoke Greek. Later extended to Latin, of course, and then to the mistakes in grammar and usage which non-native speakers make when essaying any strange language, and then to whatever mistakes seem specially barbaric to us. It is also sometimes used to refer to usages from an earlier or more "barbaric" period in the same language, as when a Renaissance poet would use a Middle English word, for example.

Bonner points out that "Under Stoic influence, it became accepted that a barbarism was a fault in the use of a single word, and a solecism was one arising in words in conjunction, that is, an error of syntax" (*Education in Ancient Rome*, p. 198). The *Ad Herennium* makes this distinction, as does Quintilian, who discusses both categories at length (I.v.5–54), and concedes to poets their deliberate use *metri causa* — when they become not faults but *metaplasmos . . . et schemata* respectively (I.viii.14). Donatus reproduces the Stoic distinction and also, with that characteristic zeal to catalogue errors and vices of language which he has bequeathed to a grateful posterity, the distinction between barbarism and metaplasm (*Ars maior*, III, 1–4), the second a deliberate change allowed by poetic license.

See also **Solecismus**.

Barbarolexis (bar ba ro LEX is) — **Barbarismus**.

Bathos (BA thos; G. "depth"). *See* **Pathos**.

Bdelygma (bdel YG ma; G. "nausea, sickness; filth, nastiness") — **Abominatio**.
    Expression of hatred, usually short. As Emilia to Othello: "O gull! O dolt! / As ignorant as dirt!" (*Othello*, V, ii).

Benedictio (ben e DIC ti o; L. "extolling, praising, lauding") — **Eulogia**.

Benevolentia — **Philophronesis**.

Bitter Taunt. Puttenham's term for **Sarcasmus**.

Blazon — **Effictio**.

Bomphiologia (bom phi o LO gi a; G. "booming, buzzing words"); alt. sp. **Bomphilogia**.
    Bombastic speech; "using such bombasted words, as seem altogether farced full of wind, being a great deal too high and lofty for the matter" (Puttenham). Peacham gives, as one example, Terence's boasting soldier, Thraso. Shakespeare's Ancient Pistol will do as well:

> "Solus," egregious dog? O viper vile!
> The "solus" in thy most mervailous face;
> The "solus" in thy teeth, and in thy throat,
> And in thy hateful lungs, yea, in thy maw, perdy,
> And, which is worse, within thy nasty mouth!
> I do retort the "solus" in thy bowels;
> For I can take, and Pistol's cock is up,
> And flashing fire will follow.
>
> (*Henry V*, II, i)

See further discussion at **Macrologia**.

Brachylogia (bra chy LO gi a; G. "brevity in speech or writing") — **Asyndeton; Cutted Comma.**
1. Omission of conjunctions between single words: "Beguil'd, divorced, wronged, spited, slain!"
2. Brevity of diction; abbreviated construction; word or words omitted. A modern theorist differentiated this use from **Ellipsis** in that the elements missing are more subtly, less artificially, omitted in ellipsis: "The corps goeth before, we follow after, we come to the grave, she is put into the fire, a lamentation is made" (Peacham).

Brevitas (BRE vi tas; L. "shortness").
Concise expression.

> He is about to be struck down. A dark hand, gloved at first in folly, now intervenes. Exit Czar.
>
> (Churchill, *The World Crisis*)

Broad Floute. Puttenham's term for **Antiphrasis.**

Bugbear Style — Skotison.

Cacemphaton (cac EM pha ton; G. "ill-sounding") — **Aischrologia; Foule Speech; Turpis locutio.**
1. Scurrilous jest; lewd allusion or double entendre, as when the blues singer Big Bill Broonzy sings, "I'm gonna squeeze your lemon, baby, 'till the good juice comes."
2. Sounds combined for harsh effect. So Peacham: "when there come many syllables of one sound together in one sentence, like a continual jarring upon one string, thus, neither honour nor nobility, could move a naughty niggardly noddy."

Cacosistaton (ca co SIS ta ton; G. "badly constructed").
An argument that can serve as well on either side of a question.

Cacosyntheton (ca co SYN the ton; G. "ill-composed") — **Male collocatum; Misplacer.**
Awkward transposition of the parts of a sentence. Puttenham's example: "In my years lusty, many a deed doughty did I." Or Churchill's famous "This is the kind of nonsense up with which I shall not put." Or, as in this only partially successful syntactical gymnastic from Kingsley Amis's *I Want It Now*: "Now and again it felt rather like that. It was now, or again, now."
See also **Hysteron proteron.**

Cacozelia (ca co ZE li a; G. "unhappy imitation; affectation") —
Fonde Affectation; Mala affectio.
Studied affectation of style; affected diction made up of adaptation
of Latin words or inkhorn terms, as when Hamlet parodies Osric:

> Sir, his definement suffers no perdition in you; though, I know, to
> divide him inventorially would dozy th' arithmetic of memory, and yet
> but yaw neither in respect of his quick sail. But, in the verity of ex-
> tolment, I take him to be a soul of great article, and his infusion of
> such dearth and rareness as, to make true diction of him, his sem-
> blable is his mirror, and who else would trace him, his umbrage, noth-
> ing more. . . . The concernancy, sir? Why do we wrap the gentleman
> in our more rawer breath?
>
> *(Hamlet, V, ii)*

See also **Soraismus.**

Caesum (CAE sum; L. "something cut off") — **Comma.**

Canonical Syllogism.
The irreducible common form of the various types of **Syllogism,**
either universal or particular.

Casus pro casu (CA su; L. "one case for another") — **Antiptosis.**

Catachresis (ca ta CHRE sis; G. "misuse, misapplication") — **Abuse;**
Abusio.
1. Implied metaphor, using words wrenched from common usage, as when Hamlet says, "I will speak daggers to her."
2. A second definition seems slightly different but perhaps is not:
an extravagant, unexpected, farfetched metaphor, as when a weeping woman's eyes become Niagara Falls. Pope gives these examples
in the *Peri Bathous:*

> Mow the Beard,
> Shave the Grass,
> Pin the Plank,
> Nail my sleeve.

Catacosmesis (ca ta cos ME sis; G. "arrangement, order") —
Anticlimax. Ordering words in descending importance; opposite of
Climax. Some see an unwitting instance in the Yale University
motto: "For God, for Country, and for Yale."

Cataplexis (ca ta PLEX is; G. "amazement, consternation").
Threatening punishment, misfortune, or disaster:

> Hence,
> Horrible villain! or I'll spurn thine eyes
> Like balls from me; I'll unhair thy head!
> Thou shalt be whipp'd with wire, and stew'd in brine,
> Smarting in ling'ring pickle.
>
> (*Antony and Cleopatra*, II, v)

See also **Ominatio; Paraenesis**.

Categoria (ca te go RI a; G. "accusation, assertion, prediction") — **Accusatio**.

Reproaching a person with his wickedness to his face. So Prince Hal to Falstaff:

> These lies are like their father that begets them — gross as a mountain, open, palpable. Why, thou clay-brained guts, thou knotty-pated fool, thou whoreson obscene greasy, tallow-catch —
>
> (*1 Henry IV*, II, iv)

Categorical Propositions.

Four forms:

(1) Universal Affirmative: All politicians are corrupt.
(2) Universal Negative: No politician is corrupt.
(3) Particular Affirmative: Some politicians are corrupt.
(4) Particular Negative: Some politicians are not corrupt.

Quality of proposition: Affirmative or Negative. Quantity of proposition: Universal or Particular. Also called "Simple" propositions, as opposed to Disjunctive and Hypothetical, which are called "Compound."

See also **Square of Opposition**.

Causes.

Logicians distinguish four:

(1) material (for example, the metal from which a car is made)
(2) formal (the design of the car)
(3) efficient (the assembling of the car)
(4) final (the purpose of the car: transportation)

See also **Necessary Cause; Sufficient Cause**.

Ceratin (ce RA tin; G. "the fallacy called the Horns").

An argument so couched that, seemingly, all possibilities equally prove it true (or false). A variety of **Dilemma**. The "horns" of a dilemma are called *ceratinae* (G. "made of horn").

See also **Crocodilinae**.

Certitudo (cer ti TU do; L. "certainty") — **Asphalia**.

Changeling. Puttenham's term for **Hypallage**.

Characterismus (cha rac ter IS mus; G. "marking with a distinctive sign") — **Notatio**.
   Description of the body or mind; a type of **Enargia**. See **Effictio** for an example.

Charientismus (cha ri en TIS mus; G. "wit, graceful jest") — **Privie Nippe**.
   Type of **Irony**; clothing a disagreeable sense with agreeable expressions; soothing over a difficulty, or turning aside antagonism with a joke:

> *King.* Have you heard the argument? Is there no offense in't?
> *Hamlet.* No, no, they do but jest, poison in jest; no offense i' the world.
> (*Hamlet*, III, ii)

Robert Redford on the place whence he derived his living: "If you stay in Beverly Hills too long, you become a Mercedes."

Chiasmus (chi AS mus; G. "crossing") — **Commutatio**.
   The ABBA pattern of mirror inversion. So an exasperated university president remarks: "Anyone who thinks he has a solution does not comprehend the problem and anyone who comprehends the problem does not have a solution." The term is derived from the Greek letter X (chi) whose shape, if the two halves of the construction are rendered in separate verses, it resembles:

The figure has been popular in advertising. A breakfast cereal warns us: "The question isn't whether Grape Nuts are good enough for you, it's whether you are good enough for Grape Nuts." And the Mark Cross leather shop, when they were still purveyors to the horsey rich, bragged: "Everything for the horse except the rider, and everything for the rider except the horse." Knut Rockne's famous instance was popularized by John Dean during the Watergate scandal: "When the going gets tough, the tough get going."
   Chiasmus seems to set up a natural internal dynamic that draws the parts closer together, as if the second element wanted to flip over and back over the first, condensing the assertion back toward the compression of **Oxymoron** and **Pun**. The ABBA form seems to exhaust the possibilities of argument, as when Samuel Johnson destroyed an aspiring author with, "Your manuscript is both good and original; but the part that is good is not original, and the part that is original is not good."

See also **Antimetabole.**

Chleuasmos (chleu AS mos; G. "mockery, irony") — **Epicertomesis.**
A sarcastic reply that mocks an opponent and leaves him no answer.

> *Don Juan* (placidly) . . . Yes: a funeral was always a festivity in black,
> especially the funeral of a relative. At all events, family ties are rarely
> kept up here [in Hell]. Your father is quite accustomed to this: he will
> not expect any devotion from you.
> *Ana.* Wretch: I wore mourning for him all my life.
> *Don Juan.* Yes: it became you.
>
> (Shaw, *Man and Superman,* Act III)

Chorographia (cho ro GRA phi a; G. "description of a country").
Description of a nation; a type of **Enargia**. A description of England:

> This royal throne of kings, this scepter'd isle,
> This earth of majesty, this seat of Mars,
> This other Eden, demi-paradise,
> This fortress built by Nature for herself
> Against infection and the hand of war,
> This happy breed of men, this little world,
> This precious stone set in the silver sea,
> Which serves it in the office of a wall
> Or as a moat defensive to a house,
> Against the envy of less happier lands
> This blessed plot, this earth, this realm, this England. . . .
>
> (*Richard II*, II, i)

A description of America:

> The American people, taking one thing with another, constitute the
> most timorous, sniveling, poltroonish, ignominious mob of serfs and
> goose-steppers ever gathered under one flag in Christendom since the
> end of the Middle Ages.
>
> (H. L. Mencken)

Chreia (CHREI a; G. rhet. "pregnant sentence or maxim, often illustrated by an anecdote"); alt. sp. **Chria.**
1. A scrap of papyrus from Oxyrhynchus defines a chreia as "a concise and praiseworthy reminiscence about some character." A full modern definition: "a saying or action that is expressed concisely, attributed to a character, and regarded as useful for living" (Hock and O'Neil, pp. 9, 26). Some examples:

> "Grief," as Dr. Johnson said, "is a species of idleness."

> Alexander the Macedonian king, on being urged by his friends to
> amass money, said: "but it didn't help even Croesus."

Lord Melbourne once remarked that "Things are coming to a pretty pass when religion is allowed to invade private life."

2. Elaboration of a chreia into a short essay was one of the stock exercises in the **Progymnasmata**. Elaboration was done according to a list of topics: praise of the character, paraphrase of the saying, explanation of the saying, analogy, historical example, and citation of authority. Textbooks today still sometimes recommend that we begin an essay with a proverb or provocative quotation.

Chronographia (chro no GRA phi a; G. "time-writing") — **Counterfait Time**.

A type of **Enargia**. Description of time, as when Romeo says:

> Look love, what envious streaks
> Do lace the severing clouds in yonder East.
> Night's candles are burnt out, and jocund day
> Stands tiptoe on the misty mountain tops.
>
> (*Romeo and Juliet*, III, v)

Ciceronian Style.

The phrase has been used in many ways. It has meant the oratorical style, par excellence; the style that makes maximum use of the **Period**; the full, or amplified, style; the "pure" style of Cicero's orations, which English Humanists aimed to imitate — the touchstone, that is, of classical Latinity; the ornamental, or Asiatic, style, one that uses the "schemes of thought" (see **Trope** and **Asianism**).

Here is an example from the *Philippics* which is Ciceronian in its power, but not in the mannerisms sometimes associated with his name:

> Does Marcus Antonius want peace? Let him lay down his arms, make his petition, ask our pardon [*arma deponat, roget, deprecetur*]. Nobody will give him a fairer hearing than I, though in recommending himself to traitors he has preferred my enmity to my friendship. Obviously no concessions are possible while he is making war. If he petitions us, perhaps there will be something we can concede. But to send envoys to a man on whom twelve days ago you passed a judgment of the weightiest and sternest character is — not levity but, to speak my mind, stark lunacy.
>
> (*Philippics* 5.3, trans. Shackleton Bailey)

See also **Senecan Style**, and **Style** in chapter 2.

Circuitio (cir cu IT i o; L. "going around"); alt. sp. **Circumitio** — **Periphrasis**.

Circumductum (cir cum DUC tum).

Latin equivalent of **Colon**. Sometimes **Macrologia**.

Circumlocution (L. "speaking around") — **Periphrasis**.

Civill Jest. One of Puttenham's terms for **Asteismus**.

Clausula (CLAU su la; L. "conclusion, end").
   1. The conclusion or final cadence of a **Period**.
   2. A logically complete utterance; what we would call a sentence.

Climax (G. "ladder") — **Anabasis**; **Ascensus**; **Gradatio**; **Marching Figure**.
   Mounting by degrees through linked words or phrases, usually of increasing weight and in parallel construction:

> . . . of this wine may be verified that merry induction, that good wine makes good blood, good blood causeth good humours, good humours cause good thoughts, good thoughts bring forth good works, good works carry a man to heaven, ergo good wine carry a man to heaven.
> (Howell, *Familiar Letters*)

See also **Anadiplosis**; **Auxesis**.

Close Conceit. Puttenham's term for **Noema**.

Cohortatio (co hor TA ti o; L. "exhortation").
   Amplification that moves the hearer's indignation, as when the horrors of an enemy's barbarities are dwelt upon to promote patriotism:

> Behind them, behind the armies and fleets of Britain and France, gather a group of shattered states and bludgeoned races: the Czechs, the Poles, the Norwegians, the Danes, the Dutch, the Belgians — upon all of whom the long night of barbarism will descend unbroken even by a star of hope, unless we conquer, as conquer we must — as conquer we shall.
> (Churchill's radio address, "A Solemn Hour")

Colon (G. "limb; clause"; pl. *cola*) — **Circumductum**; **Member**; **Membrum orationis**.
   The second of the three elements in the classical theory of the **Period**, a theory of prose rhythm originated by the Peripatetics. More generally, an independent clause that yet depends on the remainder of the sentence for its meaning. Halfway between a **Comma** and a period in length.

Colors (of rhetoric).
   1. Sometimes, generally, all the figures.
   2. More narrowly, and usually, the **Easy Ornaments** or **Schemes**. Perhaps the colors might be most appropriately defined as a general

term for devices used as superficial decoration (rather than metaphorical creation of meaning) of a discourse. *See also* **Difficult Ornament**.

3. Quintilian uses the Latin word *color* to mean the particular slant or gloss one seeks to give an argument or a sequence of events.

Comma (G. "that which is cut off, e.g., short clause"; pl. *commata*) — **Caesum; Dependens; Incisum**.

1. The first and shortest of the three elements — the other two are **Colon** and **Period** — in the classical theory of prose rhythm originated by the Peripatetics. More generally, in Greek and Latin prose theory, a short phrase or dependent clause.

2. **Hypodiastole**. A brief pause in speaking; the punctuation to mark such a pause in reading.

Commemoratio (com me mo RA ti o; L. "a calling to mind, mentioning") — **Apomnemonysis**.

Commendatio (com men DA ti o) — **Encomium**.

Commentatio (com men TA ti o; L. "study; careful preparation") — **Enthymeme**.

Commentum (com MEN tum) — **Enthymeme**.

Commiseratio (com mi se RA ti o; L. "a part of an oration intended to excite compassion") — **Conquestio; Oictos**.

Evoking pity in the audience. Several Latin words (*commiseratio, conquestio, lamentatio, misericordia*) and two Greek ones (*eleos* and *oiktos*) have been used to describe the evocation of pity in general and, in particular, to denote that part of the **Peroration**, the closing section of the oration, which seeks to evoke pity and sympathy for one's case. The appeal to pity is made "by the use of 'commonplaces' which set forth the power of fortune over all men and the weakness of the human race. When such a passage is delivered gravely and sententiously, the spirit of man is greatly abased and prepared for pity" (*De inventione*, I.liv.106). Both the *Ad Herennium* and *De inventione* warn that the appeal to pity should be brief, for "nothing dries more quickly than a tear."

See also **Indignatio**.

Commonplaces — **Koinoi topoi; Loci communes**. *See* chapter 2 at **Invention: The commonplaces**.

Commoratio (com mo RA ti o; L. "lingering") — **Abode**.

Emphasizing a strong point by repeating it several times in different words: ". . . expelled, thrust out, banished, and cast away from the city" (Peacham).

Communio (com MU ni o) — **Synonymia.**

Commutatio (com mu TA ti o; L. "change, interchange") — **Antimetabole; Chiasmus.**

Compar (COM par; L. "like, equal") — **Isocolon.**

Comparison — **Comparatio.**
Comparison in the general sense; it can be figure or argument: "The simple inherit folly: but the prudent are crowned with knowledge" (Proverbs 14:18).
See also **Syncrisis.**

Compensatio (com pen SA ti o; L. "weighing, balancing").
1. **Antisagoge.**
2. **Antanagoge.**

Complexio (com PLEX i o; L. "combination, connection") — **Symploce.**

Composition (L. "putting together").
Sometimes used in rhetoric as a general term for word arrangement. The Greek equivalent term is *synthesis*, the Latin *compositio*.

Compound Proposition.
One that contains two elements.

Comprehensio (L. "seizing with the hands") — **Period.**

Comprobatio (com pro BA ti o; L. "approval") — **Conciliatio.**
Complimenting one's judges or hearers to win their confidence. So Northumberland to the future Henry IV:

> Believe me, noble lord,
> I am a stranger here in Gloucestershire. . . .
> And yet your fair discourse hath been as sugar,
> Making the hard way sweet and delectable.
> > (*Richard II*, II, iii)

Concessio (con CES si o; L. "allowing, granting") — **Epitrope; Permissio.**
The speaker concedes a point, either to hurt the adversary directly or to prepare for a more important argument:

Falstaff. Boy, tell him I am deaf.
Page. You must speak louder. My master is deaf.
Justice. I am sure he is, to the hearing of anything good.

(*2 Henry IV*, I, ii)

See also **Synchoresis.**

Conciliatio (con ci li A ti o; L. "making friendly, winning over").
1. **Comprobatio.**
2. **Euphemismus (2).**

Conclusion (L. *conclusio*, "shutting up, closing").
1. **Peroration.**
2. **Period.**
3. General sense: a brief summary.

Conductio (con DUC ti o; L. "bringing together") — **Congeries.**

Conduplicatio (con du pli CA ti o; L. "doubling, repetition").
Repetition of a word or words in succeeding clauses, (1) for amplification or emphasis: "You are promoting riots, Gracchus, yes, civil and internal riots"; or (2) to express emotion: "You were not moved when his mother embraced your knees? You were not moved?" (*Ad Herennium*, IV.xxviii.38).

Conexio (co NEX i o; L. "binding together, close union") — **Ploce.**

Conexum (co NEX um) — **Symploce.**

Confessio — **Paromologia.**

Confirmation (L. *confirmatio*) — **Proof.**

Conformatio (con for MA ti o; L. "form, configuration") — **Prosopopoeia.**

Confusio (con FU si o; L. "confusion") — **Synchisis.**

Confutation (L. *confutatio*) — **Refutation.**

Congeries (CON ge ries; L. "heap, pile") — **Conductio; Frequentatio; Heaping Figure; Symphoresis; Synathroesmus.**
Word heaps; when "we lay on such [a] load and so go to it by heaps, as if we would win the game by multitude of words and speeches, not all of one but of divers matter and sense, . . . as he that said

> To muse in mind how faire, how wise, how good,
> How brave, how free, how courteous and how true,
> My Lady is doth but inflame my blood."
>
> (Puttenham, p. 236)

> O flittring Flockes of grisly ghostes that sit in silent seat
> O ougsome Bugges, O Goblins grym of Hell I you intreat:
> O lowring Chaos dungeon blynde, and dreadful darkened pit. . . .
>
> (Seneca's *Medea*, trans. John Studley)

See also **Accumulatio; Systrophe.**

Conglobatio (con glo BA ti o; L. "heaping together") — **Systrophe.**

Conjunctio (con JUNC ti o; L. "joining together").
Clauses or phrases expressing similar ideas are held together by placing the verb between them: "Either with disease physical beauty fades, or with age" (*Ad Herennium*, IV.xxvii.38). See **Zeugma.**

Conquestio (con QUES ti o; L. "a violent complaining or bewailing") — **Commiseratio.**

Consenting Close. Puttenham's term for **Epiphonema.**

Consolatio (con so LA ti o; L. "consoling, comforting") — **Paramythia.**
Consoling one who grieves; a stylized letter or essay of condolence.

Consonance.
Resemblance of stressed consonant-sounds where the associated vowels differ. So Churchill said that Asquith "reigns supine, sodden and supreme." The term has also been taken to mean a kind of reverse **Alliteration**, in which terminal rather than initial consonants are repeated. An example might be this passage from Thomas Campion's *A Book of Ayres*:

> When thou must home to shades of underground,
> And there arriv'd, a new admired guest,
> The beauteous spirits do ingirt thee round.

Constantia (con STAN ti a; L. "steadiness, firmness") — **Eustathia.**

Constitutio (con sti TU ti o) — **Issue.**

Consummatio (con sum MA ti o; L. "summing up") — **Diallage.**

Contentio (con TEN ti o; L. "contest, strife; comparison, contrast").

1. **Antithesis.**
2. **Antistasis.**

Continuatio (con ti nu A ti o; L. "connection, continuation") —
Period.

Contractio (con TRAC ti o; L. "drawing together; shortening") —
Systole.

Contradictories.
   Two mutually exclusive **Propositions**: they cannot *both* be true;
they cannot *both* be false:

   All judges are lawyers.
   Some judges are not lawyers.

Contraposition — **Antithesis.**

Contraries.
   Two **Propositions** that cannot both be true, though they may both
be false:

   All policemen are honest.
   No policeman is honest.

Contrarium (con TRA ri um) — **Enantiosis.**
   One of two opposite statements is used to prove the other: "Now
how should you expect one who has ever been hostile to his own
interests to be friendly to another's?" (*Ad Herennium*, IV.xviii.25).

Controversia (con tro VER si a).
   In Roman oratorical training, a mock lawcourt oration, often on an
impossibly intricate situation which taxed the student's wit and
imagination. A favorite subject, for example, was the conflict between the letter and the intent of the law. The controversia came
after training in the suasoria. Like all other rehearsal-orations, these
often employed an impersonation or speech in character (**Prosopopoeia**).
   See also **Declamatio; Progymnasmata; Suasoria.**

Conversio (con VER si o; L. "turning around"); alt. sp. **Conversum** — **Antistrophe (1).**

Coople Clause. Puttenham's term for **Polysyndeton.**

Copia (CO pi a; L. "abundance").

Expansive richness of utterance as an educational technique and stylistic goal. (Quintilian's phrase is *copia rerum ac verborum*.) The great monument to this ambition is Erasmus's *De copia*, where a stock of standard variations is offered for a stock of standard themes. As variations on the commonplace of brevity, "in short," for example, Erasmus offers: "to put it briefly," "finally, in short," "in brief," "to say once and for all," "to define in a word," "why keep you with much talk," "why more?" and several others (see *Collected Works of Erasmus*, vol. 23, pp. xxxv ff.; vol. 24 passim).

See also **Amplificatio**.

Copulatio (co pu LA ti o; L. "coupling, joining") — **Ploce**.

Correctio (cor REC ti o; L. "making straight, setting right").

1. **Diorismus; Epanorthosis; Epidiorthosis; Epitimesis.** Correction of a word or phrase used previously: "Call it not patience, Gaunt, it is despair" (*Richard II*, I, ii). Peacham (following Quintilian quoting Cicero [Q. IX.i.30]) postulates two kinds:

(a) correcting the word before it is uttered:

> We have brought here before you, Judges . . . not a thief but a violent robber, not an adulterer, but a breaker of all chastity . . .
>
> > (Cicero against Verres)

(b) correcting the word after it is uttered:

> Your brother, no, no brother, yet the son
> (Yet not the son, I will not call him son)
> Of him I was about to call his father . . .
>
> > (*As You Like It*, II, iii).

See also **Metanoia**.

2. **Diorthosis; Praecedens correctio; Prodiorthosis.** Preparing the way for saying something the speaker knows will be unpleasant to his auditors:

> I will begin by saying what everybody would like to ignore or forget but which must nevertheless be stated, namely, that we have sustained a total and unmitigated defeat, and that France has suffered even more than we have.
>
> > (Churchill, on the Munich Agreement)

Counterchange. Puttenham's term for **Antimetabole**.

Counterfait Action. Puttenham's term for **Pragmatographia**.

Counterfait Countenance. Puttenham's term for **Prosopographia**.

Counterfait in Personation. Puttenham's term for **Prosopopoeia**.

Counterfait Place. Puttenham's term for **Topographia.**

Counterfait Representation. Puttenham's term for **Hypotyposis;** *see* **Enargia.**

Counterfait Time. Puttenham's term for **Chronographia.**

Counterturne. Puttenham's term for **Antistrophe (1).**

Crocodilinae (cro co DI li nae) — **Crocodilities.**
A kind of **Dilemma.**

> A crocodile, having seized a woman's son, said that he would restore him, if she would tell him the truth. She replied, "You will not restore him." Was it the crocodile's duty to give him up?
>
> (Quintilian, I.x.5; p. 162 n. 2)

See also **Ceratin.**

Crosse-Couple. Puttenham's term for **Synoeciosis.**

Cuckowspell. Puttenham's term for **Epizeuxis.**

Cumulatio (cu mu LA ti o; L. "forming into a heap") — **Soraismus.**

Curry Favell. Puttenham's term for **Paradiastole.**
"Curry-favell" once meant "a flatterer," whence our corrupted version, "to curry favor."

Cursus (CUR sus).
"The cadence or *cursus* (clausula) is a special form of prose rhythm. It was invented by the Greek orators and was, originally, a kind of punctuation for oral delivery, marking the end of a clause or sentence" (*Princeton Encyclopedia of Poetry and Poetics*, p. 666; this entry contains a useful brief bibliography). In the Middle Ages, the theory came to describe patterns of stress rather than syllable length. "According to medieval theory, the *cursus* was used at the ends of the *commata, cola,* and *periodus* (or *conclusio*), the parts, large or small, of which a rhetorical period is constructed. In other words it was a conventional way of giving a beautiful flow at the end of a rhetorical unit" (Croll, *Style, Rhetoric, and Rhythm,* p. 306). There were three basic patterns or runs: *cursus planus, cursus tardus,* and *cursus velox.* In metrical terms, the *planus,* or even run, consisted of a dactyl and a trochee; the *tardus,* or slow run, of two dactyls; the *velox,* or quick run, of a dactyl and two trochees. The stressed equivalents may be represented by, respectively, "háppily márried," "cómpany pólicy," and "líberal edúcátion."

Curt Style — Senecan Style.

Cutted Comma. Puttenham's term for **Brachylogia.**

Declamatio (de cla MA ti o).

The elaborately ornamented and rehearsed speech on a fictional situation or hypothetical lawsuit which formed a central part of Roman rhetorical discipline. Fictional rehearsal speeches must be as old as rhetoric itself, of course; Greek **Progymnasmata** were smaller-scale exercises of the same sort, and they were followed by **Hypotheses,** full-scale rehearsal speeches for assembly and lawcourt. And the various modes of rehearsal orations lasted until Newtonian science called the whole rhetorical paideia into doubt. *Declamation* is as good a word as any for the genre as a whole, and we need such a word right now, when developments in the arts, in electronic text, and in educational thinking have given new life to the idea of such a rehearsal reality.

Roman declamation, according to Bonner's excellent monograph of that name, began as a voice-training exercise. After learning to raise and strengthen the voice (*anaphonesis*), the student would try out different voice-styles to fit different verbal styles and occasions. The range of imposture extended even further, as the student learned to impersonate historical and mythological characters. Such exercises were very popular in Rome and were practiced by men such as Cicero throughout adult life. They were also turned into occasions for what the Elizabethans called "tearing a cat," ranting for the fun of it, and thus got a bad name from which they have yet to recover. Yet, however abused, declamation offered a much broader education than we customarily accord it: not only in history and mythology, law and political science, but in psychology, sociology (what we might today call *role theory*, for example), and, above all, in *decorum*, the appropriate adjustment to social situations of all sorts. Declamation provided what we might call a *centrifugal* educational technique, a single central (we would say *interdisciplinary*) exercise out of which training in a number of disciplines was spun. The practice of declamation provided, that is, a model for a core-curriculum in miniature.

Declamations combined theory and practice in a way very congenial not only to the present educational temper but to the current postmodern climate in the arts, for they have obvious affinities to what we customarily call *happenings* or *participatory drama*. Occupying the same "factional" ("factual" + "fictional") ground, they invite precisely the heightened self-consciousness about ordinary behavior as intrinsically "artistic" that informs much postmodern visual and behavioral art. It is perfectly appropriate, for example, to analyze a work of participatory art like Christo Javacheff's *Running Fence* as a classical declamation. (Indeed, I have done so myself in an essay called "The Extraordinary Convergence.")

Technology as well as art has revived declamation as an educational technique. Multimedia educational systems controlled by hypertext computer programs can provide today much the same kind of centrifugal interdisciplinary training. The ubiquitous use of computer simulations in all fields of inquiry represents a return of what we might call *declamatory reality* and the educational techniques which go with it. Because they carry their "prerequisites" with them, such centrifugal declamations fit far more easily into the discontinuous university curriculum of the present day than customary linear artifacts. They may provide the framework, in an unlooked-for historical corner, for a new coherent liberal arts curriculum. (For a perceptive discussion of the expansive powers of declamatory training, see Bonner's *Education in Ancient Rome*, pp. 277ff.)

See also **Controversia; Suasoria.**

Declinatio (de cli NA ti o; L. "turning away").
   A digression.

Decorum (L. "propriety") — **To prepon.**
   As a rhetorical concept, the idea advanced in Aristotle's *Rhetoric*, and developed by Cicero, Quintilian and others, that style should suit subject, audience, speaker and occasion. No idea was more carefully worked out in rhetorical theory nor more universally acclaimed; everyone writing about rhetoric touches on it in one way or another. And from Horace — really from Aristotle — onward it forms a major theme of literary criticism as well. (For a detailed discussion and list of citations, see D'Alton, *Roman Literary Theory and Criticism*, pp. 116ff.)

   In spite of its obviousness, and venerability, the idea of decorum could use some rethinking. We might notice, for example, that decorum as a stylistic criterion finally locates itself entirely in the beholder and not the speech or text. No textual pattern per se is decorous or not. The final criterion for excess, *in*decorum, is the stylistic self-consciousness induced by the text or social situation. We know decorum is present when we don't notice it, and vice versa. Decorum is a gestalt established in the perceiving intelligence. Thus the need for it, and the criteria for it, can attain universal agreement and allegiance, and yet the concept itself remain without specifiable content.

   The number of stylistic and behavioral variables such a judgment must take into account leave the rules which are said to inform it far

behind. It becomes an intuitive judgment of the sort a modern phe-
nomenologist might examine, dependent on deep patterns of what
Michael Polanyi would call "tacit knowledge." It thus becomes —
and clearly was for classical education — not only a rhetorical criterion but a general test of basic acculturation. To know how to establish the "decorum" of a particular occasion meant that you had,
as a child or a foreigner might, learned to find your footing in that
culture. I've taken the phrase "find your footing" from Clifford
Geertz, a cultural anthropologist who locates the center of anthropology in something not too different from classical *decorum*.

From the perspective of postmodern thought, one can also see
more clearly that decorum is a *creative* as well as a *pious* concept, that
it *creates* the social reality which it reflects. Decorum, not to put too
fine an edge on it, amounts to a pious fraud, the "social trick" par
excellence. We create, with maximum self-consciousness and according to precise rules, an intricate structure of stylistic forces balanced carefully as to perceiver and perceived, and then agree to
forget that we have created it and to pretend that it is nature itself
we are engaging with. Rhetorical theory has spent endless time discussing how to adjust utterance to this preexistent social reality
without reflecting on how that reality has been *constituted* by the
idea of decorum. Like the human visual system, rhetorical decorum
is a bag of tricks which constitutes for us a world that it then presents as "just out there" awaiting our passive reception.

Further, one might even think of decorum as the origin of, and
basis for, what we usually call "common sense" or "reasonability."
Richard Harvey Brown has "reformulated" reason along these lines
in a brilliant essay, "Reason as Rhetorical: On Relations among Epistemology, Discourse, and Practice," where he argues for a "reason"
which seems to me isomorphic with the "decorum" of classical rhetoric.

With *decorum*, as so often in current thought, the basic ideas of
classical rhetoric have found new life and further development in
disciplines other than the study of formal rhetoric.

See also **Vices of Language**.

Deesis (de E sis; G. "entreaty"); alt. sp. **Deisis — Obsecratio; Obtestatio**.

Vehement supplication either of the gods or of men:

> O God of battles, steel my soldiers' hearts! . . .
>   Not today, O Lord
> Oh, not today, think not upon the fault
> My father made in compassing the crown!
>
>   (*Henry V*, IV, i)

See also **Deinosis; Ecphonesis.**

Default. Puttenham's term for **Ellipsis.**

Definer by Difference. Puttenham's term for **Horismus.**

Definiendum (de fi ni EN dum).
The term to be defined in a **Definition.**

Definiens (de FI ni ens).
The defining terms or categories in a **Definition**; they are usually called the genus term and the species term. Thus man (**Definiendum**) is defined by calling him "a rational (species) animal (genus)."

Definitio (de fi NI ti o; L. "boundary, limitation") — **Horismus.**

Definition.
Its two parts are **Definiens,** the defining term, and **Definiendum,** the term to be defined. Some common traditional types:

(1) *prescriptive* — insistence that a certain definition is the only one acceptable
(2) *stipulative* — an agreement that one of several meanings will be intended for purposes of a single debate or discourse
(3) *lexical* — as in a dictionary
(4) *negative* — defining something by proving what it is not
(5) *likeness/difference*
(6) *classificatory* — assigning the object to the smallest possible class. A classifying definition based on internal qualities is sometimes called "essential"; one based on externals, "descriptive." It is difficult, sometimes, to distinguish between them.

An adequate definition of "definition," one that would satisfactorily compensate for the deficiencies of the traditional ones, is beyond the scope of this list and of its compiler. As a partial expansion of the traditional categories just given, though, perhaps the by now old warning of Ogden and Richards (*The Meaning of Meaning,* pp. 109ff.) may be suggestive:

> There is at present no theory of Definition capable of practical application under normal circumstances. The traditional theory, in so far as it has not been lost in the barren subtleties of Genus and Differentia, and in the confusion due to the term 'Connotation,' has made little progress — chiefly on account of the barbarous superstitions about language which have gathered on the confines of logic from the earliest times. Four difficulties have stood in the way and must first be removed. (pp. 109–110)

The first of these difficulties is this: do we define words or things? The answer suggested would seem to be that we define words by suggesting synonyms, things by enumerating their properties and contrasting those properties with the properties of other things. The second of the difficulties is really a caution not to confuse the two kinds of definition distinguished in the first. The third insists that "all definitions are essentially ad hoc." "They are," these authors explain, "relevant to some purpose or situation, and consequently are applicable only over a restricted field or 'universe of discourse.'" Taken out of the field of discourse for which it was intended, the definition becomes a metaphor ("energy" for the physicist, and "energy" or the lack of it, as the schoolmaster sees it in his pupils, is the example used). The fourth difficulty is "the problem of 'intensive' as opposed to 'extensive' definition which comes to a head with the use of the terms 'denote' and 'connote'":

> . . . two symbols may be said to have the same connotation when they symbolize the same reference. An intensive or connotative definition will be one which involves no change in those characters of a referent in virtue of which it forms a context with its original sign. In an extensive definition there may be such a change. In other words when we define intensively we keep to the same sign-situation for definiendum and definiens; when we define extensively this may be changed. (pp. 111–112)

Dehortatio (de hor TA ti o).
Dissuasion; advice to the contrary:

> You are too sensible a girl, Lizzy, to fall in love merely because you are warned against it; and, therefore, I am not afraid of speaking openly. Seriously, I would have you be on your guard. Do not involve yourself, or endeavour to involve him in an affection which the want of fortune would make so very imprudent.
>
> *(Pride and Prejudice)*

Deinosis (DEI no sis; G. "exaggeration; indignation"); alt. sp. **Donysis — Indignatio.**

Deisis — Deesis.

Deliberatio (de li be RA ti o).
Evaluating possible courses of action; weighing arguments. So Shakespeare's Tarquin pauses before raping Lucrece:

> What win I if I gain the thing I seek?
> A dream, a breath, a froth of fleeting joy.
> Who buys a minute's mirth to wail a week?
> Or sells eternity to get a toy?

For one sweet grape who will the vine destroy?
  Or what fond beggar, but to touch the crown,
  Would with the sceptre straight be stroken down? . . .
                            (*The Rape of Lucrece*, 211ff.)

Deliberative Rhetoric. *See* **Rhetoric: The three branches** in chapter 2.

Delivery — **Hypocrisis**.
  The last of the traditional five parts of rhetoric, that which teaches control of voice, effective gesture, pose. See discussion in chapter 2.

Demonstratio (de mon STRA ti o; L. "pointing out, showing") — **Enargia**.
  Vivid description. "It is Ocular Demonstration when an event is so described in words that the business seems to be enacted and the subject to pass vividly before our eyes [*ante oculos*]" (*Ad Herennium*, IV.lv.68).

Dendrographia.
  Description of trees. A type of **Enargia**. So Joyce Kilmer:

I think that I shall never see
A poem as lovely as a tree.
A tree whose hungry mouth is prest
Against the sweet earth's flowing breast, . . .

Denominatio (de no mi NA ti o) — **Metonymy**.

Denumeratio (de nu me RA ti o; L. "enumeration") — **Dinumeratio**.

Denying the Antecedent (Fallacy of).
  To deny the antecedent, or first part, of a **Hypothetical Proposition**:

If John ran a four-minute mile he is a fast miler.
John did not run a four-minute mile.
Therefore, John is not a fast miler.

Opposite of **Affirming the Consequent**.

Dependens (de PEN dens; L. "hanging from") — **Comma**.

Descriptio (de SCRIP ti o) — **Pragmatographia**.

Diacope (di A co pe; G. "cleft, gash").
  1. Repetition of a word with one or a few words in between: "My heart is fixed, O God, my heart is fixed" (Peacham). Used to express

strong emotion. *See also* **Epizeuxis** (repetition without interruption, another vehement emphasizer) and **Ploce**.

2. **Tmesis**. Separation of the elements of a compound word by another word or words: "West — by God — Virginia"; "how dearly ever parted" (*Troilus and Cressida*, III, iii) for "however dearly parted."

Diaeresis (di AE re sis; G. "dividing, division"); alt. sp. **Dieresis** — **Partitio**.

1. **Dinumeratio (1)**. Dividing the genus into species in order to amplify:

> The king-becoming graces,
> As justice, verity, temp'rance, stableness,
> Bounty, perseverance, mercy, lowliness,
> Devotion, patience, courage, fortitude.

(Macbeth, IV, iii)

2. Dividing one syllable into two, especially by pronouncing two adjacent vowels; also the twin dots used above a letter to indicate such a pronunciation, as in "preëminent." The opposite of **Synaeresis**.

3. In prosody: the division made in a line or a verse when the end of a foot coincides with the end of a word.

Dialectic.

Like **Rhetoric**, a complex and vexed term. I can offer here only the general Platonic view and a tentative rejoinder. Dialectic is the famous "Socratic Method" of one-on-one question and answer. Plato's Socrates usually presents it as an interactive method of argumentation aiming at truth, as against the uninterrupted and *non*interactive speech of an orator, which aims only to bamboozle the audience. Since dialectic addresses an audience of one, it spurns those techniques of emotional appeal needed when one is addressing a large crowd. (When Somerset Maugham wrote that the intelligence quotient of a theater audience was always much lower than that of a single reader, even of the same play, it was this difference that he sought to remark.) Quintilian, like many others, quotes Zeno's famous comparison of dialectic to a closed fist and rhetoric to an open hand.

Dialectic argument thus has come to mean, in a loose sense, logical or philosophical argument, as against the emotional, crowd-pleasing persuasion of rhetoric. Dialectic is "good" argument, serious one-on-one argument that pursues truth rather than trying to mislead people. Almost, if you like, *academic* argument. And if, as one student of Plato has said, dialectic in Plato tends to mean "the ideal method of argument, *whatever* that may be," still, we all know the difference between serious argument and "mere rhetoric" when we see them. "Rhetoric" is what our opponents use. So much for what one might call "the definition according to Platonic rumor."

A stricter and more detailed argument than we have room for here would take issue with the "loose sense" sketched in the previous paragraph. Dialectic, for Plato, did not strictly pursue "truth" but tried to refine "opinion" by means of ever more explicit definitions. And for Aristotle, logic dealt with truth but dialectic, like rhetoric, still handled opinions. As these terms have been used in the broad marketplace of Western ideas, however, rhetoric and non-interactive oratory have formed one group, and lead to forming *opinion*, while dialectic and logic have formed a second group, and are commonly thought to pursue *truth*.

Plato argued for dialectic as a *philosophical* method as against the *rhetorical* methods of the Sophists. But G. B. Kerferd has recently argued that dialectic was originally a *sophistic* method: "the sophists did develop a method of argument by question and answer. This, I would say, is the only possible view based on the evidence that we have" (*The Sophistic Movement*, p. 33). If dialectic offers as its center the opportunity for opposed points of view to contend, surely this must be seen as part of *rhetoric*'s central assumption, the possibility of real two-sided argument. Plato may have gotten things upside down, as I try to suggest at the end of **Dissoi Logoi**.

Perhaps the largest-scaled contrast between rhetoric and dialectic has been offered by Walter Ong, who presents the difference as one between orality and literacy:

> To a great extent, in the ancient cultures rhetoric was related to dialectic as sound was to sight. This is not to say that rhetoric was not concerned with the clear and distinct, nor that dialectic, as the art of discourse, was not concerned with sound at all. The difference was a polar difference: rhetoric was concerned with what was resonant and closer to the auditory pole; dialectic with what was relatively silent, abstract, and diagrammatic. In this kind of view, the two arts are not the same, but neither are they sharply "distinct" from one another in any readily definable way.
>
> (*Ramus, Method, and the Decay of Dialogue*, p. 280)

Sister Miriam Joseph gives an excellent short summary of the Aristotelian logic/dialectic/rhetoric relationship in *Shakespeare's Use of the Arts of Language*, pp. 18–19.

Diallage (di AL la ge; G. "interchange") — Consummatio.

Bringing several arguments to establish a single point.

Dialogismus (di a log IS mus; G. "debate, discussion") — **Right Reasoner**.

Speaking in another person's character.

> They will say to me, "A Minister of Supply is not necessary, for all is going well." I deny it. "The position is satisfactory." It is not true. "All is proceeding according to plan." We know what that means.
> (Churchill to Parliament on preparations for World War II)

See also **Enargia; Ethopoeia (2); Prosopopoeia; Sermocinatio**.

Dialysis (di A ly sis; G. "separation, dissolution").

1. **Dismembrer**. One argues from a series of disjunctive (compound hypothetical) propositions (e.g., "Either you ran out of gas or you ran out of money") directly to a conclusion. Henry V says before Agincourt:

> If we are mark'd to die, we are enow
> To do our country loss; and if to live,
> The fewer men, the greater share of honour.
> God's will! I pray thee wish not one man more.
> (*Henry V*, IV, iii)

See also **Dilemma (2)**.

2. The *Ad Herennium* calls this figure **Divisio**. A statement of a problem followed by particularization of the alternatives:

> Answer him fair with yea, or nay,
> If it be yea: I shall be fain.
> If it be nay: friends as before.
> (Wyatt)

Dialyton (di A ly ton; G. "dissolved; separated").

1. **Asyndeton**.

2. May also mean — generally — emphasizing a word by setting it off from the rest of the sentence in other ways besides asyndeton.

Diaphora (di A pho ra; G. "dislocation, difference, disagreement").

1. **Ploce**.

2. Repetition of a common word rather than a proper name to signify qualities of, as well as naming, the person: "'What man is there living, that would not have pitied that case if he had been a man'; in the latter place man signifieth humanity, or the pitiful affection that is in man" (Peacham).

Diaporesis (di a po RE sis; G. "perplexity; doubting") — **Aporia**.

Diastole (di A sto le; G. "distinction, separation") — **Ectasis**. Lengthening a syllable or vowel usually short; opposite of **Systole**.

Diasyrmus (di a SYR mus; G. "disparagement, ridicule") —
Elevatio.

Disparagement of opponent's argument through a base similitude. "He fights with leaden daggers; i.e., he has weak arguments" (Peacham).

See also **Apodioxis**.

Diatyposis (di a ty PO sis; G. "vivid description; system").
  1. **Enargia**.
  2. **Informatio; Testamentum**. Recommending useful precepts to someone else (Peacham's definition), as in Polonius's advice to Laertes:

> And these few precepts in thy memory
> Look thou character. Give thy thoughts no tongue,
> Nor any unproportioned thought his act.
> Be thou familiar, but by no means vulgar.
> Those friends thou hast, and their adoption tried,
> Grapple them unto thy soul with hoops of steel . . .
>
> (*Hamlet*, I, iii)

Diazeugma (di a ZEUG ma; G. "disjoining").
  One subject with many verbs:

> He bites his lip and starts;
> Stops on a sudden, looks upon the ground,
> Then lays his finger on his temple; straight
> Springs out into fast gait, then stops again,
> Strikes his breast hard . . .
>
> (*Henry VIII*, III, ii)

An inverted form of **Zeugma**.

Dicaeologia (di cae o LO gi a; G. "plea in defense"); alt. sp.
Dichologia — **Anangeon; Excuse; Necessum**.

Defending one's words or acts with reasonable excuses; excusing by necessity; defending the justice of one's cause as briefly as possible. So the Defendant in a breach of promise suit in Gilbert and Sullivan's *Trial by Jury* pleads:

> Oh, gentlemen, listen, I pray,
>   Though I own that my heart has been ranging,
> Of nature the laws I obey,
>   For nature is constantly changing.

Dictamen (dic TA men) — **Ars dictaminis**.

Dieresis — **Diaeresis**.

Difficult Ornament — Ornatus difficilis.

The distinction between easy and difficult ornaments parallels that often made between **Schemes** and **Tropes**: the easy ornaments were those that involved superficial patterns of sound or arrangement; the hard ornaments involved some real change in meaning, some metaphorical substitution. As with scheme and trope, it is easy to distinguish extremes. **Alliteration** is easy, **Synecdoche** difficult or hard. But distinction is harder with various kinds of **Paronomasia**, for example. Examples of easy ornaments would be various devices of repetition of both letter and word. It may be generally acceptable to say that the easy ornaments were ornaments pure and simple; the difficult ones effected a fundamental change in meaning. The *Rhetorica ad Herennium* lists ten difficult figures: **Allegory, Antonomasia, Catachresis, Hyperbaton, Hyperbole, Metaphor, Metonymy, Onomatopoeia, Periphrasis, Synecdoche.**

See also **Style: The figures** in chapter 2.

Digestion.

An orderly enumeration of the points to be discussed, the implications of a question, etc.

See also **Dinumeratio.**

Digression — Egressio; Excessus; Excursus; Parecbasis; Straggler.

The various terms have both a technical and a general meaning. The technical: a tale, or interpolated anecdote, which follows the **Division** and illustrates or amplifies some point in it. Quintilian thinks the position of the anecdote is not crucial. The general: any digressive tale or interpolation, especially one prepared in advance on a commonplace subject, and inserted at the appropriate time.

See also **Paradiegesis.**

Dilemma (G. "double proposition").

1. General definition: Any technique of argument which offers an opponent a choice, or a series of them, all of which are unacceptable. The counterargument ("taking the dilemma by the horns") is to deny the premise by which choice is restricted to unacceptable alternatives. For example, the boss argues: I will not give you a raise; either it will make you lazy and less efficient, or avaricious and less content. The employee replies: No, it will make me more energetic, because less discontent.

2. Logic: a **Syllogism** in which the major premise is a **Compound Hypothetical Proposition** and the minor a **Disjunctive Proposition**. If the conclusion is a disjunctive proposition, the syllogism is called *complex*; if the conclusion is a **Categorical Proposition**, *simple*. For example, if welfare legislation feeds the people, they will grow lazy;

if it does not feed the people, it will be a failure. It either will or will not feed the people. Therefore, the legislation will either make people lazy or it will be a failure. A dilemma with the minor premise left out makes the figure **Dialysis**.

See also **Ceratin; Crocodilinae.**

Diminutio (di mi NU ti o; L. "decrease, lessening") — **Meiosis.**

Dinumeratio (di nu me RA ti o; L. "enumeration") — **Denumeratio; Enumeratio.**

1. **Diaeresis (1)** — **Eutrepismus; Ordinatio.** Dividing a subject into subheadings; amplifying a general fact or idea by giving all of its details; division of subject into adjuncts, cause into effects, antecedent into consequents.

> How do I love thee? Let me count the ways.
> I love thee to the depth and breadth and height
> My soul can reach, when feeling out of sight
> For the ends of Being and ideal Grace.
> I love thee to the level of everyday's
> Most quiet need, by sun and candlelight.
> I love thee freely, as men strive for Right;
> I love thee purely, as they turn from Praise.
> I love thee with the passion put to use
> In my old griefs, and with my childhood's faith.
> I love thee with a love I seemed to lose
> With my lost saints, — I love thee with the breath,
> Smiles, tears, of all my life! — and, if God choose,
> I shall but love thee better after death.
> (Elizabeth Barrett Browning)

See also **Digestion; Distribution.**

2. **Anacephalaeosis; Anamnesis.** A summary or recapitulation, intended to refresh the hearer's memory.

Further discussion. A tangled cluster of terms surrounds dinumeratio. Let me hazard an "executive summary":

(1) Denumeratio is a misreading/misspelling of dinumeratio. Retire it.

(2) Dinumeratio and enumeratio are synonyms for the same set of patterns.

(3) Two basic meanings, both having to do with subdividing a single subject into subheads, emerge from the tradition: the first describes the act "coming," when one is opening out the matter to be discussed; the second describes it "going," when one is summarizing what one has said by summarizing its parts.

(a) The first or "coming" sense associates the two terms with the **Division**, the stage of an oration where one opens out one's argument. Cicero (*De oratore*, III.liv.207) uses dinumeratio to describe an "enumeration of points." Quintilian, in the long quotation from the *De oratore* in book IX (i.26ff.), picks up and subsumes this meaning.

(b) The second or "going" sense associates the two terms with the **Peroration**, or summing-up stage, of an oration, as the *Ad Herennium* argues: "The Summing Up [*enumeratio*] gathers together and recalls the points we have made" (II.xxx.47).

(4) Both dinumeratio and enumeratio have been used to describe both the "coming" and the "going" meanings, and various synonyms have been associated with both terms in both meanings.

Diorismus (di or IS mus; G. "distinction, definition") — **Correctio (1)**.

Diorthosis (di or THO sis; G. "making straight") — **Correctio (2)**.

Director. Puttenham's term for Greek **Gnome**. The synonymous Latin **Sententia** he Englishes as **Sage Sayer**.

Dirimens copulatio (DI ri mens   co pu LA ti o; L. "a joining together that interrupts").

A wonderfully lascivious-sounding but obscure, nonclassical, and probably dispensable term. It sounds as if it should be a synonym for *coitus interruptus* but really seems to mean, as Peacham uses it, a series of minus/plus, not-only/but-also comparisons: "When we bring forth one sentence, with an exception before it, and immediately join another after it, that seemeth greater." Peacham quotes, as an example, Cicero thanking the Roman people after his return from exile: "You have not only taken away my calamity, but also seem to augment my dignity." And St. Paul:

> For he is the minister of God to thee for good. But if thou do that which is evil, be afraid; for he beareth not the sword in vain: for he is the minister of God, a revenger to execute wrath upon him that doeth evil. Wherefore ye must needs be subject, not only for wrath, but also for conscience sake.
>
> (Romans 13:4–5)

If I understand the term, this is also an example:

> What of that? It is not death that matters, but the fear of death. It is not killing and dying that degrades us, but base living.
>
> (Shaw, *Man and Superman*, Act III)

See **Auxesis** for fuller discussion, and also **Progressio**.

Disabler. Puttenham's term for **Meiosis**.

Disdainefull. Puttenham's term for **Insultatio**.

Disjunctio (dis JUNC ti o; L. "separation").
1. Use of different verbs to express similar ideas in successive clauses. The *Ad Herennium* gives this example: "By the Roman people, Numantia was destroyed, Carthage razed, Corinth demolished, Fregellae overthrown." The focus of disjunctio is on the relation of the similarly positioned verbs (here, in the Latin, *delevit, sustulit, disiecit, evertit*). *See also* **Hypozeuxis; Zeugma**.
2. Logic: the relation between two or more alternatives of a **Disjunctive Proposition**.

Disjunctive Proposition (Disjunction).

A **Proposition** composed of two propositions, one of which must be true and the other of which sometimes may be true: "Either his car broke down or he forgot our appointment."

Disjunctive (or Alternative) Syllogism.

One containing a disjunctive proposition (see preceding entry).

Dismembrer. Puttenham's term for **Dialysis**.

Dispositio (dis po SI ti o) — **Arrangement**.

Dissimilitude (L. "unlikeness") — **Syncrisis**.

Dissimulatio (dis si mu LA ti o; L. "dissembling, concealment") — **Irony**.

Dissoi logoi (DIS soi LO goi; G. "double arguments").
So schooled are we in the truism that every argument has two sides that it comes as a surprise to find the Greeks *inventing* two-sided argument: it was a pedagogical and philosophical technique called *dissoi logoi*, the art of constructing opposing arguments for a single question. The name comes from an anonymous sophistic treatise of ca. 4th century B.C. "The essential feature," Kerferd writes, "was not simply the occurrence of opposing arguments but the fact that both opposing arguments could be expressed by a single speaker, as it were *within* a single complex argument" (*The Sophistic Movement*, p. 84). Such an argumentative procedure could

force any question into an **Aporia** by pointing out that each side was true within the terms that it had chosen to develop the argument. Both sides depended, ultimately, on language and its imperfect correspondence to the "outside world," whatever one might think that world to be. A form of this analytical technique has recently been revived under the name of "Deconstruction." Or, the parties could agree to accept one position as superior, even though it manifestly depended on human argument and not Divine Truth. It is from this accommodation to antithetical structure that Anglo-Saxon jurisprudence descends: we arrange social issues into diametrically opposed questions, arrange a dramatic display of their conflict, and (since the law cannot afford aporia as a conclusion to social disputes) accept the jury-audience's verdict as a defining truth, a precedent for future disputation.

This point deserves a closer look. Genuine two-sided argument is not the same thing as finding out the "real" truth by looking at all sides of the question. That procedure, which we normally think of as "philosophical" argument, does not *allow* really two-sided argument. The truth is whole and one — *one-sided* — though we may be forced to use argument to elicit it. Truth, in such a view, is absolute and independent of the world of sense — Plato's Truth. Rhetoric, in contrast, built upon *this* world, not a world of Ideas, and in this world the same thing presents itself in different truths. A mile is longer to a child than to an adult runner. In such a world, two-sided argument allows us to adjudicate, harmonize, these contending views. The formal two-sided procedures of Western jurisprudence are just such a formal, social, invented procedure for dealing with an uncertain world. Again, the jury's verdict may approach the Truth asymptotically — as most of us hope it does — but it can never be more than an interim report from a reality always rendered multiplex through the changing scales of sentient perception, human and other.

This distinction may cast a little light on the perennially paradoxical problem of defining **Dialectic**. Plato, and most philosophers thereafter, have preferred to think of themselves as pursuing, by whatever means, a truth which is finally True, finally *one-sided*. Sometimes those "whatever means" include techniques which look like genuine two-sided argument, but finally are not. The shifting meanings of dialectic may preserve as their center a final allegiance to one-sided argument, however pursued. Rhetoric, on the other hand, is pledged to two-sided argument; that, finally, is its reason for being, the *techne* which Plato refused to accord it. This does not mean that two-sided debate does not aspire to truth, or that it thinks of thought itself as one long hopeless aporia. That kind of existential self-pity has indeed emerged in some modern Deconstructionists, but it had no part in the classical allegiance to genuine two-sided argument.

Rhetoric thus accepts the validity of elenchic interchange in a different spirit from that dramatized in the Platonic dialogues. There really are two sides to the question, rather than Socrates on one side and various stooges allegorizing Error on the other. Thus Plato's Socrates may have got things upside down. It is the philosophical use of dialectic which lacks genuine interaction, which presents argument as essentially a display of one side of the question. In that universe, finally there is only one side.

Two-sided argument in its strong form also helps us to define what verbal "ornamentation" in general really is. If we think that the truth is already known, "one-sided," then all rhetorical figuration is called into question as "ornamental," finally or at least hopefully unnecessary. (Nobody, Aristotle observes in the *Rhetoric*, uses rhetoric to teach geometry.) This is the position which led Bishop Sprat to fulminate against figurative language in the *History of the Royal Society of London* ("Who can behold, without indignation, how many mists and uncertainties, these specious *Tropes* and *Figures* have brought on our Knowledge?"). But if truth is established through real two-sided argument, then the tropes and figures become not specious but potentially, at least, truth-telling — not, that is, "ornamental" at all.

See also **Elenchus**.

Dissolutio (dis so LU ti o) — **Asyndeton**.

Distinctio (dis TINC ti o).
Explicit reference to various meanings of a word, thereby removing ambiguities: "Remove all scruples with distinction, as being charged that you have brought very light reasons, you may answer, if by *light* you mean *clear*, I am glad you do see them; if by light you mean *of no weight*, I am sorry you do not feel them" (Hoskyns).

Distributed Term (of a **Syllogism**).
Refers to all members of a class designated by a term.

Distribution — **Distributor; Divisio; Merismus.**
Dividing the whole into its parts.

> Two things he feared, but the third was death;
> That fierce young mans vnruly maistery;
> His money, which he lov'd as liuing breath;

> And his faire wife, whom honest long he kept vneath.
>
> (Spenser, *Faerie Queene*, III, x, 2)

See also **Dinumeratio.**

Divisio (di VI si o).
1. Division into kinds or classes. "I pass with relief from the tossing sea of Cause and Theory to the firm ground of Result and Fact" (Churchill, *The Story of the Malakand Field Force*). *See also* **Dialysis (2); Dinumeratio.**
2. **Division.**

Division; alt. sp. **Divisio — Partitio; Proposition.**
The third part of a six-part classical oration. It set forth points stipulated (agreed on by both sides) and points to be contested. See **Arrangement: The parts of an oration** in chapter 2. *See also* **Dinumeratio** (*Further discussion*, 3a); **Exposition.**

Domain (of a **Proposition**).
The group of all entities that can serve as the subject of a proposition. Thus, in the proposition "_____ loves Joan," all those who might love Joan are the domain of the proposition. Entities that would render the proposition nonsensical or false are usually excluded from the domain (e.g., "apples" in the example). More largely, we might say that the domain of the argument is that class of objects about which the argument can make a meaningful statement.

Donysis — Deinosis.

Doubler. Puttenham's term for **Ploce.**

Double Supply. Puttenham's term for **Syllepsis.**

Doublet — Epizeuxis.

Doubtfull. Puttenham's term for **Aporia.**

Drie Mock. Puttenham's term for **Irony.**

Dubitatio (du bi TA ti o; L. "wavering in opinion") — **Aporia.**

Duplicatio (du pli CA ti o) — **Anadiplosis.**

Easy Ornament — Ornatus facilis.
Opposite of **Difficult Ornament.**
See also **Style: The figures** in chapter 2.

Eccho Sounde. Puttenham's term for **Epanalepsis.**

Eclipsis — Ellipsis.

Ecphonesis (ec pho NE sis; G. "exclamation"); alt. sp. **Ecpho-nema** — Epecphonesis; Epiphonesis; Exclamatio; Outcrie.
Exclamation expressing emotion. Peacham's examples: "O lamen-table estate! O cursed misery! O wicked impudency! O joy incom-parable! O rare and singular beauty!"
See also **Apostrophe; Paeanismus.**

Ecphrasis (EC phra sis; G. "description").
A self-contained description, often on a commonplace subject, which could be inserted at a fitting place in a discourse. It was one of the exercises of the **Progymnasmata,** and could deal with per-sons, events, times, places, etc. Thus a kind of **Enargia.**

Ectasis (EK ta sis) — **Diastole.**

Effictio (ef FIC ti o; L. "fashioning") — **Blazon.**
Personal description (outward appearance); the head-to-toe (in that order) itemization of a heroine's charms, common in earlier English poetry:

> My Lady's hair is threads of beaten gold,
>   Her front the purest Chrystal eye hath seen:
> Her eyes the brightest stars the heavens hold,
>   Her cheeks red roses such as seld have been:
> Her pretty lips of red vermillion dye,
>   Her hands of ivory the purest white:
> Her blush Aurora, or the morning sky,
>   Her breast displays two silver fountains bright,
> The Spheres her voice, her grace the Graces three,
>   Her body is the Saint that I adore,
> Her smiles and favors sweet as honey be,
>   Her feet fair Thetis praiseth evermore.
> But ah the worst and last is yet behind,
>   For of a Gryphon she doth bear the mind.
>   (Bartholomew Griffin, *Fidessa*, 39)

Egressio (e GRES si o; L. "going out") — **Digression.**

Eicon — Icon.

Eidolopoeia (ei do lo po EI a; G. "formation of [often mental] im-ages").

Presenting a dead person as speaking, or the speech thus assigned.

> But if the cause be not good, the king himself hath a heavy reckoning to make when all those legs and arms and heads, chopped off in a battle, shall join together at the latter day and cry all, "We died at such a place," some swearing, some crying for a surgeon, some upon their wives left poor behind them, some upon the debts they owe, some upon their children rawly left.
>
> (*Henry V*, IV, i)

Eironeia — Irony.

Elenchus (e LEN chus; G. "cross-examining, testing; argument of refutation").

Aggressive argumentative exchange and cross-examination; argument for the fun of argument. Plato's Socrates reenacted a special Platonic version: "[Elenchus] constitutes perhaps the most striking aspect of the behaviour of Socrates. It consists typically of eliciting an answer to a question, such as what is Courage, and then securing assent to further statements which are visibly inconsistent with the answer given to the first question. On rare occasions this leads to something approaching an acceptable modification of the first answer. But far more often the Dialogue closes with the participants in a state of *Aporia*, unable to see any way forward or any escape from the contradictory views in which they are enmeshed" (Kerferd, *The Sophistic Movement*, pp. 65–66).

See also **Dialectic; Dissoi logoi; Rhetoric**.

Elevatio (e le VA ti o; L. rhet. "disparaging") — **Diasyrmus**.

Ellipsis (el LIP sis; G. "defect; omission"); alt. sp. **Eclipsis — Brachylogia (2); Default**.

Omission of a word easily supplied: "And he to England shall along with you" (*Hamlet*, III, iii).

Elocutio (el o CU ti o; L. "utterance, expression") — **Lexis**.

The Latin term for **Style**, the third of the five parts of rhetoric.

See also **Phrasis**.

Emphasis — Significatio.

Enallage (en AL la ge; G. "interchange") — **Exchange**.

Substitution of one case, person, gender, number, tense, mood, part of speech, for another. Word play of this sort was very common in inflected languages like Latin or Greek, which can make changes in case, gender, number, etc. and still easily preserve the root word. As Puttenham said, Greek and Latin had "divers cases, moods, tenses, genders, with variable terminations, by reason whereof, they changed not the very word, but kept the word, and changed the shape . . . only, using one case for another, or tense, or person, or gender, or number, or mood. We, having no such variety of accidents, have little or no use of this figure. They called it *Enallage*" (p. 171).

Other critics before and since, because they wanted English to behave like Latin and Greek, have found a use for this figure and for others (e.g. **Anthimeria; Antiptosis**) which depend for their effect on change of inflection. Renaissance theorists especially were eager to impose inflections, or figures describing them, onto English, just as they tried to impose quantitative classical poetic meters on verse. Thus we confront a confusing cluster of terms whose relationship with each other is far from clear and which, when exemplified in English, often seem either simply mistakes or a looser idiom than we now permit ourselves.

If all figures of language can also be vices (see **Vices of Language**), this cluster seems closer to the border between effect and mistake than most. But the ordinary student will not go far wrong in using enallage as a general term for the whole broad range of substitutions, intentional or not. If intentionality is relevant, one can always mention it.

Sister Miriam Joseph cites, as examples of enallage, as shift in person or case of pronoun, the following Shakespearean examples: "Is she as tall as me?" (*Anthony and Cleopatra*, III, iii); "And hang more praise upon deceased I" (*Sonnet* 72). And she instances use of a singular verb with a plural subject: "Is there not wars? Is there not employment?" (*2 Henry IV*, I, ii). But surely these represent simply a looser usage than ours. And we can think of any subject-verb disagreement as the same thing exactly, though Sister Miriam insists that enallage is "the *deliberate* use of one case, person . . . for another" [emphasis mine]. But what of these examples given by Peacham? "*Gender:* It is a wicked daughter that despises his mother. Wind is loud, she bloweth cold. *Person:* Here he is, what have you to say for him? *for* Here I am."

Alleotheta, Anthimeria, Antiptosis, and **Anthypallage** all belong in this cluster, and the examples usually given of at least the first three seem as often mistakes as intended effects. Alleotheta, like enallage, is a *general* term for substitution of case, gender, number, tense, etc. Peacham makes it the central term and enallage derivative. Anthimeria is a less general term than either, the use of one part of speech for another. Antiptosis substitutes one case for another; here especially the English examples seem forced. Anthyp-allage, as used by Demetrius, has the clearest meaning — a change of grammatical case in order to produce a special poetic effect — but is also the least reproducible in English.

Enallage is sometimes made synonymous with **Permutatio**, fol-lowing a red herring spawned by Quintilian (IX.iii.7), but we should forget this if possible; things are complicated enough. Likewise with Peacham's making **Hendiadys** a kind of anthimeria.

Enantiosis (en an ti O sis; G. "opposition").
1. **Irony.**
2. **Contrarium.**

Enargia (en AR gi a; G. "vividness, distinctness").

A generic term for visually powerful, vivid description which re-creates something or someone, as several theorists say, "before your very eyes." The most representative use of this term which I have found is Dionysius of Halicarnassus's description of Lysias's powers of description (*Critical Essays*, "Lysias," 7). Lysias, Dionysius writes, makes his listener feel that he can "see the actions which are being described going on and that he is meeting face-to-face the characters in the orator's story." Such visual, person-to-person immediacy — the impact we feel, perhaps, in live television at its best — was par-ticularized by the theorists into the terms listed below. It includes:

General synonyms: **Demonstratio; Diatyposis; Hypotyposis** (the main synonym).

Vivid characterization: **Characterismus; Dialogismus; Ethopoeia; Mimesis; Pathopoeia; Prosopopoeia.**

Vivid description: **Anemographia; Chorographia; Chronographia; Dendrographia; Geographia; Hydrographia; Pragmatographia; Prosopographia; Topographia.**

See also **Ecphrasis; Energia.**

Encomium (G. "eulogy"); alt. sp. **Ecomium — Commendatio.**
Praise of a person or thing by extolling inherent qualities.

See also **Comprobatio; Eulogia; Laudatio.**

Endiadis — Hendiadys.

Energia (en er GI a; G. "activity"; rhet. "vigor of style").

A general term for vigor, vividness, energy in expression. Aris-totle uses the term (*Rhetoric*, III, 1411b22ff.) in the course of dis-cussing how to make description vivid by bringing it "before your eyes" (πρὸ ὀμμάτων), a phrase he uses three times in four lines. The general term *energia* has thus since Aristotle retained a sense of visual vividness, of a word or phrase which makes us *see* what is taking place. It came early to overlap with **Enargia**, a term with a somewhat narrower meaning. Quintilian uses energia to mean vigor — everything in writing that is not flat or lifeless — but in a context where he is discussing forming visual pictures (φαντασία *in concipiendis visionibus*, VIII.iii.88–89). Puttenham says enargia delights the ear but energia the mind (III, iii), in which case we have an isomorph of the scheme/trope distinction (see **Trope**). Both terms, when used in discussions of seventeenth-century English prose style, sometimes overlap and/or coincide with the "point" of the **Pointed Style**.

Perhaps it would make sense to use enargia as the basic umbrella term for the various special terms for vigorous ocular demonstration, and energia as a more general term for vigor and verve, of whatever sort, in expression.

Enigma (G. "allusive or obscure speech"); alt. sp. **Aenigma**.
   A riddle.

See also **Noema; Schematismus.**

Enthymeme (EN thy meme; G. "thought, piece of reasoning") — **Aggressio; Commentatio; Commentum; Epicheireme.**
   1. Maintaining the truth of a **Proposition** from the assumed truth of its contrary.

> If it be great praise to please good men;
> Surely to please evil men it is a great shame.
>
> (Sherry)

   2. Logic: abridged **Syllogism**, one of the terms being omitted as understood.
   3. Rhetoric: Aristotle uses the term to mean a "syllogism" in which the premises are only generally true, a rhetorical, or probable, syllogism. If they are absolutely true (scientifically proved) the proper term is syllogism. Thinking that Aristotle meant enthymeme to refer to the shortened form of any syllogism, later theorists called the rhetorical syllogism in full form epicheireme (see Quintilian, V.x.1–19 and xiv.14). Prevailing usage today seems to make enthymeme equivalent to rhetorical syllogism or shortened syllogism of any sort, and to ignore epicheireme. The enthymeme and the example were, for Aristotle, the two fundamental logical tools of rhetoric.

Further discussion. The syllogism/epicheireme distinction seems similar to the distinction now current in artificial intelligence circles between *information* and *knowledge*. Jeremy Campbell points out that "memory is organized in the brain in such a way that large amounts of relevant world knowledge are triggered almost instantly by a very small quantity of incoming data" (*The Improbable Machine*, p. 48). It is upon the ways of leveraging a small amount of data into a large amount of information that the distinction has turned, the brevity or omitted premise of the enthymeme pointing to this essential but often "illogical" leverage.

Ong sees the leveraging, or bargaining on the basis of shared tacit assumptions, in terms of the subconscious:

> It [the enthymeme] is thought of as concluding because of something unexpressed, unarticulated: *enthymema* primarily signifies something within one's soul, mind, heart, feelings, hence something not uttered or "outered" and to this extent not a fully conscious argument, legitimate though it may be. Aristotle's term here thus clearly acknowledges the operation of something at least very like what we today would call a subconscious element.
>
> (*Rhetoric, Romance, and Technology*, p. 12)

Michael Polanyi's theory of "tacit bargaining" would seem to depart from this kind of argument.

See also **Aetiologia.**

Entrance — **Exordium.**

Enumeratio (e nu me RA ti o) — **Dinumeratio.**

Epagoge (EP a go ge; G. "bringing in"; log. "argument by induction") — **Inductio.**

An inductive argument, or a series of them: "a form of argument which leads the person with whom one is arguing to give assent to certain undisputed facts: through this assent it wins his approval of a doubtful proposition because this resembles the facts to which he has assented" (Cicero, *De inventione*, I.xxxi.51). The argument Cicero uses as illustration:

> . . . in a dialogue by Aeschines Socraticus Socrates reveals that Aspasia reasoned thus with Xenophon's wife and with Xenophon himself: "Please tell me, madam, if your neighbor had a better gold ornament than you have, would you prefer that one or your own?" "That one," she replied. "Now, if she had dresses and other feminine finery more expensive than you have, would you prefer yours or hers?" "Hers, of course," she replied. "Well, now, if she had a better husband than you have, would you prefer your husband or hers?"

Epanadiplosis (e pa na di PLO sis; G. "doubling") — **Epanalepsis.**

Epanalepsis (e pa na LEP sis; G. "resumption, repetition") — **Eccho Sounde; Epanadiplosis; Repetitio; Slowe Returne.**

Repetition at the end of a clause or sentence of the word or phrase with which it began: "I might, unhappy word, O me, I might" (Sidney, *Astrophil and Stella*, 33).

Epanaphora (e pa NA pho ra; G. "carrying back").
Intensive **Anaphora.**

Epanodos (e PA no dos; G. "return; recapitulation, fuller statement of a point").
    1. **Regressio; Retire.** Like **Prolepsis (2)**, a general statement is expanded by discussing it part by part, with the further qualification for epanodos that the terms used in the summary are specifically repeated in the fuller discussion that follows:

> A strife is grown between *Vertue* and *Love*,
>   While each pretends that *Stella* must be his.
>   Her eyes, her lips, her all, saith *Love* do this,
> Since they do weare his badge, most firmely prove.
> But *Vertue* thus that title doth disprove,
>   That *Stella* (O deare name) that *Stella* is
>   That vertuous soule, sure heire of heav'nly blisse.
> (Sidney, Astrophil and Stella, 52)

    2. **Ploce.**
    3. For Quintilian **Polyptoton**, too, is a type of epanodos (IX.iii.36).

Epanorthosis (e pa nor THO sis; G. "setting straight") — **Correctio (1).**

Epecphonesis (e pec pho NE sis) — **Ecphonesis.**

Epembasis (e PEM ba sis; G. "attack, advance") — **Anaphora.**

Epenthesis (e PEN the sis; G. "insertion") — **Interpositio.**
    Addition of a letter, sound, or syllable to the middle of a word: "Lie blist'ring fore the visitating sun" (*Two Noble Kinsmen*, I, i).

Epergesis (e PER ge sis) — **Epexegesis.**

Epexegesis (e pex e GE sis; G. "explanation"); alt. sp. **Epergesis** — **Explanatio.**
    Adding words or phrases to further clarify or specify a statement already made: "For I know that in me (that is, in my flesh) dwelleth no good thing" (Romans 7:18).

Epexergasia — **Exergasia.**

Epezeugmenon (e pe ZEUG me non; G. "joined").
1. **Zeugma.**
2. Minor premise of a **Disjunctive Syllogism.**

Ephodos (EPH o dos; G. "[means of] approach") — **Insinuatio.**

Epicertomesis (e pi cer to ME sis; G. "sarcasm, taunt") — **Chleuasmos.**

Epicheireme (e pi chei REME; G. "dialectical proof") — **Aggressio.**
See **Enthymeme.**
See also **Apodixis (2).**

Epicrisis (e PI cri sis; G. "judgment") — **Adjudicatio.**
The speaker quotes a passage and comments on it:

> When I warned them that Britain would fight on alone, whatever they [Vichy France] did, their generals told their Prime Minister and his divided Cabinet, "In three weeks England will have her neck wrung like a chicken." Some chicken! Some neck!
> (Churchill to the Canadian parliament during WWII)

Epideictic (e pi DEIC tic; G. lit. "fit for displaying or showing off").
See **Rhetoric: The three branches** in chapter 2.

Epidiorthosis (e pi di or THO sis) — **Correctio (1).**

Epilogue (G. *epilogos*, "reasoning"; rhet. "peroration of a speech").
1. **Peroration.**
2. Inferring what will follow from what has been spoken or done before:

> Did you perceive
> He did solicit you in free contempt
> When he did need your loves, and do you think
> That his contempt shall not be bruising to you,
> When he hath power to crush?
> (*Coriolanus*, II, iii)

Epimone (e PI mo ne; G. "tarrying, delay") — **Love Burden; Perseverantia.**
Frequent repetition of a phrase or question, in order to dwell on a point, as in Anthony's choral repetition of "And Brutus is an honorable man" in his "Friends, Romans, countrymen" speech (*Julius Caesar*, iii, ii). Or in the following example:

> So downe he fell, and forth his life did breath,
> That vanisht into smoke and cloudes swift;
> So downe he fell, that th'earth him vnderneath

> Did grone, as feeble so great load to lift;
> So downe he fell, as an huge rockie clift,
> Whose false foundation waues haue washt away,
> With dreadfull poyse is from the mayneland rift,
> And rolling downe, great *Neptune* doth dismay;
> So downe he fell, and like an heaped mountaine lay.
>
> (Spenser, *Faerie Queene*, I, xi, 54)

Epiphonema (e pi pho NE ma; G. "witty saying; phrase added by way of ornament or as a finishing touch") — **Acclamatio; Consenting Close; Surclose.**

Striking epigrammatic or sententious utterance to summarize and conclude a passage, poem, or speech:

> Justice Holmes talks in one of his little speeches about the feelings of a man who has come to the end of a very long life and a long service on the bench and looks back over what he has done and finds it so distressingly small, and he ends up by saying words that I should like to leave with you. He said, "Alas, gentlemen, we cannot live our dreams. We are lucky enough if we can give a sample of our best and if we can know in our hearts that it was nobly done."
>
> (Dean Acheson, *Grapes from Thorns*, p. 98)

Epiphonesis (e pi pho NE sis; G. "acclamation") — **Ecphonesis.**

Epiphora (e PI pho ra; G. lit. "a bringing to or upon") — **Antistrophe (1).**

Epiplexis (e pi PLEX is; G. "rebuke") — **Epitimesis; Percontatio.**

Asking questions in order to reproach or upbraid, rather than to elicit information, as Cicero does in his first speech against Catiline:

> In the name of heaven, Catilina, how long do you propose to exploit our patience? Do you really suppose that your lunatic activities are going to escape our retaliation for evermore? Are there to be no limits to this audacious, uncontrollable swaggering?
>
> (trans. Michael Grant)

See also **Erotesis.**

Epiploce (e pi PLO ce; G. "plaiting together") — **Ploce.**

The etymology would seem to imply a series in some particular (perhaps climactic) order. The *Princeton Encyclopedia of Poetry and Poetics* defines it as a term "applied by ancient metricians to alternative possibilities of regarding a metrical sequence."

Epistrophe (e PI stro phe; G. "turning about") — **Antistrophe (1).**

Epitheton (e PI the ton; G. "attributed"); alt. sp. **Epithet** — **Appositum; Attribution; Qualifier.**

Qualifying the subject with an appropriate adjective; an adjective that frequently or habitually accompanies a certain noun:

> O sir, we quarrel in print, by the book, as you have books for good manners. I will name you the degrees. The first, the Retort Courteous; the second, the Quip Modest; the third, the Reply Churlish; the fourth, the Reproof Valiant; the fifth, the Countercheck Quarrelsome; the sixth, the Lie with Circumstance; the seventh, the Lie Direct.
>
> (*As You Like It*, V, iv)

Epitimesis (e pi ti ME sis; G. "censure, criticism").
   1. **Epiplexis.**
   2. **Correctio (1).**

Epitrochasmus (e pi tro CHAS mus; G. "rapid succession of statements") — **Percursio.**
   A swift movement from one statement to the next; rapid touching on many different points.

> All Kings, and all their favorites,
> All glory of honours, beauties, wits,
> The sun itself, which makes times, as they pass,
> Is elder by a year, now, than it was
> When thou and I first one another saw:
> All other things, to their destruction draw,
> Only our love hath no decay.
>
> (Donne, *The Anniversary*)

Epitrope (e PI tro pe; G. "[grant of] power to decide").
   1. **Concessio; Permissio.** Conceding agreement or permission to an opponent, often ironically, as in the following exchange in Shaw's *Man and Superman*:

> *Doña Ana.* Don Juan: a word against chastity is an insult to me.
> *Don Juan.* I say nothing against your chastity, Señora, since it took the form of a husband and twelve children. What more could you have done had you been the most abandoned of women?
> *Doña Ana.* I could have had twelve husbands and no children, that's what I could have done. . . .
> *The Statue.* Bravo Ana! Juan: you are floored, quelled, annihilated.
> *Don Juan.* No: for though that difference is the true essential difference — *Doña Ana has, I admit, gone straight to the real point* — yet it is not a difference of love or chastity, or even constancy. . . . [emphasis mine]

   2. **Anacoenosis.**

Epizeuxis (e pi ZEUX is; G. "fastening together; repetition") — **Cuckowspell; Doublet; Geminatio; Underlay.**

Emphatic repetition of a word with no other words between. Poe's "The Bells" wins the prize here:

> To the swinging and the ringing
>> Of the bells, bells, bells —
>> Of the bells, bells, bells, bells,
>> Bells, bells, bells —

See also **Palilogia (2).**

Eristic (e RIS tic; G. "quarrel").
"[A]s Plato uses the term, eristic means 'seeking victory in argument', and the art which cultivates and provides appropriate means and devices for so doing. Concern for the truth is not a necessary part of the art . . ." (Kerferd, p. 62).

See also **Dialectic.**

Erotema — Erotesis.

Erotesis (e ro TE sis; G. "a questioning") — **Interrogatio; Questioner.**
A "rhetorical question," one which implies an answer but does not give or lead us to expect one, as when Laertes rants about Ophelia's madness: "Do you see this, O God?" (*Hamlet*, IV, v).

See also **Epiplexis; Hypophora; Ratiocinatio.**

Ethopoeia (e tho po EI a; G. "delineation of character") — **Notatio.**
1. Type of **Enargia**: description of natural propensities, manners, affections, virtues and vices in order to flatter or reproach; character portrayal generally.
2. Putting oneself in the place of another, so as to both understand and express that person's feelings more vividly, e.g., thinking like a jewel thief, if you are defending one. The Greek orator Lysias was supposed to have been the first to develop this technique fully; it does not seem too far removed from "method" acting, or indeed from naturalistic acting of any sort. The term might be used, though to my knowledge it never has been, to describe the "acting" of a character in a play-within-a-play, Falstaff "playing" the king in *1 Henry IV*, for example.

See also **Controversia; Dialogismus; Prosopopoeia; Sermocinatio.**

Ethos (E thos; G. "disposition, character"). *See* **Pathos.**

Etiologia — Aetiologia.

Eucharistia (eu char IS ti a; G. "a thanksgiving"); alt. sp. **Eucharista — Gratiarum actio.**

Giving thanks; prayer of thanksgiving.

Euche (EU che; G. "prayer, vow") — **Precatio; Votum**.
1. Vow or oath to keep a promise. *See also* **Eustathia**.
2. Prayer for evil; curse.

Eulogia (eu LO gi a; G. "praise, blessing") — **Benedictio**.
Commending or blessing a person or thing.

> And he opened his mouth, and taught them, saying,
> Blessed are the poor in spirit: for theirs is the kingdom of heaven.
> Blessed are they that mourn: for they shall be comforted.
> Blessed are the meek, for they shall inherit the earth.
>
> (Matt. 5:2–5)

See also **Comprobatio; Encomium**.

Euphemismus (eu phe MIS mus; G. "use of an auspicious word for an inauspicious one")
1. Prognostication of good; opposite of **Ominatio**.
2. **Conciliatio; Paradiastole; Soother**. Euphemism; circumlocution to palliate something unpleasant, "pass away" for "die." Not "poison ivy" but, as Cole Porter put it, "the ivy you touch with a glove."

See also **Comprobatio**.

Euphuism.
Originally the elaborately patterned prose style of John Lyly's prose romance *Euphues* (1579), euphuism has now come to mean any highly figured, Asiatic style. It emphasizes the figures of words that create balance, and makes frequent use of antithesis, paradox, repetitive patterns with single words, sound-plays of various sorts, amplification of every kind, sententiae and especially the "unnatural natural history" or simile from traditional natural history.

Lyly's style has been studied largely to be deplored. The central charge has been that it is wholly ornamental, a bag of superficial verbal tricks which exists for its own sake rather than to create meaning, as modern critics customarily expect highly figurative language to justify itself by doing. Recently this verdict has undergone some modification, however. G. K. Hunter (*John Lyly: The Humanist as Courtier*) has argued that Lyly's patterned prose brought a new discipline and symmetry to the resources of English prose. Jonas Barish ("The Prose Style of John Lyly") has tried to show how some of the figures are used, what particular purposes Lyly had in mind. And several scholars have called attention to the self-consciously dramatic contexts of much Elizabethan rhetorical prose, contexts in which characters are meant to be seen as speaking "rhetorically."

(For a modern example, see the example illustrating **Exuscitatio** below.) In this connection one might cite Northrop Frye's clever observation on the self-consciousness of the euphuistic style: "Euphuism . . . is easy to parody, but in euphuism itself there is a curious quality that is really a kind of self-parody. Its ingenuity makes it witty, and the wit may be conscious or, at times, unconscious" (*The Well-Tempered Critic*, pp. 64–65).

In any event, euphuism must remain the rhetorical prose style par excellence, and the strongest warning that understanding a rhetorical style in a fictional matrix requires a fuller range of critical equipment than the rhetorical theorist by himself can provide. An example from *Euphues*:

> True it is Philautus that he which toucheth the nettle tenderly, is soonest stung, that the fly which playeth with the fire is singed in the flame, that he that dallieth with women is drawn to his woe. And as the adamant draweth the heavy iron, the harp the fleet dolphin, so beauty allureth the chaste mind to live, & the wisest wit to lust: The example whereof I would it were no less profitable than the experience to me is like to be perilous. The vine watered with wine is soon withered, the blossom in the fattest ground is quickly blasted, the goat the fatter she is the less fertile she is; yea, man the more witty he is the less happy he is.

See also **Asianism.**

Eustathia (eu sta THI a; G. "stability, tranquility") — **Constantia.** Pledge of constancy.

> For certes, fresshe wommanliche wif,
> This dar I seye, that trouth and diligence,
> That shal ye fynden in me al my lif;
> N'y wol nat, certein, breken youre defence;
> And if I do, present or in absence,
> For love of God, lat sle me with the dede,
> If that it like unto youre wommanhede.
> *(Troilus and Criseide*, III, 1296–1302)

See also **Euche (1).**

Eutrepismus (eu tre PIS mus; G. "preparation") — **Dinumeratio.**

Even. Puttenham's term for **Parison**; *see* **Isocolon.**

Exacerbatio (ex a cer BA ti o; L. "exasperation") — **Sarcasmus.**

Exargasia — **Exergasia.**

Excessus (ex CES sus) — **Digression.**

Exchange. Puttenham's term for **Enallage.**

Exclamatio (ex cla MA ti o) — **Ecphonesis.**

Excursus (ex CUR sus) — **Digression.**

Excusatio (ex cu SA ti o) — **Pareuresis.**

Excuse — **Dicaeologia.**

Execratio (ex e CRA ti o) — **Ara.**

Exemplum (ex EM plum; L. "pattern, model") — **Paradigma.**
   An example cited, either true or mythical; an illustrative story or anecdote. Mythical example:

> Such first was *Bacchus*, that with furious might
> All th'East before vntam'd did ouerronne,
> And wrong repressed, and establisht right,
> Which lawlesse men had formerly fordonne.
> There Iustice first her princely rule begonne.
> Next *Hercules* his like ensample shewed,
> Who all the West with equall conquest wonne,
> And monstrous tyrants with his club subdewed;
> The club of Iustice dread, with kingly powre endewed.
> (Spenser, *Faerie Queene*, V, i, 2)

Illustrative anecdote:

> At the time of the Russian entry into the war, he [Churchill] was suddenly asked by someone, "What will govern your policy toward Russia?" He stared at his toes reflectively for only a few seconds before he said solemnly, "The baboon in his native habitat is a creature who harms no one. The baboon in a cage at the zoo is a creature who is the object of profound interest and sometimes commiseration from the spectators. The baboon in bed with your wife or sister is something which no one can regard without profound horror and disgust. These three sentences I trust will indicate the ideas which will govern my policy towards Russia."
> (Gen. Raymond Lee, *The London Journal, 1940–41,* p. 466)

See also **Paradiegesis; Simile.**

Exergasia (ex er GA si a; G. "working out, treatment"); alt. sp.
Exargasia — **Epexergasia; Expolitio; Gorgious.**
   Repeating the same thought in many figures:

> I take thy hand — this hand,
> As soft as dove's down and as white as it,
> Or Ethiopian's tooth, or the fann'd snow that's bolted
> By the northern blasts twice o'er.
> (*The Winter's Tale,* IV, iv)

Exgressus (ex GRES sus) — **Digression**.

Exordium (ex OR di um; L. "beginning") — **Entrance; Prooemium**.
The first part of a classical oration. It caught the audience's interest while introducing the subject. It was sometimes divided into the direct (L. *principium*; G. *prooimion*) and the indirect (L. *insinuatio*; G. *ephodos*). See **Arrangement: The parts of an oration** in chapter 2.

Expeditio (ex pe DI ti o; L. rhet. "proof by elimination") — **Apophasis (2); Speedie Dispatcher**.
Rejection of all but one of various alternatives:

> There is no remedy for love, none you can drink or eat, no song you can sing, nothing but kisses and embraces and the coming together with naked bodies.
>
> (Longus, *Daphnis and Chloe*, V.7)

Experientia (ex pe ri EN ti a; L. "proof, trial") — **Apodixis**.

Explanatio (ex pla NA ti o) — **Epexegesis**.

Expolitio (ex po LI ti o; L. "polishing, adorning, embellishing") — **Exergasia**.

Exposition (L. *expositio*).
A seemingly straightforward but actually most confusing term. Let me, as an executive decision, specify two main meanings, beyond which it does not seem needful for most users to go.
1. The *Ad Herennium* defines it in the following way. The *divisio* or **Division**, the third part of a formal oration, has two parts. The first part a modern lawyer might call the stipulation: the contending parties set down what points they agree on and what points are to be disputed. The second part then deals with the points to be disputed, and it, in turn, has two parts. The first, called *enumeratio*, numbers the points to be disputed. The second, the *expositio*, sets out these points: "The Exposition consists in setting forth, briefly and completely, the points we intend to discuss" (*Expositio est cum res quibus de rebus dicturi sumus exponimus breviter et absolute*, I.x.17). The exposition, then, is the second part of the second part of the division:
Part 1. Stipulation about what is agreed and what must be disputed.
Part 2a. Enumeration of points of disagreement.
Part 2b. Brief exposition of these points.

If the enumeration is omitted, the exposition becomes the entire second part of the division, and the most important part, the part that deals with what people disagree about. This is what the term means in the *De inventione* (I.xxii.31), when Cicero is discussing the third part of the oration (which he calls the *partitio*): *Altera est in qua rerum earum de quibus erimus dicturi breviter* exposition *ponitur distributa.*

2. The more obvious sense of the Latin word *expositio*, "a setting forth, exposition," is used by rhetorical writers (see the Lewis and Short entries, s.v.) as an ordinary word, not a special term, to mean a general setting forth of a topic, a narration or explanation. "Exposition" is a fine English translation.

Further discussion. After this, things get more complicated. The two words *narratio* and *expositio* occur in a single sentence in *De inventione* (I.xix.27): *Narratio est rerum gestarum aut ut gestarum expositio* ("The *narrative* is an *exposition* of events that have occurred or are supposed to have occurred"). Thus exposition comes to mean the *second* part of an oration as well as the third. Quintilian uses the term in this sense to refer to the second part of the oration (III.ix.7), the **Narration** (which, since he uses a five-part overall scheme, he does not of course distinguish from division anyway).

Perhaps it would make sense to use "Exposition" only in its general Latin and English sense and refer to the second or third parts of an oration, or parts thereof, by one of their other Latin names.

Or, following a suggestive note by Harry Caplan, the famous editor of the *Ad Herennium*, we might exploit another and hitherto hidden meaning. In a note to *expositio* in the vexed passage cited above, Caplan gives as a Greek equivalent the word ἔκθεσις. For both the Greek word and the Latin, the first meaning is a particular kind of "exposure," the "exposure of a child." Perhaps we can use "exposition" to refer to "killing a baby" in the same metaphorical sense in which Elizabethan dramatists referred to "tearing a cat." Dickens was fond of exposition in this sense, employing it often when the monthly-part sales of a novel indicated declining reader interest.

Exprobatio (ex pro BA ti o; L. "reproach") — **Onedismus.**

Extension.
   Roughly, denotation of a term; in logic, all the subclasses of a given class.

Extenuatio (ex te nu A ti o) — **Meiosis.**

Exuperatio (ex u pe RA tio) — **Hyperbole.**

Exuscitatio (ex us ci TA ti o; L. "awakening, arousing").
Emotional utterance that seeks to move hearers to a like feeling. Here is Thomas Dekker, urging on us the pleasures of country life:

> Hast thou a desire to rule, get up to the mountains, and thou shalt see the greatest trees stand trembling before thee to do thee reverence, those maist thou call thy Nobles. . . . Wouldest thou behold battles? Step into the fields, there shalt thou see excellent combats between the standing Corn and the Winds. Art thou a tyrant and delightest in the fall of the Great ones? Muster then thy Harvesters together, and down with those proud Summer Lords.
>
> (*The Pelican Book of English Prose*, 1.261)

Fable (L. *fabula*, "discourse, narrative, story") — **Apologue**.
A short allegorical story that points a lesson or moral; the characters are frequently animals.

See also **Exemplum; Progymnasmata; Simile.**

Fallacy (Logical).
Two forms: (1) Formal — violates rules of **Syllogism**; (2) Informal (or material) — of *relevance* or of *ambiguity*.
  (a) Fallacies of *relevance:*
    Argumentum ad baculum (appeal to force).
    Argumentum ad hominem (disparage the character of the speaker, instead of attacking his arguments).
    Argumentum ad ignorantiam (argue that a proposition is true because it has never been proved false).
    Argumentum ad misericordiam (appeal to pity).
    Argumentum ad populum (play on the feelings of the audience).
    Argumentum ad verecundiam (appeal to traditional values).
    Converse accident (fallacious generalization on the basis of unrepresentative sample).
    Post hoc, propter hoc (because A occurs before B, A is the cause of B: confusion of temporal and causal sequence).
    Petitio principii (assuming as a premise the conclusion to be proved — "begging the question").
    Rigged question (the terms of the question require admission as part of any answer: Have you stopped beating your wife?).
    Ignoratio elenchi (an argument which proves a conclusion different from the one intended).
  (b) Fallacies of *ambiguity:*
    Equivocation (deliberate confusion of two or more meanings of a word).
    Amphiboly (argument from grammatically ambiguous premise).
    Accent (change of stress or emphasis to change meaning).
    Composition (taking a part for the whole).

Division (taking the whole for a part).
(The last two are sometimes called **Secundum quid**.)
(This summary is drawn from chapter 3 of Copi's *Introduction to Logic*. Copi notes that Aristotle enumerated thirteen types of fallacies, and that the fullest list known to him contains well over one hundred.)

False Semblant. Puttenham's term for **Allegory**.

Far-Fet. Puttenham's term for **Metalepsis**.

Fictio (FIC ti o; L. "invention").
Attributing rational actions and speech to nonrational creatures.

> With how sad steps, ô Moone, thou climb'st the skies,
>   How silently, and with how wanne a face,
>   What, may it be that even in heav'nly place
> That busie archer his sharpe arrowes tries?
> Sure, if that long with *Love* acquainted eyes
>   Can judge of *Love*, thou feel'st a Lover's case;
>   I reade it in thy lookes, thy languisht grace,
> To me that feele the like, thy state descries.
>   (Sidney, *Astrophil and Stella*, 31)

Figure.
A general term for any striking or unusual configuration of words or phrases.
See also **Style**, **Trope**, and chapter 2.

Figures of Rhetoric.
"Every definition," Erasmus tells us, "is a misfortune." Certainly the lists of rhetorical terms which have appeared since the beginnings of formal rhetoric — which have from time to time seemed to *be* formal rhetoric — have been viewed as one long series of misfortunes. As every historian of rhetoric points out, even the historians of figures seem to hate the figures. Almost no one has a good thing to say about them, but almost no one could resist arguing about them and, if possible (and often if not), adding a new term to the list. In a self-conscious age like our own, the very existence of the terminology, and of lists of it like this one, deserves a comment. Why has the nomenclature loomed so large and confused so many?
Perhaps the confusion began because Rome was bilingual. The Greek rhetorical terminology put on a Latin doubleture, and then in the Renaissance both sets of terms absorbed the numinosity of classical culture itself. No wonder Puttenham's wonderful terms hadn't a chance. They must have seemed — they still seem to us —

somehow *impious*. It is those confusing, conflicting, overlapping Greek and Latin terms that we cling to. Everyone from Quintilian onward, of course, has complained about the imprecision and proliferation, regretting the absence of a clear, brief, and definitive set of terms, a nomenclature fixed once and for all. Curtius remarks, for example: "The study of figures has never been satisfactorily systematized. . . . This lack of a settled terminology, and, in short, the endless variations in enumerating and defining the figures, are to be explained historically by contacts between various schools" (*European Literature and the Latin Middle Ages*, p. 45).

To counteract this historical drift, some critics have suggested informal basic classifications. W. K. Wimsatt, Jr., for example, practiced the reduction this way:

> To put the matter simply yet, I believe, essentially: the figures of speech found in classical prose and poetry and described by Aristotle and the Roman rhetoricians, though multiplied during the centuries and often confused, fell into a few classes of main importance: 1. logical patterns of parallel and contrast in syllable, word, and phrase; 2. metaphoric meanings (often and correctly taken as figures of thought); and 3. a series of non-logical phonetic auxiliaries of metaphor, variously graded as pun, "turn" (or *traductio*), and alliteration.
>
> (*Alexander Pope: Selected Poetry and Prose*, p. xxix)

And Alexander Bain had suggested a not wholly dissimilar three-part categorization in the previous century:

> A classification of the more important Figures may be based on the three leading divisions of the Human Understanding . . . :
>
> (1) Discrimination, or Feeling of Difference, Contrast, Relativity. . . .
> (2) Similarity, or the Feeling of Agreement. . . .
> (3) Retentiveness, or Acquisition.
>
> (*English Composition and Rhetoric*, pp. 135–136)

But needful as such historical and classificatory thinking is, it may overlook the central point about the nomenclature of rhetorical figuration: that the confusion has been a *creative* one. We have *needed* to create it. The vast pool of terms for verbal ornamentation has acted like a gene pool for the rhetorical imagination, stimulating us to look at language in another way. When Gombrich wants to find out how Constable's painting of *Wivenhoe Park* creates the illusion of life, he superimposes a grid upon it, to break up the three-dimensional illusion into a series of surface squares which can then be studied in a new way. Doesn't rhetorical terminology work in much this way, testifying to a kind of verbal attention which looks *at* the verbal surface rather than *through* it? The figures have worked historically to teach a way of seeing — have supplied, if you will, a theory of reader response. If, as the postmodern Derridean theorists argue, rhetorical analysis is required for all kinds of reading, philosophical and ordinary as well as poetical, might we not argue that the terms have formed the central theory for such a general theory of verbal attention?

The act of inventing ever more finely tuned discriminatory figures has formed an excuse for a different activity altogether, the establishment of a domain of expressivity opposite to argumentation. We continually underestimate the degree of self-consciousness with which the world before Newton spoke and listened, read and wrote. Speeches were also entertainments, and it was the doctrine of the figures, the ability to create them and to spot them on the wing, that set up the oscillation between argumentation and ornamentation which has always provided the *diastole* and *systole* of the Western verbal imagination. As a dozen different fields of inquiry are telling us in one way or another today, ornament matters. It is not "merely ornamental." It feeds a genuine human hunger, the hunger for style. The great Greek scholar Eric Havelock once wrote that "Our species seems to have an inner biologic motivation which seeks to vary its own forms of expression" (*The Liberal Temper in Greek Politics*, p. 30). The rhetorical figures have been the central testimony, for language, to this inner motivation. Perhaps we should not repine that they have been so many and so various. Much has been done with such variety.

We might also project rhetorical figures onto a yet larger scale. They may represent a basic evolutionary strategy for our species. The biologist Edward O. Wilson writes: "The brain depends upon elegance to compensate for its own small size and short lifetime. As the cerebral cortex grew from apish dimensions through hundreds of thousands of years of evolution, it was forced to rely on tricks to enlarge memory and speed computation. The mind therefore specializes on analogy and metaphor, on a sweeping together of chaotic sensory experience into workable categories labeled by words and stacked into hierarchies for quick recovery" (*Biophilia*, p. 60). Such a raison d'être for figured language would make it finally into a kind of data-compression, an immensely rapid substitute for iterative searching. As such, it would be a part of our original evolutionary equipment, not an add-on; essential rather than ornamental.

Fleering Frumpe. Puttenham's term for **Mycterismus**.

Flitting Figure. Puttenham's term for **Metastasis**.

Fonde Affectation. Puttenham's term for **Cacozelia**.

Forrein Speech. Puttenham's term for **Barbarismus.**

Foule Speech. Puttenham's term for **Cacemphaton.**

Frequentatio (fre quen TA ti o; L. "crowding together") — **Congeries.**

Geminatio (ge mi NA ti o; L. "doubling") — **Epizeuxis.**

Geographia (ge o GRA phi a).
Description of the earth. A type of **Enargia.**

> Earth, ocean, air, beloved brotherhood!
> lf our great Mother has imbued my soul
> With aught of natural piety to feel
> Your love, and recompense the boon with mine;
> If dewy morn, and odorous noon, and even,
> With sunset and its gorgeous ministers,
> And solemn midnight's tingling silentness;
> If autumn's hollow sighs in the sere wood,
> And winter robing with pure snow and crowns
> Of starry ice the grey grass and bare boughs;
> If spring's voluptuous pantings when she breathes
> Her first sweet kisses, have been dear to me;
> If no bright bird, insect, or gentle beast
> I consciously have injured, but still loved
> And cherished these my kindred; then forgive
> This boast, beloved brethren, and withdraw
> No portion of your wonted favour now!
>
> (Shelley, *Alastor*)

Gnome ([g]NOME; G. "thought, judgment, opinion") — **Proverb.**

Gorgiac Figures.
   A term sometimes used to describe **Antithesis, Isocolon, Homoioteleuton**, and like figures of parallelism, balance, and contrast which Gorgias is said to have invented.

Gorgious. Puttenham's term for **Exergasia.**

Gradatio (gra DA ti o) — **Climax.**

Graecismus (grae CIS mus; from L. *graecus*, "Greek").
   Use of Greek idiom or grammatical or orthographical features in writing or speaking English.

Gratiarum actio (gra ti AR um   AC ti o) — **Eucharistia.**

Heaping Figure. Puttenham's term for **Synathroesmus**; *see* **Congeries.**

Hebraism.
Use of Hebrew idiom or grammatical or orthographical features in writing or speaking English.

Hendiadys (hen DI a dys; G. "one by means of two"); alt. sp. **Endiadis, Hendiasys — Twinnes.**
Expression of an idea by two nouns connected by "and" instead of a noun and its qualifier: "by length of time and siege" for "by a long siege." Puttenham offers as an example: "Not you, coy dame, your lowers and your looks," for "your lowering looks." Peacham, ignoring the derivation of the term, defines it as the substituting, for an adjective, of a substantive with the same meaning: "a man of great wisdom" for "a wise man." This redefinition would make it a kind of **Anthimeria.**

Heterogenium (he te ro GE ni um; G. "of a different kind") — **Apoplanesis.**

Heuresis (HEU re sis; G. "discovery, invention") — **Invention.**

Hirmus (HIR mus; G. "series, sequence"); alt. sp. **Heirmos, Hirmos, Hyrmos, Irmus — Long Loose; Period.**
Originally a philosophical term; used by Stoic grammarians and apparently first applied to rhetoric by Donatus.

Homiologia (ho mi o LO gi a; G. "uniformity of style") — **Sermo ubique sui similis.**
The etymologically correct spelling would be *homoiologia.* Tedious, redundant, unvaried style.
See also **Macrologia.**

Homoeoprophoron (ho moe o PRO pho ron; G. "similar in pronunciation") — **Alliteration.**

Homoeosis (ho moe O sis; G. "likeness, resemblance"); alt. sp. **Omiosis — Simile.**

Homoioptoton (ho moi OP to ton; G. "in a like case, with a similar inflexion"); alt. sp. **Homoeoptoton — Simile casibus; Similiter cadens.**
In classical rhetorical theory, the use in a sentence or verse of various words in the same case and with similar case endings. Lack-

ing a real series of inflections, English uses the term loosely, often making it synonymous with **Homoioteleuton**, often making it mean simply rhyme. So Wilson, in the *Arte of Rhetorique*, gives this example: "By great travail is gotten much avail, by earnest affection men learn discretion." For a fuller discussion, see the following entry.

Homoioteleuton (ho moi o te LEU ton; G. "like ending") — **Like Loose; Simile determinatione; Similiter desinens**.

In English, the use of similar endings to words, phrases, or sentences. Peacham gives this example: "Eloquent is he who can invent excellently, dispose evidently, figure diversely, remember perfectly." Sister Miriam Joseph cites a passage from *Two Gentlemen of Verona* which shows the pattern (rather forced in the third instance) at the beginning rather than the end of the clause or line: "How churlishly I chid Lucetta hence / When willingly I would have had her here! / How angerly I taught my brow to frown . . ." (I, ii). Puttenham (p. 173) offers a more varied example:

> Mischances ought not to be lamented
> But rather by wisdom in time prevented.
> For such mishaps as be remediless,
> To sorrow them it is but foolishness.
> Yet are we all so frail of nature,
> As to be grieved with every displeasure.

Further discussion. The confusion of homoioteleuton with **Homoioptoton** stems not only from adapting the two terms from a highly inflected language to one much less so, but from confusion in classical theory itself.

The author of *Rhetorica ad Herennium*, in his discussion of these two terms (IV.xx.28), remarks that they resemble one another very much (*inter se vehementer conveniunt*). They certainly do. He separates the two on the basis of the kind of ending: homoioptoton (*Similiter cadens*) is a figure of similar case-endings; homoioteleuton (*Similiter desinens*) is a figure of similar endings for indeclinable words, words with invariant terminations (*tametsi casus non insunt in verbis*).

As an example of homoioptoton, he gives this: *Hominem laudem egentem virtutis, abundantem felicitatis?* ("Am I to praise a man with plenty of luck but little virtue?" [my translation]).

As examples of homoioteleuton, he gives: *Turpiter audes facere, nequiter studes dicere; vivis invidiose, delinquis studiose, loqueris odiose* ("You dare to act dishonourably, you strive to talk despicably; you live hatefully, you sin zealously, you speak offensively") and *Audaciter territas, humiliter placas* ("Blusteringly you threaten; cringingly you appease").

But these examples of homoioteleuton include variant as well as invariant forms. The adverbs (*Turpiter/nequiter* and *invidiose/studiose/odiose*) do not vary, but the verbs (*audes/studes* and *vivis/delinquis/loqueris*) are inflected, change endings just as nouns and adjectives do. We must infer that homoioptoton applies only to nouns and adjectives. The example which the *Ad Herennium* author goes on to use confirms the conclusion: *Perditissima ratio est amorem petere, pudorem fugere, diligere formam, neglegere famam* ("A most depraved proceeding it is to seek love but shun respect, cherish beauty but neglect fame"). This example, he tells us, combines both homoioptoton and homoioteleuton; the noun forms (*amorem, pudorem, formam, famam*) represent the first, and the verb forms (*petere, fugere, diligere, neglegere*), which are all infinitives, the second. He remarks of this example that writers who use these figures well usually mix the two in the same construction, as here.

Quintilian's discussion of these two terms (IX.iii.77–80) forms part of a larger discussion of **Gorgiac Figures** like **Isocolon** and **Parison**, figures which often reinforce their similar parallel structures with similar sounds in similar places. He thus approaches homoioptoton and homoioteleuton thinking primarily of *location* rather than of *the nature of the termination*. That approach may explain why he confuses these two definitional criteria in the course of a rather sloppy discussion.

Homoioteleuton occurs when clauses have the same endings (*ut clausula similiter cadat, syllabis iisdem in ultimam partem collatis: ὁμοιοτέλευτον vocant*). It usually occurs in a **Tricolon**, he says, and gives this example: *vicit pudorem libido, timorem audacia, rationem amentia* ("Desire overcame shame, brazenness overcame fear, mindlessness overcame mind" [my translation]). But here, of course, we have inflected nouns in the same case — exactly the criterion, for the *Ad Herennium* author, of homoioptoton! Quintilian then goes on to define homoioptoton as involving words in the same case, whether their endings are alike or not (*etiamsi dissimilia sint quae declinentur*). Then positionality enters, when he argues that homoioptoton does not always occur at the end of a sentence (and, by implication, homoioteleuton does), but may be at the beginning or in the middle.

A prose stylist in an inflected language inevitably creates sound resemblances by the nature of the language. Sometimes these seem inelegant or obtrusive and alterations are made. Thus a writer might find *magnarum terrarum* an inelegant jingle and choose an adjective of another declension, *grandium*, say, to avoid the sound similarity. Or, of course, the resemblance might be intentionally sought. It was overuse of such ornament, as by Gorgias, that formed the departure point for Quintilian's discussion. The overfine distinctions between these two terms may make more sense if we think of them as a basic prose strategy for an inflected language, especially for ones so self-conscious about ornamentation as classical Greek and Latin. (This strategy has been traced by Karl Polheim in *Die lateinische Reimprosa*.)

The Tudor theorists seem to have followed the *Ad Herennium*. Puttenham gives a string of "-ly" adverbs as exemplifying homoioteleuton, which thus means similar endings in uninflected words, or rhyme. Wilson identifies homoioptoton as similar inflections. Yet neither specifies exactly the distinctions the *Ad Herennium* author draws — naturally enough since, fine drawn for Latin, they make no sense at all for English. Since the issue of inflections is not crucial in English, we might differentiate between the two terms on the basis of position, using homoioptoton to mean similar termination of a pair or series of words within a sentence or verse, homoioteleuton to mean a similar closing of several sentences or verses. Or, more simply, we could use homoioteleuton to mean similar endings of all sorts in English, and reserve homoioptoton for discussions of Greek and Latin.

Horismus (ho RIS mus; G. "marking out by boundaries, limitation") — **Definer by Difference; Definitio.**

In logic, a clear, brief, pithy definition, as when Shaw tells us that "Economy is the art of making the most of life." In rhetoric, a definition by opposites, as when Proudhon tells us that "Property is theft." Puttenham describes the difference between logical and rhetorical meanings thus: ". . . wisdom is a prudent and witty foresight . . . this definition is Logical. The Orator useth another manner of definition, thus: Is this wisdom? no it is a certain subtle knavish crafty wit, it is no industry, as you call it, but a certain busy brain-sickness" (p. 231).

Humiliatio (hu mi li A ti o) — **Tapinosis.**

Hydrographia (hy dro GRA phi a).

Description of water. A type of **Enargia**. So Nicholas Monsarrat's description of the Atlantic Ocean, in *The Cruel Sea:*

> First, the ocean, the steep Atlantic stream. The map will tell you what that looks like: three-cornered, three thousand miles across and a thousand fathoms deep, bounded by the European coastline and half of Africa, and the vast American continent on the other side: open at

the top, like a champagne glass, and at the bottom, like a municipal rubbish-dumper.

Hypallage (hy PAL la ge; G. "interchange, exchange") — **Changeling**.

1. Awkward or humorous changing of agreement or application of words, as with Bottom playing Pyramus:

> I see a voice. Now will I to the chink,
> To spy and I can hear my Thisby's face.
> *(A Midsummer Night's Dream,* V, i)

2. **Metonymy**.

3. Gram., "a change in the relation of words by which a word, instead of agreeing with the case it logically qualifies, is made to agree grammatically with another case" (Smyth, *Greek Grammar*, p. 678).

4. Sometimes used to describe a deliberately misapplied epithet, as when, in a well-rehearsed mistake, Churchill referred to the "infernal combustion engine."

Hyperbaton (hy PER ba ton; G. "transposed") — **Transcensio; Transgressio; Transiectio; Trespasser**.

1. A generic figure of various forms of departure from ordinary word order, including **Anastrophe; Cacosyntheton; Epergesis; Hypallage; Hysterologia; Hysteron Proteron; Parenthesis; Tmesis**.

2. Separation of words usually belonging together. Churchill's humorous illustration of "good usage" is an example: "This is the kind of impertinence up with which I will not put." Quintilian (VIII.vi.65) offers an orthodox Latin example, in which *duas* is stressed by its separation from *partes: animadverti, iudices, omnem accusatoris orationem in duas divisam esse partes* ("I noted, gentlemen, that the speech of the accuser was divided into two parts").

Hyperbole (hy PER bo le; G. "excess, exaggeration") — **Exuperatio; Loud Lyer; Overreacher; Superlatio**.

Exaggerated or extravagant terms used for emphasis and not intended to be understood literally; self-conscious exaggeration.

> For instance, of a Lion;
> He roared so loud, and looked so wondrous grim,
> His very shadow durst not follow him.
> (Pope, *Peri Bathous*)

Hyperzeugma (hy per ZEUG ma).

Opposite of **Zeugma**. Each phrase has its own verb. Churchill's famous speech uses both verbs and prepositions:

We shall go on to the end, we shall fight in France, we shall fight on the seas and oceans, we shall fight with growing confidence and growing strength in the air, we shall defend our island, whatever the cost may be, we shall fight on the beaches, we shall fight on the landing grounds, we shall fight in the fields and in the streets, we shall fight in the hills; we shall never surrender.

> (House of Commons, 4 June 1940)

Hypocrisis (hy PO cri sis; G. "reply; [orator's] delivery") — **Delivery**.

Hypodiastole (hy po di A sto le) — **Comma (2)**.

Hypophora (hy PO pho ra) — **Anthypophora; Antiphora; Apocrisis; Rogatio; Subjectio**.

Asking questions and immediately answering them:

> Who taught me to curl myself inside a buttercup? Iolanthe! Who taught me to swing upon a cobweb? Iolanthe! Who taught me to dive into a dewdrop — to nestle in a nutshell — to gambol upon gossamer? Iolanthe!
>
> (Gilbert and Sullivan, *Iolanthe*)

Or the Devil's marvelous rant in Shaw's *Man and Superman:*

> Man measures his strength by his destructiveness. What is his religion? An excuse for hating me. What is his law? An excuse for hanging you. What is his morality? Gentility! . . . What is his art? An excuse for gloating over pictures of slaughter.

Two different uses of the figure have been discriminated by some theorists. Peacham, for example, says that we can "make the oration very pleasant" or "confute" our opponent. Sonnino makes this difference into two terms, one which simply asks and answers questions (*rogatio*) and another which does so in order to disarm or discredit our opponents in advance. Since this adversarial use is called *subjectio* by the *Ad Herennium* author (IV.xxiii.33), she calls the second term by this name. This discrimination seems to me needless and confusing. The basic term — asking questions and immediately answering them — is clear enough though, Heaven knows, variously described.

See also **Erotesis; Ratiocinatio**.

Hypotaxis (hy po TAX is; G. "subjection").

An arrangement of clauses or phrases in a dependent or subordinate relationship, as in this Johnsonian structure:

> No place affords a more striking conviction of the vanity of human hopes, than a public library; for who can see the wall crowded on every side by mighty volumes, the works of laborious meditation and

accurate enquiry, now scarcely known but by the catalogue, and preserved only to increase the pomp of learning, without considering how many hours have been wasted in vain endeavours, how often imagination has anticipated the praises of futurity, how many statues have risen to the eye of vanity, how many ideal converts have elevated zeal, how often wit has exulted in the eternal infamy of his antagonists, and ambition delighted in the gradual advances of her authority, the immutability of his decrees, and the perpetuity of her power?

(*Rambler*, 106)

Opposite of **Parataxis**.

Hypothesis (G. "the subject under discussion").

One of the two categories into which the Greek rhetorician Hermagoras of Temnos divided the subjects of rhetoric. It was a specific subject, concerned with individual people, places, etc. For example, "Is Hamlet responsible for Polonius's death?" The Latin term is *causa*. The opposite category is **Thesis**.

Hypothetical (or Conditional) Propositions.

A hypothetical proposition is composed of an "if" clause, called the antecedent or *protasis*, and a "then" clause, called the consequent or *apodosis:* "If there is an inner logic to rhetorical terminology, it certainly escapes me."

Hypothetical Syllogism.

A syllogism that contains only **Hypothetical Propositions** is called a pure hypothetical syllogism. If it also contains **Categorical Propositions** it is a mixed hypothetical syllogism.

Hypotyposis (hy po ty PO sis; G. "sketch, outline, pattern") — Enargia.

Hypozeugma (hy po ZEUG ma; G. "being under a yoke") — Rerewarder.

A type of **Zeugma** in which the last clause of a sentence uses a verb which is understood in the others: "Hours, days, weeks, months, and years do pass away" (Sherry).

Hypozeuxis (hy po ZEUX is) — Substitute.

Every clause in a sentence has its own subject and verb.

> Madam, the guests are come, supper serv'd up, you call'd, my young lady ask'd for, the nurse curs'd in the pantry, and everything in extremity.
>
> (*Romeo and Juliet*, I, iii)

See also **Zeugma**.

Hysterologia (hys te ro LO gi a).

Form of **Hyperbaton**.

1. A phrase is interposed between a preposition and its object: "I ran after with as much speed as I could, the thief that had undone me" (Peacham).

2. Sherry makes the term mean **Hysteron proteron**: "When that is done afterwards, is set in speaking in the former place, as: pluck off my boots and spurs." He gives **Prepostera locutio** as the Latin equivalent.

Hysteron proteron (HYS te ron   PRO te ron; G. "the latter [put as] the former") — **Preposterous**.

Form of **Hyperbaton**: syntax or sense out of normal logical or temporal order.

> Th'Antoniad, the Egyptian admiral,
> With all their sixty, fly and turn the rudder.
> > *(Antony and Cleopatra*, III, x)

See also **Anastrophe**.

Icon (I con; G. "likeness, image, portrait"); alt. sp. **Eicon** — **Resemblance by Imagerie**.

Painting resemblance by imagery, as when Richard II describes himself:

> Down, down I come, like glist'ring Phaeton,
> Wanting the manage of unruly jades.
> > *(Richard II*, III, iii)

See also **Image; Simile**.

Ignoratio elenchi (ig no RA ti o   e LEN chi; L. "ignorance" + G. "confutation").

An argument which proves a conclusion different from the one intended. See **Fallacy (Logical)**, and chapter 2 at **Invention: Ten invalid topics**.

Illusio (il LU si o; L. "mocking, jeering") — **Irony**.

Image (L. *imago*, "imitation, copy, likeness").

A thing that represents something else; a symbol, emblem, representation. The term "imagery," as it is used today in literary criticism, was not part of the traditional rhetorical nomenclature. The pictorial (visual image-making) part of its meaning was expressed by the various subdivisions of **Enargia**; the more common of its present

meanings, figurative expression generally, was divided up into a long list of figures — not all of them **Tropes**, of course.
See also **Icon**.

Imminutio (im mi NU ti o; L. "lessening, weakening") — **Meiosis**.

Impartener. Puttenham's term for **Anacoenosis**.

Impossibilia (im pos si BI li a) — **Adynata**.

Imprecatio (im pre CA ti o) — **Ara**.

Improprietas (im pro PRI e tas) — **Acyrologia**.

Inartificial Proofs.
Those external to the case and supplied by such things as documents, witnesses, etc. — what we would today call "evidence."
See also **Artificial Proofs; Proof**.

Incisum — **Comma**.

Incongruitie. Puttenham's term for **Solecismus**.

Incrementum (in cre MEN tum) — **Auxesis (2)**.

Indignatio (in dig NA ti o; L. "indignation, displeasure") — **Aganactesis; Deinosis**.
Arousing the audience's scorn and indignation. Cicero in the *De inventione* (I.lii.98) divides the **Peroration** or conclusion of a speech into three parts: the summing-up, the *indignatio*, or arousing of ill-will toward the opponent, and the *conquestio* or arousing of sympathy. Although Cicero enumerates fifteen **Topics** appropriate to indignatio (*De inventione* I.liii.100–105), Rufinianus says that it is conveyed mostly by delivery (*indignatio, quae fit maxime pronuntiatione* [Halm, p. 41]). Since the indignation was aroused by amplifying the relevant commonplaces, this section of the conclusion was sometimes, to subsequent confusion, called **Amplificatio**.
See also **Commiseratio; Pathopoeia**.

Inductio (in DUC ti o; L. "leading into") — **Epagoge**.

Inductive Proof.
Argument, through the various valid forms of **Syllogism**, from an accepted fact or facts to a conclusion based on them; argument from the particular to the general; scientific reasoning.

Informatio (in for MA ti o; L. "representation, sketch, outline") — **Diatyposis (2)**.

Insertour. Puttenham's term for **Parenthesis**.

Insinuatio (in si nu A ti o; L. "winding or stealing into") — **Ephodos**.
The "Subtle Approach," one of the two kinds of openings or introductions. The other is **Prooemium**, or Direct Opening. See **Exordium**.

Insultatio (in sul TA ti o; L. "scoffing, reviling") — **Disdainefull**.
Derisive, ironical abuse of a person to his face. As Hamlet says to his mother:

> Look on this picture, and on this,
> The counterfeit presentment of two brothers.
> See what a grace was seated on this brow:
> Hyperion's curls, the front of Jove himself . . .
> This was your husband. Look you now what follows.
> Here is your husband, like a mildewed ear
> Blasting his wholesome brother. Have you eyes?
> Could you on this fair mountain leave to feed,
> And batten on this moor? Ha! Have you eyes?
>
> (*Hamlet*, III, iv)

Intellectio (in tel LEC ti o) — **Synecdoche**.

Interclusio (in ter CLU si o) — **Parenthesis**.

Interjectio — **Parenthesis**.

Interpellatio (in ter pel LA ti o; L. "interruption") — **Aposiopesis; Interruptio**.

Interpositio (in ter po SI ti o; L. "placing between").
1. **Parenthesis**.
2. **Epenthesis**.

Interpretatio (in ter pre TA ti o) — **Synonymia**.

Interrogatio (in ter ro GA ti o) — **Erotesis**.

Interruptio (in ter RUP ti o) — **Aposiopesis**.

Invention (L. *inventio*; G. *heuresis*).

The first of the five traditional parts of rhetorical theory, concerned with the finding and elaboration of arguments. Aristotle felt that factual **Proof** lay outside the art of rhetoric and so an inquiry into the facts of the case was not part of invention. Roman theorists such as Cicero and Quintilian disagreed. First, the speaker investigated the facts of the case. Then he determined the central **Issue** of the case. Then he explored the available means of persuasion. See **Invention** in chapter 2.

Inversio (in VER si o; L. "inversion") — **Allegory**.

Irmus — **Hirmus**.

Irony; alt. sp. **Eironeia** — **Dissimulatio**; **Drie Mock**; **Enantiosis**; **Illusio**.
1. Implying a meaning opposite to the literal meaning. Thus in *Pride and Prejudice*, Mr. Bennet: "I admire all my three sons-in-law highly. Wickham, perhaps, is my favourite."
2. Speaking in derision or mockery:

> . . . it was said by a French king, to one that praid his reward, showing how he had been cut in the face at a certain battle fought in his service: ye may see, quoth the king, what it is to run away and look backwards.
>
> (Puttenham, p. 189)

Generally speaking, the more sophisticated the irony, the more is implied, the less stated. **Trope** irony has been called franker than **Scheme** irony because in "scheme" irony the disguise is obvious rather than confessed, but this distinction seems no stronger than the suspect trope/scheme distinction itself. Many subcategories of irony have been needed, and of course many rhetorical terms point to irony of some sort. Anyone can do the same as needed by simply qualifying the word with the appropriate adjective.

Specifically rhetorical irony presents few problems. Puttenham's "drie mock" pretty well describes the phenomenon. One kind of rhetorical irony, however, may need further attention. There can be relatively few rhetorical situations where the target of persuasion is utterly ignorant of the designs someone has on him — the relationship of persuader and persuaded is almost always self-conscious to some degree. If the persuader wants to overcome any implicit sales resistance (especially from a sophisticated audience), one of the ways he will do it is to acknowledge that he *is* trying to talk his audience into something. By this, he hopes to gain their trust for as long as the soft sell takes. When he does this, he really acknowledges that his rhetorical maneuvering is ironical, that it says one thing while it tries to do another. At the same time, a second irony is present, since the pitchman is still far from laying all his cards on the table. The point to be made is that every rhetorical posture except the most naive involves an ironical coloration, of some kind or another, of the speaker's **Ethos**.

From the literary critic's point of view, irony and **Allegory** ought to bear some relation, since irony is clearly a particular, 180-degree-reversed, instance of allegory's double meaning. That is, the ironist depends on an allegorical habit of mind in his reader, a habit that will juxtapose surface and real meanings. For one suggestion as to how they might be related, see **Pun**.

See also **Charientismus; Metonymy**.

Isocolon (i so CO lon; G. "of equal members or clauses") — **Compar; Even; Parimembre; Parison**.

Phrases of approximately equal length and corresponding structure. Churchill, speaking about the life of a politician, combines this figure with **Pun** and **Climax**: "He is asked to stand, he wants to sit, and he is expected to lie." Bacon's laconic "Never complain, never explain" has served generations of later statesmen. Sometimes the similar elements are built into larger structures:

> Your reasons at dinner have been sharp and sententious; pleasant without scurrility, witty without affection, audacious without impudency, learned without opinion, and strange without heresy.
>
> (*Love's Labor's Lost*, V, i)

A narrower definition (e.g., *Ad Herennium*, IV.xx) calls for the clauses to have the same number of syllables.

Issue — **Constitutio; Stasis; Status**.

The complicated definitions of this term came from an effort to schematize *what an argument was about*. Cicero argued that the whole matter was contained in three questions: Does it exist? (*Sitne?*); What is it? (*Quid sit?*); What kind of thing is it? (*Quale sit?*). The modern equivalent of this concise method is the journalist's litany, Who? What? When? Why? Where? For rhetorical theorists, the question has usually been a lot more complicated.

Hermagoras, it is generally thought, introduced the theorizing about the *staseis* or issues. He divided oratorical argument into general **Theses** and particular **Hypotheses**. Theorists debated whether the issues of a thesis were the same as those of a hypothesis; Quintilian concluded that they were. Whether it applied to both or only to particular cases, the "issue" was the subject of a debate or the point of contention in a legal action. Hermagoras seems to have distinguished four types:

(1) conjectural (G. στοχασμός; L. *status* or *constitutio coniecturalis*): dispute over a fact. "Was the deed done?"
(2) definitional (G. ὅρος; L. *definitiva* or *proprietas*): dispute over a definition. "What *kind* of deed was done?"
(3) qualitative (G. ποιότης; L. *generalis* or *qualitas*): dispute over the value, quality, or nature of an act. "Was it a *legal* deed?"
(4) translative (G. μετάληψις; L. *translativa* or *translatio*): dispute over moving the issue from one court or jurisdiction to another. "Are we trying the case in the right court?"

The *Rhetorica ad Herennium* (I.xi.18–19) distinguishes three types: conjectural, legal ("some controversy turns upon the letter of a text"), juridical (dispute about fact).

The definition and use of the issues is an extremely vexing problem. One of the fullest discussions is Quintilian's (III.vi; there is also a discussion early in book VII), but the Loeb translator warns of it, "This chapter is highly technical and of little interest for the most part to any save professed students of the technique of the ancient schools of rhetoric." For the undeterred, there are excellent modern discussions in Bonner, *Roman Declamation*, especially pp. 12ff., and in Kennedy, *The Art of Persuasion in Greece*, pp. 305–314; see also Howell, *Logic and Rhetoric in England*, pp. 70–71, and Grube, *The Greek and Roman Critics*, pp. 142–144.

Iteratio (i te RA ti o; L. "repetition").
1. **Anaphora**.
2. **Palilogia (2)**.

Ius iurandum (ius iu RAN dum) — **Orcos**.

Judicial Rhetoric. *See* **Rhetoric: The three branches** in chapter 2.

Junctio (JUNC ti o; L. "joining") — **Zeugma**.

Kairos (kai ROS).
The Greek word for time, place, circumstances of a subject. Gorgias maintained that since there was no absolute truth, two antithetical statements could be made on any subject: only by reference to *kairos* could one decide which side to take.

Koinoi topoi (KOI noi TOP oi; G. "commonplaces") — **Commonplaces; Loci communes**. *See* chapter 2 at **Invention: The commonplaces**.

Koinonia (koi NO ni a; G. "association, partnership").
Consulting with one's opponent or with the judges.
See also **Comprobatio**.

Koinotes (KOI no tes; G. "sharing in common") — **Symploce**.

Lamentatio (la men TA ti o; L. "wailing, weeping") — **Threnos**.

Laudatio (lau DA ti o) — **Panegyric**.

Laws of Thought.
Those who use this term give three:
(1) Principle of Identity — if a statement is true, it is true.
(2) Principle of Contradiction — no statement can be both true and false.
(3) Principle of Excluded Middle — any statement must be either true or false.

Leptologia (lep to LO gi a; G. "subtle argument; quibbling").
Subtle speaking; quibbling. Surely Churchill gets the brass ring here:

> I rise to commit an irregularity. The intervention I make is without precedent, and the reason for that intervention is also without precedent, and the fact that the reason for my intervention is without precedent is the reason why I must ask for a precedent for my intervention.

Lexis (LEX is; G. "speech; diction, word") — **Elocutio**.
See also **Style**.

Licentia (li CEN ti a; L. "freedom; boldness, presumption") — **Parrhesia**.

Licentious. Puttenham's term for **Parrhesia**.

Like Letter. Puttenham's term for **Parimion**.

Like Loose. Puttenham's term for **Homoioteleuton**.

Literal Level. *See* **Allegory**.

Litotes (LI to tes; G. "plainness, simplicity") — **Antenantiosis; Moderatour**.
Denial of the contrary; understatement that intensifies, as when a politician once said to his garrulous subordinate, "A period of silence from you would now be not unwelcome." In litotes, "more is understood than is said," as in "He is not the wisest man in the

world" when we mean "He is a fool" (Peacham). Sister Miriam Joseph remarks: "Litotes is related to what the logicians call equipollence or obversion, which consists in expressing a thought by denying its contradictory" (p. 323).

Loci communes (LO ci com MU nes) — **Commonplaces; Koinoi topoi.** *See* chapter 2 at **Invention: The commonplaces.**

Loci positio (po SI ti o) — **Topothesia.**

Logic.
The rules of formal reasoning. It includes all the devices for persuasion that Aristotle includes under the third group of ways to persuade — "proving the case." The other two are: establishing the speaker as a man of trust, and playing on the emotions of the audience.

Logos (LO gos; G. "word; thought").
A word of many meanings in Greek, and the now-frequent use of it in criticism of literature and the arts does not always make clear what meaning is intended. Three related but different areas of meaning dwelt in *logos*. It referred to language itself, to the thinking which language expressed, and to the conceptually knowable part of the world which language could express: language, thought, world. See Kerferd's excellent discussion of this word in *The Sophistic Movement*, pp. 83ff.
See also **Proof; Rhetoric.**

Long Language. Puttenham's term for **Macrologia.**

Long Loose. Puttenham's term for **Hirmus.**

Loose Language. Puttenham's term for **Asyndeton.**

Loud Lyer. Puttenham's second term for **Hyperbole.**

Love Burden. Puttenham's term for **Epimone.**

Macrologia (ma cro LO gi a; G. "speaking at length") — **Long Language; Sermo superfluus.**
Long-winded speech; using more words than necessary. So Polonius's famous exercise in brevity:

> My liege and madam, to expostulate
> What majesty should be, what duty is,
> Why day is day, night night, and time is time,

Were nothing but to waste night, day, and time.
Therefore, since brevity is the soul of wit,
And tediousness the limbs and outward flourishes,
I will be brief.

(Hamlet, II, ii)

Further discussion. The terms for longwindedness — what we might call the "Polonian figures," after their great Shakespearean practitioner, Polonius — I am upon thorns to differentiate. Most theorists list them as separate, though often overlapping, terms, and I have followed that practice here. But I would hate to be cross-examined on the differences between them. One group of terms seems to cluster around "needless repetition," and another around what we might today call "overwriting," an overelaborated style. The "needless repetition" group would include **Macrologia, Perissologia, Pleonasmus**, and **Tautologia**; the "overwriting" group, **Asianism, Bomphiologia, Periergia**, and **Poicilogia**, and perhaps **Homiologia** as well. But even this distinction is hard to maintain; the example I have given above, the very locus classicus of longwindedness, illustrates both areas of meaning. A third area, the various terms for circumlocution, seems to me different altogether, and so I have not cross-referenced the relevant terms.

Mala affectio (MA la   af FEC ti o; L. "unfavorable impression, attitude, propensity") — **Cacozelia**.

Malapropism.

A form of **Cacozelia**: vulgar error through an attempt to seem learned; not, properly speaking, a rhetorical term. The word commemorates Mrs. Malaprop, a character in Sheridan's *The Rivals* (1775): "Now don't attempt to extirpate yourself from the matter: you know I have proof controvertible of it." Modern Malaprops, happily, are still with us, as in, "Unless I get my husband's money very soon, I will be forced to lead an immortal life." Also sometimes **Acyrologia**.

Male collocatum (MA le   col lo CA tum; L. "badly grouped") — **Cacosyntheton**.

Male figuratum (fi gu RA tum) — **Aschematiston**.

Marching Figure. Puttenham's term for **Climax**.

Martyria (mar TYR i a; G. "testimony, evidence") — **Testatio**.

Confirming something by one's own experience, as when Horatio says of the ghost:

> Before my God, I might not this believe
> Without the sensible and true avouch
> Of mine own eyes.

> (*Hamlet*, I, i)

See also **Apodixis**.

Maxim (L. "greatest [proposition]") — **Proverb**.

Mediate Inference.

One drawn in a **Syllogism** that has two premises; inference from one premise is called *immediate*.

Megaloprepeia (me ga lo pre PEI a; G. "magnificence").

Elevation and gravity of style; *gravitas*. For Demetrius (*On Style*, 36), the name for the high style. See chapter 2 at **Style: The three types**.

Meiosis (mei O sis; G. "lessening") — **Diminutio; Disabler; Extenuatio; Imminutio.**

To belittle, often through a trope of one word; use a degrading epithet: "childish carriage" for "Rolls Royce," or Oscar Wilde's description of an English country gentleman fox-hunting as "the unspeakable in full pursuit of the uneatable." Quintilian tells us it can also refer to a naturally meager style, or one intentionally and aggressively plain; in the first case it is not a figure, in the second, it is (VIII.iii.50). Sometimes it overlaps with **Litotes**.

See also **Tapinosis**.

Membrum orationis (MEM brum o ra ti O nis); alt. sp. **Member — Colon.**

Memory (L. *memoria*; G. *mneme*).

The fourth of the traditional five parts of rhetoric, that which discusses devices to aid and improve the memory. One common device was a "memory theater" in which the various features of a well-known room or hall were associated each with a separate point the speaker sought to remember (see Yates, *The Art of Memory*). See chapter 2 at **Memory**.

Mempsis (MEMP sis; G. "blaming, reproach; complaint") — **Querimonia**.

Complaining against injuries and pleading for help.

> How long wilt thou forget me, O Lord? For ever?
> How long wilt thou hide thy face from me?
> How long shall I take counsel in my soul,

Having sorrow in my heart daily? How long shall mine enemy be
    exalted over me?
Consider and hear me, O Lord my God:
Lighten mine eyes, lest I sleep the sleep of death.
                                          (Psalm 13:1–3)

Merismus (me RIS mus; G. "division") — **Distribution.**

Merry Scoffe. One of Puttenham's terms for **Asteismus.**

Mesozeugma (me so ZEUG ma; G. "yoking in the middle"); alt. sp.
Mezozeugma — **Middlemarcher.**

A type of **Zeugma** which places in the middle of a construction the
common verb on which two or more words or clauses depend:
"And now a bubble *burst*, and now a world."

Metabasis (me TA ba sis; G. "change, shifting, transition") —
Transitio.

Figure of transition: brief statement of what has been said and
what will follow; a "linking summary" (Taylor). "You know how he
has just been conducting himself towards his fatherland; now consider what kind of son he has been to his parents" (*Rhetorica ad
Herennium*, IV.xxvi.36).

Metalepsis (me ta LEP sis; G. "substitution") — **Far-Fet; Trans ump-
tio.**

Present effect attributed to a remote cause: "The ship is sinking:
damn the forest where the mast grew." The remote cause, because
several causal steps intervene between it and the result, seems less
like a cause than a metaphor substituted for a cause. Peacham's
example: "Virgil by ears of corn signifieth harvests, by harvests,
summers, and by summers, years." Quintilian is perhaps right
when he calls it a **Trope** we should know about but seldom have
occasion to use since, he says, it is used by the Greeks but rarely in
Latin. The Greeks certainly did use the word *metalepsis*, since it has
thirteen different meanings in Liddell and Scott, including ones special to grammar, rhetoric (see **Issue**), and dialectic. In that playful
spirit, I submit a short amplification.

Quintilian (VIII.vi.37ff.) calls it a transition from one trope to another: "The commonest example is the following: *cano* [sing] is a
synonym for *canto* [chant] and *canto* for *dico* [speak], therefore *cano*
is a synonym for *dico*, the intermediate step being provided by
canto." The main element would thus seem to be omission of a
central term in an extended metaphor or series of them, a kind of
compressed chain of metaphorical reasoning. So Sister Miriam Jo-

seph: "Cause and effect are related productively, antecedent and consequent temporally. The conditional or hypothetical proposition states the relation of antecedent and consequent." Perelman (*New Rhetoric*, p. 181) argues that it "can facilitate the transposition of values into facts. 'He forgets' for 'he is ungrateful.' " If I have absorbed the collective wisdom about this trope, the following passage from Howell's *Familiar Letters* ought to be one:

> . . . of this wine may be verified that merry induction, that good wine makes good blood, good blood causeth good humours, good humours cause good thoughts, good thoughts bring forth good works, good works carry a man to heaven, ergo good wine carry a man to heaven.

Metanoia (me ta NOI a; G. "change of mind or heart; correction"); alt. sp. **Metania — Penitent**.

Qualification of a statement by recalling it and expressing it in a better way, often by using a negative.

> Gentlemen, my part is done; yours is about to commence. . . . Oh, how awful is your responsibility! . . . I do conjure you, not as fathers, but as husbands; — not as husbands, but as citizens; — not as citizens, but as men; — not as men, but as Christians. . . .
> (Charles Phillips, *Speeches* [1817], quoted in David Mellinkoff, *Conscience of a Lawyer*, pp. 46–47)

See also **Correctio (1)**.

Metaphor (G. "transference") — **Translatio; Transport**.

Changing a word from its literal meaning to one not properly applicable but analogous to it; assertion of identity rather than, as with **Simile**, likeness. (Quintilian, however, minimizes the differences between the two: "On the whole *metaphor* is a shorter form of *simile*" [VIII.vi.8].)

Aristotle's explanation of how a metaphor works conceives of metaphor not only as comparison between two elements but creation of a third, new meaning: "We all naturally find it agreeable to get hold of new ideas easily: words express ideas, and therefore those words are the most agreeable that enable us to get hold of new ideas. Now strange words simply puzzle us; ordinary words convey only what we know already; it is from metaphor that we can best get hold of something fresh" (*Rhetoric*, III, 1410b). Kenneth Burke develops this argument: "It is precisely through metaphor that our perspectives, or analogical extensions, are made — a world without metaphor would be a world without purpose" (*Permanence and Change*, p. 194). Quintilian calls it "the most beautiful of tropes," praising it for accomplishing "the supremely difficult task of providing a name for everything" (VIII.vi.4–5). Roman Jakobson has

100

singled out metaphor and **Metonymy** as the two main engines of rhetorical language, passing down to modern critical thinking a basic distinction between metaphor as indicating similarity and metonymy as revealing contiguity. And Northrop Frye has made the distinction into an oral/literate one, arguing that metaphor is an *oral* device, metonymy a *literate* one: "The basis of expression here is moving from the metaphorical, with its sense of identity of life or power or energy between man and nature ('this is that'), to a relationship that is rather metonymic ('this is put for that'). Specifically, words are 'put for' thoughts, and are the outward expressions of an inner reality" (*The Great Code*, pp. 7–8). Vico called metaphor a fable in brief, which leads us to think of it as allegory-in-miniature, in the same way that we might think of **Pun** as irony-in-miniature. And finally, Christine Brooke-Rose (in *A Grammar of Metaphor*, pp. 23–24), after surveying all the definitions, settles on this plain definition: "metaphor . . . is any replacement of one word by another, or any identification of one thing, concept or person with any other."

Perhaps it is metaphor's intrinsic *instability* which has attracted so much recent attention: to appreciate the metaphoricality of a metaphor we must posit a nonmetaphorical, normative "reality" against which to project the metaphorical transformation. The oscillation of the two reality states, normative and transformative, provides the essential bounded instability of a bistable illusion.

Metaplasm (ME ta plasm; G. "a changed form").

"Metaplasm is a transformation of letters or syllables in single words, contrary to the common fashion of writing or speaking, either for cause of necessity, or else to make the verse more fine" (Peacham). A generic term: see **Antisthecon; Aphaeresis; Apocope; Diaeresis; Diastole; Ellipsis; Epenthesis; Metathesis; Paragoge; Prothesis; Synaeresis; Synaloepha; Syncope; Systole.**

See also **Barbarismus.**

Metastasis (me TA sta sis; G. "removal; change") — **Flitting Figure; Remove; Transmotio.**

1. Passing over an issue quickly. The cleverest, self-confessed, example must be Churchill's reply to reporters at a news conference: "I think 'No comment' is a splendid expression. I am using it again and again. I got it from Sumner Welles."

2. Turning back an insult or objection against the person who made it:

> *Oliver:* Get you with him, you old dog!
> *Adam:* Is 'old dog' my reward? Most true, I have lost my teeth in your service.

> (*As You Like It*, I, i)

Metathesis (me TA the sis; G. "transposition, change") — **Antisthecon; Transposition.**
Type of **Metaplasm**: transposition of a letter out of normal order in a word — "morden" for "modern." An Australian judge recently used the figure when he commented, "If I had my way with Germaine Greer's followers, I would put them all behind bras."

Metonymy (me TO ny my; G. "change of name") — **Denominatio; Hypallage (2); Misnamer; Transmutation; Transnominatio.**
There are four types, corresponding to the four **Causes**: substitution of cause for effect or effect for cause, proper name for one of its qualities or vice versa; so the Wife of Bath is spoken of as half Venus and half Mars to denote her unique mixture of love and strife. Kenneth Burke (in Appendix D to *A Grammar of Motives*) includes metonymy in his list of four "master tropes." Each, he points out, can perform a function considerably wider than its formal rhetorical definition might indicate:

> For *metaphor* we could substitute *perspective*;
> For *metonymy* we could substitute *reduction*;
> For *synecdoche* we could substitute *representation*;
> For *irony* we could substitute *dialectic*.

Perhaps metonymy has received attention in postmodern critical thinking because it is an affair finally of scale-manipulation, and manipulating scale in time and space undergirds much postmodern art and music. Or perhaps, since collage has stood at the center of the postmodern art world, the juxtaposition of metonymy has been felt to be the central instance of the transforming power of metaphor.
See also **Alloiosis; Irony; Metaphor; Synecdoche.**

Mezozeugma — **Mesozeugma.**

Middlemarcher. Puttenham's term for **Mesozeugma.**

Mimesis (mi ME sis; G. "imitation").
Imitation of gesture, pronunciation, or utterance; self-conscious role-playing, as when a rhapsode reenacts the poem he is reciting. A generic term.
See also **Dialogismus; Ethopoeia; Prosopopoeia; Sermocinatio**, *inter alia.*

Mingle Mangle. Puttenham's term for **Soraismus.**

Misnamer. Puttenham's term for **Metonymy.**

Misplacer. Puttenham's term for **Cacosyntheton.**

Mneme (MNE me; G.) — **Memory.**

Moderatour. Puttenham's term for **Litotes.**

Moral Level. *See* **Allegory.**

Mycterismus (myc te RIS mus; G. "turning up the nose, sneering at") — **Fleering Frumpe; Subsannatio.**
Mockery of an opponent, accompanied by a gesture. Thus when an opponent in Parliament asked Churchill, "Must you fall asleep when I am speaking?" Churchill replied, "No, it is purely voluntary."

Narration (L. *narratio*) — **Praecognitio; Prothesis.**
The second part of a six-part classical oration. It gives the audience the history of the problem. See chapter 2 at **Arrangement: The parts of an oration.**

Necessary Cause.
A **Cause** in the absence of which the result *cannot* happen.

Necessum (ne CES sum; L. "unavoidable, inevitable") — **Dicaeologia.**

Negatio (ne GA ti o; L. "denial") — **Apophasis (1).**

Newnamer. Puttenham's term for **Onomatopoeia.**

Nicknamer. Puttenham's term for **Prosonomasia.**

Noema (no E ma; G. "thought, idea").
Deliberately obscure speech. Puttenham calls this **Close Conceit.** "In the United States there is more space where nobody is than where anybody is. This is what makes America what it is" (Gertrude Stein, *The Geographical History of America*).
See also **Enigma; Schematismus.**

Nominatio (no mi NA ti o; L. "naming").
1. **Antonomasia.**
2. **Onomatopoeia.**

Nominis fictio (NO mi nis FIC ti o; L. "feigning of a name") — **Onomatopoeia**.

Non sequitur (SE qui tur; L. "it does not follow").
A statement that bears no relationship to the context preceding.

Notatio (no TA ti o; L. "marking, observing, describing") — **Characterismus; Ethopoeia**.

Obsecratio (ob se CRA ti o; L. "imploring") — **Deesis**.

Obtestatio (ob tes TA ti o; L. "calling [the gods] to witness") — **Deesis**.

Obticentia (ob ti CEN ti a; L. "pause, sudden break") — **Aposiopesis**.

Occultatio (oc cul TA ti o; L. "concealment; insinuation, suggestion") — **Occupatio; Paralepsis; Parasiopesis; Praeteritio**.
Emphasizing something by pointedly seeming to pass over it, as in introducing a guest speaker one says, "I will not dwell here on the twenty books and the thirty articles Professor X has written, nor his forty years as Dean, nor his many illustrious pupils, but only say that last year in Africa he killed ten men with his spear."
An erroneous reading in the *Ad Herennium* has led to the currency of **Occupatio** as a synonym. After a thorough discussion of this error in the tradition, my colleague H. A. Kelly has urged that "the term *occupatio* should be retired from present-day use as a rhetorical term." Let us by all means do so; reducing the number even by one helps clarify the muddle. (See "*Occupatio* as Negative Narration: A Mistake for *Occultatio/Praeteritio*," *Journal of Modern Philology*, 74 [1976–77], 311–315.)

Occupatio (oc cu PA ti o) — **Occultatio**.

Oictos (OIC tos; G. "pity, compassion"); alt. sp. **Oictros** (Taylor misreads this as "cictros" in Sherry) — **Commiseratio**.

Ominatio (o mi NA ti o).
Prophecy of evil.
See also **Cataplexis; Paraenesis**.

Omiosis — **Homoeosis**.

Onedismus (o ne DIS mus; G. "reproach") — **Exprobatio**.
Reproaching someone as ungrateful or impious.

Onomaton (o NO ma ton; G. "words; nouns") — **Scesis onomaton**.

Onomatopoeia (on o ma to po EI a; G. "the making of words") — **Newnamer; Nominatio; Nominis fictio; Procreatio**.
Use or invention of words that sound like their meaning: "the murmur of innumerable bees," the wind "soughing" (*sooing, sowing, suffing*, according to taste or tree) in the trees.

Oppositio (op po SI ti o) — **Antithesis**.

Optatio (op TA ti o; L. "a wish").
A wish exclaimed: "A horse! my kingdom for a horse!"

Oraculum (o RA cu lum; L. "oracle, prophecy").
The "quoting" of God's words or commandments.

Oratory.
Public speech. **Rhetoric**, on the other hand, usually means the *theory* of oratory. There are three types of oratory, corresponding to the three branches of rhetoric:
(1) deliberative
(2) judicial or forensic
(3) epideictic
See chapter 2 at **Rhetoric: The three branches**.

Orcos (OR cos; G. "oath") — **Ius iurandum**.
An oath.

Ordinatio (or di NA ti o; L. "setting in order, regulating") — **Dinumeratio (1)**.

Ordo artificialis (OR do   ar ti fi ci A lis). *See* **Ordo naturalis**.

Ordo naturalis (na tu RA lis).
The term for the *ab ovo* opening (beginning from the beginning, "from the egg") of a narrative, common from the *Rhetorica ad Herennium* onward. The opposite term, for the *in medias res* opening (beginning in the middle of things), was **Ordo artificialis**.

Ornatus difficilis (or NA tus   dif FI ci lis) — **Difficult Ornament**.

Outcrie. Puttenham's term for **Ecphonesis**.

Outis — **Utis**.

Over Labour. Puttenham's term for **Periergia.**

Overreacher. Puttenham's second term for **Hyperbole.**

Oxymoron (ox y MO ron; G. "a witty, paradoxical saying," lit. "pointedly foolish").
   A condensed paradox, Milton's "darkness visible" for example, or "Everything screams in silence here" in Yevtushenko's "Babi Yar." We use this figure every day: "act natural!," "fast asleep," "civil war," "jumbo shrimp," "pretty ugly," even a "hard water" which is not yet "dry ice." It easily generates an ironic charge, as in "Ivy League football," "academic administration," "business ethics," "airline food," "apartment living," or "military intelligence."
   See also **Synoeciosis.**

Padeuteria (from G. *paideuterion*, "school").
   "A poem giving thanks to teachers for what we have been taught, or to God for our teachers" (quoted from Scaliger by Sonnino, p. 230). A genre which has often suffered from neglect but cannot be too strongly recommended.

Paeanismus (pae a NIS mus; G. "singing of the victory hymn").
   An exclamation of joy; a type of **Ecphonesis.**

> O, joy unbounded,
> With wealth surrounded,
> The knell is sounded
>   Of grief and woe.
>
> (Gilbert and Sullivan, *Trial by Jury*)

Palilogia (pa li LO gi a; G. "recapitulation").
   1. **Anadiplosis.**
   2. **Iteratio.** Repetition for vehemence or fullness.

Palindrome (G. "running back again").
   Words, phrases, or sentences which make sense read backwards as well as forwards: "Able was I ere I saw Elba"; "Madam, I'm Adam." A palindrome would seem to represent the compressed extreme of a **Chiasmus.**

Panegyric — Laudatio.
   Formal and ornate praise of person or deed. See **Rhetoric: The three branches** in chapter 2.

Parable (G. "a placing beside"); alt. sp. **Parabola — Resemblance Misticall.**

Teaching a moral by means of an extended metaphor:

> Consider the lilies of the field, how they grow; they toil not, neither do they spin: and yet I say unto you, that even Solomon in all his glory was not arrayed like one of these.
>
> (Matt. 6:28–29)

See also **Allegory; Simile.**

Paradiastole (pa ra di A sto le; G. rhet., "a putting together of dissimilar things") — **Curry Favell; Euphemismus (2)**.

"When we make the best of a bad thing . . . call an unthrift, a liberal Gentleman; the foolish-hardy, valiant or courageous; the niggard, thrifty" (Puttenham, pp. 184–185).

Paradiegesis (pa ra di e GE sis; G. "incidental narrative").

A narrative **Digression** used to introduce one's argument. Usually classed as a type of **Narration**, but Peacham calls it a special form of **Insinuatio**. Thus Churchill prefaces his discussion of the European situation created by the Munich agreement with this digression:

> In my holiday I thought it was a chance to study the reign of King Ethelred the Unready. The House will remember that that was a period of great misfortune, in which, from the strong position which we had gained under the descendants of King Alfred, we fell very swiftly into chaos. It was the period of Danegeld and of foreign pressure. I must say that the rugged words of the *Anglo-Saxon Chronicle*, written a thousand years ago, seem to me apposite. . . . I think the words apply very much to our treatment of Germany and our relations with her. "All these calamities fell upon us because of evil counsel, because tribute was not offered to them at the right time nor yet were they resisted; but when they had done the most evil, then was peace made with them."
>
> (House of Commons, 5 October 1938)

Paradigma (pa ra DIG ma; G. "model, example, lesson") — **Exemplum**.

Paradox (G. "contrary to opinion or expectation") — **Synoeciosis; Wondrer**.

A seemingly self-contradictory statement, which yet is shown to be (sometimes in a surprising way) true: "She makes the black night bright by smiling on it."

See also **Oxymoron.**

Paraenesis (pa RAE ne sis; G. "exhortation; advice") — **Admonitio**.
Warning of impending evil.

See also **Cataplexis; Ominatio.**

Paragoge (PA ra go ge; G. "leading past") — **Proparalepsis**.
Adding a letter or syllable to the end of a word: "beforne" for "before." See **Metaplasm**.

Paralepsis (pa ra LEP sis; G. "disregard, omission"); alt. sp. **Paralipsis** — **Occultatio; Passager**.

Paralogia (pa ra LO gi a; G. "fraudulent reasoning") — **Paromologia**.

Paramologia — **Paromologia**.

Paramythia (pa ra MYTH i a; G. "encouragement; consolation") — **Consolatio**.

Parasiopesis (pa ra si o PE sis; G. "omission, passing over in silence") — **Occultatio**.

Parataxis (pa ra TAX is; G. "placing side by side").
Clauses or phrases arranged independently (a coordinate, rather than a subordinate, construction), sometimes, as here, without the customary connectives: "I came, I saw, I conquered." Opposite of **Hypotaxis**. Eric Havelock has argued that parataxis is essentially an *oral* syntax, as opposed to the *literate* balance and subordination of hypotaxis.

Parathesis (pa ra THE sis; G. "putting beside") — **Parenthesis**.

Parecbasis (pa REC ba sis; G. "deviation, digression") — **Digression**.

Paregmenon (pa REG me non; G. "led aside, changed") — **Polyptoton**.

Parelcon (pa REL con; G. "redundant").
Addition of superfluous words; using two words where only one would normally stand: "for why" instead of "why."

Paremptosis (pa rem PTO sis) — **Parenthesis**.

Parenthesis (G. "insertion") — **Insertour; Interclusio; Interjectio; Interpositio; Parathesis; Paremptosis**.
Form of **Hyperbaton**: a word, phrase, or sentence inserted as an aside in a sentence complete in itself.

Pareuresis (pa REU re sis; G. "pretext") — **Adinventio; Excusatio**.

1. Offering an excuse of such weight that it overcomes all objections.

> By being so long in the lowest form [at Harrow] I gained an immense advantage over the cleverer boys. . . . I got into my bones the essential structure of the ordinary British sentence — which is a noble thing.
>> (Churchill, *My Early Life*)

2. Inventing a false pretext.

> What, upon compulsion? 'Zounds, an I were at the strappado, or all the racks in the world, I would not tell you on compulsion. Give you a reason on compulsion! If reasons were as plentiful as blackberries, I would give no man a reason upon compulsion, I.
>> (*1 Henry IV*, II, iv)

Parimembre (pa ri MEM bre) — **Isocolon**.

Parimia — **Paroemia**. *See* **Proverb**.

Parimion — **Paroemion**.

Parison (PA ri son; G. "evenly balanced"); alt. sp. **Parisosis** — **Isocolon**.

Paroemia (pa ROE mi a; G. "byword, proverb"); alt. sp. **Parimia** — **Proverb**.

Paroemion (pa ROE mi on; G. "closely resembling"); alt. sp. **Parimion, Paromoeon** — **Like Letter**.

A resolute **Alliteration**, in which every word in a phrase or sentence begins with the same letter:

> The preyful princess pierc'd and prick'd a pretty pleasing pricket.
>> (*Love's Labor's Lost*, IV, ii)

> Gaunt as the ghastliest of glimpses that gleam through the gloom of the gloaming when ghosts go aghast . . .
>> (Swinburne, *Nephelidia*)

Paromoiosis (pa ro moi O sis; G. "assimilation, assonance, comparison"); alt. sp. **Paromoeosis**.

"Parallelism of sound between the words of two clauses either approximately or exactly equal in size. This similarity in sound may appear at the beginning, at the end (*homoioteleuton*), in the interior, or it may pervade the whole" (Smyth, *Greek Grammar*, p. 681). Lausberg defines it as the highest degree of **Isocolon**, extending the correspondences of both words and parts of the sentence.

> Do not let us speak of darker days; let us speak rather of sterner days. These are not dark days: these are great days.
>> (Churchill, "To the Boys of Harrow School")

Paromologia (pa ro mo LO gi a); alt. sp. **Paramologia** — **Admittance; Confessio; Paralogia**.

Conceding a point either from conviction of its truth or to use it to strengthen one's own argument; giving away a weaker point in order to take a stronger:

> I deny not but I have heretofore used you in causes secret, in matters weighty and of counsel, that I have found you friendly, faithfull and ready, but what is all that to the purpose, when in a thing so important, and matter nearly concerning me, as whereon dependeth the safeguard of my whole house and family, I have found you in both negligent and untrusty.
>
> (Day)

Thus Bunthorne confesses to Patience,

> Let me tell you a secret. I am not as bilious as I look. . . . There is more innocent fun within me than a casual spectator would imagine. . . . If you are fond of touch-and-go jocularity — this is the shop for it.
>
> (Gilbert and Sullivan, *Patience*, Act I)

Paronomasia (pa ro no MA si a; G. "play upon words which sound alike") — **Adnominatio; Pun; Skesis**.

Punning; playing on the sounds and meanings of words; unlike **Antanaclasis** in that the words punned on are similar but not identical in sound. Falstaff includes both kinds in jesting with Prince Hal: "Were it not here apparent that thou art heir apparent . . ." (*1 Henry IV*, I, ii). Cicero (*De oratore*, II.lxiii.256) gives **Assonance** as a synonym for paronomasia, but although both assonance and **Consonance**, as well as **Alliteration**, might be thought of as kinds of paronomasia, the synonymity has not been accepted.

See also **Prosonomasia**.

Parrhesia (par RHE si a; G. "free-spokenness, frankness"); alt. sp. **Parresia** — **Licentia; Licentious**.

1. Candid speech. Fraunce cites Sidney:

> I therefore say to thee, O just Judge, that I, and only I, was the worker of *Basilius'* death: they were these hands that gave unto him that poisonous potion, that has brought death to him, and loss to Arcadia.

2. Begging pardon in advance for necessary candor. *See also* **Correctio (2)**.

Partitio (par TI ti o; L. "division; logical division into parts").
1. **Division**.
2. **Diaeresis**.

Passager. Puttenham's term for **Paralepsis;** *see* **Occultatio.**

Pathopoeia (pa tho po EI a; G. "excitement of the passions"); alt.
sp. **Pathopopeia** — **Pathos.**
General term for arousing passion or emotion.
See also, e.g., **Deesis; Ecphonesis; Indignatio; Oictos.**

Pathos (PA thos; G. "emotion; experience").
This term has been used both for techniques of stirring emotion
(especially in a law court) and for the emotions themselves. Further,
both the emotions a speaker feels *himself* and those he seeks to
evoke in others have some claim to the term. As an additional com-
plication, some writers maintain that the term applies to only certain, or a certain range of, emotions. Thus, Quintilian tells us
(VI.ii.1ff.) that "the more cautious writers" distinguish between pathos, which describes the more violent emotions, and **Ethos,** which
refers to the calmer ones. The more violent emotions, too, are likely
to be transitory, the calmer ones continuous. It seems a reasonably
accurate simplification to say that ethos is the character, or set of
emotions, which a speaker reenacts in order to affect an audience,
and pathos the emotion that the speaker aims to induce in his audience. The Renaissance theorists, however, did not make precisely
this distinction. Pathos (or **Pathopoeia**) was likely to refer to any
emotional appeal, ethos (**Ethopoeia**) simply to a description of character, or of characteristics, for whatever purpose and of whatever
kind.
The term **Bathos** has, since Pope's *Peri Bathous,* sometimes been
used to describe the emotional appeal that, intentionally or not,
evokes laughter rather than transport, which sinks rather than
soars: "The Taste of the Bathos is implanted by Nature itself in the
soul of man."

Penitent. Puttenham's term for **Metanoia.**

Percontatio (per con TA ti o; L. "questioning, inquiry") — **Epiplexis.**

Percursio (per CUR si o; L. "a rapid survey") — **Epitrochasmus.**

Periergia (pe ri ER gi a; G. "overelaboration") — **Over Labour; Sedulitas superflua.**
"When in a small matter, there is so much labor bestowed, and
too many words and figures used" (Peacham). Quintilian makes a
case for periergia as, specifically, superfluous elaboration of a point.
If so, the juvenile Jane Austen scores in miniature by describing a

flowered lawn as "a verdant Lawn enamelled with a variety of variegated flowers" ("Frederic & Elfrida"). See further discussion at **Macrologia**.

Period — Ambitus; Comprehensio; Conclusion; Continuatio; Hirmus; Periodic Sentence.

The third and longest element in the classical theory of the period, a theory of prose rhythm originated by the Peripatetics. Quintilian (IX.iv.19ff.) distinguishes two styles: "There are then in the first place two kinds of style: the one is closely welded and woven together, while the other is of a looser texture such as is found in dialogues and letters." The first, or "compact," is for him the one to which the **Comma–Colon–Period** theory of prose rhythm properly applies. Others apply it especially to formal oratorical or declamatory occasions. The basic unit of measurement is the period. If this grows too long, however, some see the colon or "member" as the basic unit (see Croll, *Style, Rhetoric, and Rhythm*, pp. 324 ff.). Its parts are *cola*; the components of the cola are short often parenthetical elements, the *commata*. The exact nature of these divisions is very variously defined and defies simplification. (They are not to be confused with the punctuation marks that later took over their names, of course.) Perhaps the following comments will help.

The period for Aristotle (*Rhetoric*, III, 1409a–b ff.):

> By a period I mean a portion of speech that has in itself a beginning and an end, being at the same time not too big to be taken in at a glance. . . . The period must . . . not be completed until the sense is complete. . . .
>
> A Period may be either divided into several members or simple. The period of several members is a portion of speech (1) complete in itself, (2) divided into parts, and (3) easily delivered at a single breath. . . . A member is one of the two parts of such a period. By a 'simple' period, I mean that which has only one member. The members, and the whole periods, should be neither curt nor long.
>
> The periodic style which is divided into members is of two kinds. It is either simply divided . . . or it is antithetical. . . .

Demetrius's *On Style* distinguishes three types of period, corresponding roughly to the traditional levels of **Style**: (1) historical (low) — plain, simple, suited to description; (2) conversational (middle) — loosest, least periodic; (3) rhetorical (high) — ornamental, highly periodic.

Generally speaking, one might say that the period expresses a complete thought self-sufficiently; beyond this, it must have at least two members. (Cicero insists it must not be longer than four iambic trimeters.) "Periodic sentence" is a very rough English equivalent; it describes a long sentence that consists of a number of elements, often balanced or antithetical, and existing in perfectly clear syntactical relationship to one another. The phrase "suspended syntax" is often used to describe it, since the syntactical pattern, and so the sense, is not completed, is "suspended," until the end. The effect of the periodic sentence is often to throw the interest forward, create a mild suspense. So Dr. Johnson on Shakespeare's annotators:

> I could have written longer notes, for the art of writing notes is not of difficult attainment. The work is performed, first by railing at the stupidity, negligence, ignorance, and asinine tastelessness of the former editors, and showing, from all that goes before and all that follows, the inelegance and absurdity of the old reading; then by proposing something which to superficial readers would seem specious, but which the editor rejects with indignation; then by producing the true reading, with a long paraphrase, and concluding with loud declamations on the discovery and a sober wish for the advancement and prosperity of genuine criticism.

The climactic member need not be at the end, however. Sometimes it is at the center, whence the terms "circuitus" and "round composition."

Baxandall has called attention to the central importance of the periodic sentence for Renaissance humanists:

> The pattern of the grand neo-classical sentence was the period: that is, the sentence combining a number of thoughts and statements in a number of balanced clauses. . . . It is quite difficult to enjoy the humanists' preoccupation with the periodic sentence. . . . But one cannot come to historical terms with the humanists' verbal performance without recognizing how supremely important it was for them, and in how many different ways. The periodic sentence is the basic art form of the early humanists. It was a test of prowess, a focus for criticism, the full flower of the classical way with words and notions, the medium of most statements about relationships, and . . . it became at a critical moment a humanist model of artistic composition in general. (pp. 20–21)

It became, he later points out, a central school exercise:

> [T]he notion of *compositio* is a very precise metaphor transferring to painting a model of organization derived from rhetoric itself. *Compositio* was a technical concept every schoolboy in a humanist school had been taught to apply to language. It did not mean what we mean by literary composition, but rather the putting together of the single evolved sentence or period, this being done within the framework of a four-level hierarchy of elements: words go to make up phrases, phrases to make clauses, clauses to make sentences. (p. 131)

The long, formal periodic structure even today still provides the best example of how print can tension the figures of position into larger patterns of hierarchical and antithetical balance.

Periodic Sentence — Period.

Periphrasis (pe RI phra sis; G. "circumlocution") — **Ambage; Circu(m)itio.**
Circumlocution, as when Sir Winston Churchill is said to have replied to an impertinent question, "The answer to your question, sir, is in the plural, and they bounce."

Perissologia (pe ris so LO gi a; G. "wordiness; elaborate writing").
Sherry specifies that perissologia applies to the repetition of thoughts, whereas **Pleonasmus**, and hence **Macrologia**, apply to words. A difficult distinction to sustain, perhaps.

Peristasis (pe RI sta sis; G. "circumstances, situation").
Amplifying by describing attendant circumstances.

Peristrophe (pe RI stro phe; G. "a turning around").
Converting an opponent's argument to one's own use. So when Churchill was asked what precautions should be taken if Prime Minister Stanley Baldwin were to die in office, he replied: "Embalm, bury, and cremate. Take no chances!"
See also **Paromologia.**

Permissio (per MIS si o) — **Concessio; Epitrope (1).**

Permutatio (per mu TA ti o; L. "change, substitution").
A changeling which lives up to its name.
1. **Allegory.**
2. **Enallage.**
3. **Antimetabole.**

Peroration — Conclusion; Epilogue.
The last part of the six-part classical oration. This conclusion was often an impassioned summary, not simply a review of previous arguments. The *Ad Herennium* tells us the Greeks divided the conclusion into summing up (*enumeratio*), amplification (*amplificatio*), and appeal to pity (*commiseratio*) (II.xxx.47). See chapter 2 at **Arrangement: The parts of an oration.**
See also **Dinumeratio (3b).**

Perseverantia (per se ve RAN ti a; L. "constancy") — **Epimone.**

Personification — Prosopopoeia.

Persuasion.

The goal of **Rhetoric**. Aristotle (*Rhetoric*, I, 1356a) lists three modes of persuasion:

(1) *ethos,* or the demonstration of the speaker's good character

(2) *pathos,* or playing on the audience's feelings

(3) *logos,* what today we would call "proof" of some sort

See **Proof.**

Perversio (per VER si o; L. "inversion") — **Anastrophe.**

Petitio principii (pe TI ti o   prin CI pi i; L. "begging the question").

The premise and conclusion say the same thing in different words, or the premise needs proof as much as the conclusion. One might argue, for example, that poverty is a good thing, since the right to starve is a Basic American Freedom. Chaim Perelman has remarked that "on the level of formal logic the accusation of begging the question is meaningless. It could indeed be maintained that any formally correct deduction consists of a *petitio principii* and the principle of identity, affirming that any proposition implies itself, then becomes a formalization of the *petitio principii.* Actually, the *petitio principii,* which does not concern the truth but the adherence of the interlocutors to the presupposed premises, is not an error of logic, but of rhetoric" (*The New Rhetoric,* p. 112).

See also **Fallacy (Logical).**

Philophronesis (phi lo phro NE sis; G. "kind treatment") — **Benevolentia.**

Attempt to mitigate anger by gentle speech and humble submission. So Prince Hal apologizes to his father for past misdeeds:

> So please your majesty, I would I could
> Quit all offenses with as clear excuse
> As well as I am doubtless I can purge
> Myself of many I am charged withal.
> Yet such extenuation let me beg
> As, in reproof of many tales devised,
> Which oft the ear of greatness needs must hear
> By smiling pickthanks and base newsmongers,
> I may, for some things true wherein my youth
> Hath faulty wand'red and irregular,
> Find pardon on my true submission.
>
> (*1 Henry IV*, III, ii)

Phrasis (PHRA sis; G. "way of speaking").

The term is sometimes used to mean "diction" or "idiom," sometimes to mean **Style.**

Pistis (PIS tis; G. "argument, proof") — **Proof**.

Pleonasmus (ple o NAS mus; G. "excess") — **Superabundancia; Too Full Speech**.
Needless repetition: "I heard it with mine ears and saw it with mine eyes."
See also **Macrologia**.

Ploce (PLO ce; G. "plaiting") — **Conexio; Copulatio; Diaphora; Doubler; Epanodos; Swift Repeate; Traductio**.
Repetition of a word or a name with a new signification after the intervention of another word or words. An extreme example:

> Welfare doesn't work: work "incentives" don't work; training doesn't work; work "requirements" don't work; "work experience" doesn't work, and even workfare doesn't quite work. Only work works.

An inadvertent example:

> Women now represent about 20% of all women lawyers, but they have had a tough time cracking the lucrative upper echelons of the profession.

Peacham would confine this term to repetition of a proper name, specifying **Diaphora** for repetition of ordinary words.
See also **Antanaclasis (3); Epiploce**.

Poicilogia (poi ci LO gi a; G. "intricate wording").
Overly ornate speech. "When in the oration there is nothing rightly and properly spoken, but all is too much befigured and begayed" (Sherry).
See also **Asianism; Euphuism**; and further discussion at **Macrologia**.

Pointed Style.
This phrase is used in discussions of seventeenth-century prose style to refer to a style usually called **Senecan**, in which rhetorical figures (often **Schemes**, especially those of balance and antithesis, of word- and sound-play) are used to clarify, reinforce, "point" meaning. The effect is often epigrammatic. The "pointed style," neat and concise, witty, can be contrasted with a witty style ornamented for the sake of ornament itself, rather than for an enhancement of meaning. The noun "point" often meant the **Sententia**, or meaning, which was thus epigrammatically expressed. Seneca is usually quoted as the exemplar of the pointed style; in English, Lincoln offers a familiar example: "It is true that you may fool all the people some of the time; you can even fool some of the people all of the time; but you cannot fool all of the people all of the time." (For a fuller discussion of pointed style, see Williamson, *The Senecan Amble*, chapter 3.)

Polyptoton (po LYP to ton; G. "employment of the same word in various cases"); alt. sp. **Polyptiton — Adnominatio; Paregmenon; Traductio.**

Repetition of words from the same root but with different endings. So Churchill about the Chamberlain government: "So they go on in strange paradox, decided only to be undecided, resolved to be irresolute, adamant for drift, solid for fluidity, all-powerful to be impotent." Or, as a modern student of rhetoric has observed, "Virtuosity is some evidence of virtue."

See also **Homoioptoton.**

Polysyndeton (po ly SYN de ton) — **Coople Clause.**

Use of a conjunction between each clause; opposite of **Asyndeton.** Milton says that Satan, in his course through Chaos, "pursues his way, / And swims or sinks, or wades, or creeps, or flies" (*Paradise Lost*, II, 949–950).

Post hoc ergo propter hoc (L. "after this, therefore because of this").

Assigning the wrong cause, by mistaking a temporal for a causal relationship.

Praecedens correctio (prae CE dens cor REC ti o) — **Correctio (2).**

Praeceptio (prae CEP ti o; L. "taking beforehand") — **Prolepsis (1).**

Praecisio (prae CI si o; L. "cutting off") — **Aposiopesis.**

Praecognitio (prae cog NI ti o; L. "foreknowledge") — **Narration.**

Praeexercitamina (prae ex er ci TA mi na; L. "preparatory exercises") — **Progymnasmata.**

Praemunitio (prae mu NI ti o; L. "strengthening beforehand"); alt. sp. **Premunitio — Proparasceue.**

Defending yourself in anticipation of an attack. Churchill's speech to the House of Commons on 13 May 1940 offers one of the most memorable — and far-sighted — examples, when he warned against the misfortunes certain to come and the criticisms, equally certain, that would follow in their wake:

> I would say to the House, as I said to those who have joined the Government: "I have nothing to offer but blood, toil, tears and sweat." We have before us an ordeal of the most grievous kind. We have before us many, many long months of struggle and suffering.

See also **Correctio (2); Prolepsis (1).**

117

Praeoccupatio (prae oc cu PA ti o) — **Prolepsis (1)**.

Praeparatio (prae pa RA ti o) — **Procatasceue**.
Preparing an audience before telling them about something done. Quintilian calls it the most often used form of **Prolepsis** (IX.ii.17). Churchill's Dunkirk speech to the House of Commons (4 June 1940) exemplifies this kind of buildup to a surprise conclusion:

> When a week ago today I asked the House to fix this afternoon as the occasion for a statement, I feared it would be my hard lot to announce the greatest military disaster in our long history.

Praesumptio (prae SUMP ti o; L. "anticipation") — **Prolepsis**.

Praeteritio (prae te RI ti o; L. "a passing over"); alt. sp. **Preteritio** — **Occultatio**.

Pragmatographia (prag ma to GRA phi a; G. "description of an action, affair") — **Counterfait Action; Descriptio**.
Vivid description of an action or event; a type of **Enargia**.

> I am a rogue if I were not at half-sword with a dozen of them two hours together. I have 'scaped by miracle. I am eight times thrust through the doublet, four through the hose; my buckler cut through and through; my sword hacked like a handsaw — *ecce signum!*
> (1 *Henry IV*, II, iv)

Precatio (pre CA ti o; L. "prayer") — **Euche**.

Prepon, To (to PRE pon; G. "what is fitting") — **Decorum**.

Prepostera locutio (L. "inverted utterance") — **Hysterologia (2)**.

Preposterous. Puttenham's term for **Hysteron proteron**.

Presumptuous. Puttenham's term for **Procatalepsis**; *see* **Prolepsis**.

Preteritio — **Praeteritio**.

Principle of Contradiction.
One of the three **Laws of Thought**. It states: No statement can be both false and true.

Principle of Excluded Middle.
One of the three **Laws of Thought**. It states: Any statement must be either true or false.

Principle of Identity.
One of the three **Laws of Thought**. It states: If a statement is true, it is true.

Privie Nippe. Puttenham's term for **Charientismus**.

Probatio (pro BA ti o; L. "inspection; demonstration, proof") — **Proof.**

Procatalepsis (pro ca ta LEP sis; G. "a seizing in advance") — **Presumptuous.** *See* **Prolepsis.**

Procatasceue (pro ca ta SCEU e; G. "preparation; introduction") — **Praeparatio.**

Procreatio (pro cre A ti o) — **Onomatopoeia.**

Prodiorthosis (pro di or THO sis; G. "setting right by anticipation") — **Correctio (2).**

Proecthesis (pro EC the sis; G. "introduction, prefatory account").
1. Defending what one has done or said, by giving reasons and circumstances. Sister Miriam Joseph gives this example from *Cymbeline*:

> Mine eyes
> Were not in fault, for she was beautiful;
> Mine ears that heard her flattery; nor my heart,
> That thought her like her seeming. It had been vicious
> To have mistrusted her. Yet (O my daughter!)
> That it was folly in me thou mayst say,
> And prove it in thy feeling.
>
> (V, v)

2. Quintilian's definition differs slightly from the above: "pointing out what ought to have been done, and then what actually has been done" (IX.ii.106).

Progressio (pro GRES si o).
Building a point around a series of comparisons:

> What a boy art thou in comparison of this fellow here. Thou sleeps: he wakes: thou plays: he studies: thou art ever abroad: he is ever at home: thou never waits, he still doth his attendance: thou carest not for no body: he doeth his duty to all men: thou doest what thou canst to hurt all, and please none: he doeth what he can, to hurt none, and please all.
>
> (Wilson, p. 401)

See also **Auxesis** for fuller discussion, and **Dirimens copulatio**.

Progymnasmata (pro gym NAS ma ta; G. "preliminary exercises") — **Praeexercitamina**.

The title of (and hence generic name for) a series of rhetorical exercises which introduced students to the study of rhetoric. Several Greek progymnasmata treatises are extant; in Latin, the only complete one known is Priscian's translation, called *Praeexercitamina*, of a work attributed to Hermogenes, a second-century Greek rhetorician. Aphthonius produced a Greek version so popular that it was Latinized in the sixteenth century and used throughout Europe. These venerable drills have lasted up to the present day, where they are reincarnated less formally as the perennial topics for beginning prose composition courses. Perhaps I should amplify the discussion here slightly by quoting Bonner's economical explanation:

> Greek rhetoricians, long before Quintilian's day, had evolved a whole series of exercises in composition, each based on a stereotyped framework of rules supplied by the teacher, which, adapting the language of physical education to intellectual studies, they termed *progymnasmata*, or "preliminary training-exercises." When the series was fully developed there were about a dozen types in all, and much consideration was given to grading them in order of difficulty, for they ranged from fairly straightforward exercises based on the Fable, the Saying *(chreia)*, and the mythological Narrative to much more difficult ones, such as the Speech in Character, the Thesis, and the Discussion of a Law. They were "preliminary" in the sense that they were designed to lead up to the full-scale mock-deliberative and mock-legal speeches, called by the Greeks *hypotheses*, and by the Romans *suasoriae* and *controversiae*. Some of these exercises (e.g., the Thesis) were extremely old, and dated back to classical Greece. . . . It seems likely, therefore, that the formation of the standard set of preliminary exercises, known to us mainly from writers of the imperial period, was a gradual process, which took place during the Hellenistic Age. It must, however, have been fairly complete by the first century B.C., and maybe earlier, for already in the late Republic the set, or a good part of it, was being used by teachers of rhetoric in Latin, who called them *exercitationes* or, later, *materiae*.
>
> (*Education in Ancient Rome*, pp. 250–251)

Prolepsis (pro LEP sis; G. "preconception, anticipation").

1. **Ante occupatio; Anticipatio; Praeceptio; Praeoccupatio; Praesumptio; Procatalepsis**. Foreseeing and forestalling objections in various ways.

> But some man will say, How are the dead raised up? and with what body do they come? Thou fool, that which thou sowest is not quickened, except it die: And that which thou sowest, thou sowest not that

body shall be, but bare grain, it may chance wheat, or of some other grain.

(1 Cor. 15:35–37)

See also **Praemunitio; Praeparatio**.

2. **Propounder**. A general statement is amplified by dividing it into parts.

> If you want a receipt for that popular mystery,
>> Known to the world as a Heavy Dragoon,
> Take all the remarkable people in history,
>> Rattle them off to a popular tune.
> The pluck of Lord Nelson on board of the *Victory* —
>> Genius of Bismarck devising a plan — . . .
> The dash of a D'Orsay, divested of quackery —
> Narrative powers of Dickens and Thackeray —
> Victor Emmanuel — peak-haunting Peveril —
> Thomas Aquinas, and Doctor Sacheverell — . . .
>> Take of these elements all that is fuscible,
>> Melt them all down in a pipkin or crucible,
>> Set them to simmer and take off the scum,
>> And a Heavy Dragoon is the residuum!

(Gilbert and Sullivan, *Patience*)

See also **Epanodos**.

Further discussion. Although prolepsis and **Procatalepsis** are sometimes discriminated by theorists, both mean foreseeing objections and answering them before they have been advanced. Prolepsis has also the second meaning indicated. The terms listed as synonyms for meaning (1) are given variously as synonyms for both terms. One theorist, the pseudo-Julius Rufinianus, gives the same meaning for both but calls procatalepsis a figure of thought and prolepsis a figure of words (Halm, pp. 48 and 60). I have adopted prolepsis as the reference term for foreseeing and forestalling objections simply because it is the shorter and better known. For those who wish to trace the story for themselves, procatalepsis is first used in the *Rhetorica ad Alexandrum* (1428b8) to mean "anticipations of arguments." Lewis and Short's citations for prolepsis center on "anticipation" as well. Quintilian uses it as in meaning (1) at IV.i.49 and IX.ii.16.

Pronominatio (pro no mi NA ti o) — **Antonomasia**.

Prooemium (pro OE mi um; G. "opening"); alt. sp. **Prooimion** — **Exordium**.

Proof.

1. **Confirmation; Pistis; Probatio**. The fourth part of a six-part classical oration. This was the main part of the speech, in which the

pros and cons of the argument were brought out. See chapter 2 at **Arrangement: The parts of an oration**.

2. More generally, proof in any form of disputation. Aristotle's *Rhetoric* (I, 1356a) isolates three kinds of persuasion available to an orator:

(1) *ethos*, or the demonstration of the speaker's good character
(2) *pathos*, or playing on the audience's feelings
(3) *logos*, what today we would call "proof" of some sort

The first two had formerly been part of the **Peroration** rather than the argument proper. Aristotle thus planted the seed of the Ramist controversy of the sixteenth century, when a group of theorists wished once again to separate the first two categories from the third.

Care should be exercised not to equate "proof" and what we might call "scientific proof." For Aristotle there were three types of reasoning (scientific demonstration, dialectic, rhetoric), and each had its own "proof." Rhetoric, for example, used the **Enthymeme**, or probable syllogism, whereas scientific demonstration used the **Syllogism**, properly so called because its conclusions were universally, not generally, true. See **Invention** in chapter 2.

Prooimion — **Prooemium**.

Proparalepsis (pro pa ra LEP sis) — **Paragoge**.

Proparasceue (pro pa ra SCEU e; G. "preparation") — **Praemunitio**.

Proportio (pro POR ti o; L. "proportion, symmetry; analogy") — **Analogy**.

Proposition (L. *propositio*).
1. **Division**.
2. Sometimes *propositio* is used simply as a figure, rather than the part of an oration, to indicate a brief proleptic summary "which compriseth in few words the sum of that matter, whereof we presently intend to speak" (Peacham).
3. In logic, a statement in which something is affirmed or denied. There are two kinds:

Primary — about things: "This is a chair."
Secondary — about other propositions: "I think this is a chair."

Propounder. Puttenham's term for **Prolepsis (2)**.

Prosapodosis (pro sa PO do sis; G. rhet. "addition that completes") — **Redditio**.

Supporting each alternative with a reason; a distributive reply: "He must either love her or leave her: love her, to stay together; leave her, to gain peace of mind."

Prosonomasia (pro so no MA si a; G. "naming, appellation") — Nicknamer.

Calling by a name or nickname; confused by some rhetoricians (following Day) with **Paronomasia**.

Prosopographia (pro so po GRA phi a; G. *prosopon*, "face; character; person") — Counterfait Countenance.

A type of **Enargia** which vividly describes the appearance of a person, imaginary or real, quick or dead. Real but dead:

> A figure like your father,
> Armèd at point exactly, cap-a-pie,
> Appears before them and with solemn march
> Goes slowly and stately by them.
>
> *(Hamlet, I, ii)*

Imaginary but alive:

> It was to weet a wilde and saluage man,
> Yet was no man, but onely like in shape,
> And eke in stature higher by a span,
> All ouergrowne with haire, that could awhape
> An hardy hart, and his wide mouth did gape
> With huge great teeth, like to a tusked Bore:
> For he liu'd all on rauin and on rape
> Of men and beasts; and fed on fleshly gore,
> The signe whereof yet stain'd his bloudy lips afore.
> (Spenser, *Faerie Queene*, IV, vii, 5)

See also **Effictio**.

Prosopopoeia (pro so po po EI a) — Conformatio; Counterfait in Personation; Personification; Sermocinatio.

1. An animal or an inanimate object is represented as having human attributes and addressed or made to speak as if it were human:

> Oft he bow'd
> His turret Crest, and sleek enamell'd Neck,
> Fawning, and lick'd the ground whereon she trod.
> His gentle dumb expression turn'd at length
> The eye of *Eve* to mark his play; he glad
> Of her attention gain'd with Serpent Tongue
> Organic, or impulse of vocal Air,
> His fraudulent temptation thus began. . . .
>
> So saying, her rash hand in evil hour
> Forth reaching to the Fruit, she pluck'd, she eat:

> Earth felt the wound, and Nature from her seat
> Sighing through all her Works gave signs of woe,
> That all was lost.

(Milton, Paradise Lost, IX, 524–531, 780–784)

2. The rhetorical exercise known as the speech in character or impersonation. In the *Praeexercitamina*, Priscian calls it *allocutio*. *See also* **Ethopoeia (2)**.

See also **Controversia; Dialogismus.**

Prothesis (PRO the sis; G. "placing before or in public").

1. Alt. sp. **Prosthesis — Appositio.** Adding a letter or syllable to the beginning of a word: "irregardless" for "regardless."

2. Aristotle's term for **Narration**. He considered it one of the two essential parts of any oration (the other was *pistis*, **Proof**).

Protrope (PRO tro pe; G. "exhortation") — **Adhortatio.**
Exhorting hearers to act by threats or promises:

> Seeming, seeming!
> I will proclaim thee, Angelo; look for 't:
> Sign me a present pardon for my brother,
> Or with an outstretch'd throat I'll tell the world aloud
> What man thou art.

(Measure for Measure, II, iv)

Proverb (L. "an old saying") — **Adage; Aphorismus; Apothegm; Gnome; Maxim; Paroemia; Sententia.**

A short, pithy statement of a general truth, one that condenses common experience into memorable form. In rhetorical education, proverbs often formed occasion or departure-point for developing a theme.

Each of the terms above is often used as a synonym for one or more of the others. They may carry various weights of authority to certain audiences — a sententia may be more weighty than an aphorism — but no firm distinctions hold. One scheme differentiates between proverbs and adages as the wisdom of a group, and apothegms, maxims and sentences as the wisdom of a single person. Another has distinguished proverb, a common saying that has become fixed (and often alliterative) in form, from a sententia, where the common wisdom has not yet found a fixed and widely accepted form; compare Quintilian's labeling of gnomes as *sententiae* (L. "judgments") because they resemble the formalism of decisions by public bodies. Another scholar defines sententia as a fine saying, proverb as a common saying; here, too, the distinction is not generally accepted. The resemblance of the proverb to the **Commonplace** or *topos* is clear enough: the proverb is a commonplace at a yet further remove of generality. It can be viewed as the last stage of generality for the **Exemplum**.

Whatever the fine differences of meaning among these terms, one common ingredient would seem to be conformity to the syntax of memory, a pronounced pattern of sight or sound that makes for natural memorization and easy recall. A proverb like "A bird in the hand is worth two in the bush" constitutes a kind of miniature memory theater (see **Memory** in chapter 2) in which the elements to be remembered are allocated to familiar elements of a visual scene. **Isocolon, Chiasmus**, and other figures of balance and antithesis are often ingredients in such memorability, and they are frequently underlined with sound patterns of some sort.

Accompanying *memorability* as a central ingredient seems to be some claim to *cultural authority*, and some kind of *witty epigrammatic compression* may perhaps be taken to form a third common theme running through the proverbial cluster. Again *perhaps* one might say that we have grown less fond of the proverbial figures and forms the further we move along the variously mensurated spectrum from orality to literacy. It is hard to imagine, for example, a modern Erasmus devoting a comparable energy to compiling and pondering a modern *Adagia*. La Rochefoucauld's enterprise, which seems akin to Erasmus's, in fact attacks the very grounds of proverbial cultural authority which Erasmus seeks to chart.

The most difficult thing for the modern reader to remember thus may be that the proverb, like the exemplum, has been for most of formal rhetoric's history a means of *proof* rather than a substantiating ornament. A second lesson for modern readers, annoyed as they often are by the solemn plethora of proverbial wisdom in the earlier literature, is the lesson Polonius teaches. In imaginative literature (and this is certainly true of imaginative literature of the English Renaissance), the proverb is, very likely, ironical. And, not infrequently, it may be so wide of the point as to be ludicrously irrelevant, a comic device. The literary use of proverbs usually is a device to introduce the commonly accepted ideas and attitudes of a society into a situation they cannot deal with. Naturally they will flounder. This common use has been seen in Polonius's case easily enough (though "to thine own self be true" still makes the purple-patch recitals by famous actors), but it is commonly ignored elsewhere in the earlier literature. Lyly's *Euphues*, for example, always teetering on the edge of proverbiality, tries to claim through its style a cultural authority denied to the vacuity of its argument. And, of course, there are plenty of modern examples of the invented and self-conscious proverb, from Blake's *Proverbs of Heaven and Hell* onward.

Oddly enough, I have found no term for this intentionally self-conscious comic or parodic proverb as a special form. Dorothy Parker was very fond of them, as in "Brevity is the soul of lingerie," or "If you laid all the Bennington girls from end to end, I wouldn't be at all surprised." My favorite example of this no-name figure has always been Claire Boothe Luce's "No good deed goes unpunished," but Churchill's famous description of Clement Atlee as "a sheep in sheep's clothing" runs a close second, and Alice Roosevelt Longworth's "If you can't say anything good about someone, sit right here by me" finds a special echo in every breast. Nor have I found a term for specially invented modern sententiae which play self-consciously upon proverbiality, like Blake's "The road of excess leads to the palace of wisdom," or "The cut worm forgives the plow." Nor for inadvertent yet inspired variations such as "Sleeping dogs never lie."

The point here for the modern student should be that the precise *kind* of proverb (or the precise term for it) matters less than the way it is used in a specific text. Perhaps the terms will have readily separable meanings only when the use of the proverb in enough different texts has been described to make the many different terms really necessary to describe the full range of use. As a final source of confusion, note that some of the synonyms for proverb are sometimes used to mean *quoting* proverbs as well as the proverbs themselves.

Prozeugma (pro ZEUG ma; G. "yoking") — **Ringleader**.

A type of **Zeugma** in which the verb is expressed in the first clause and understood in the others: "Pride oppresseth humility; hatred love; cruelty compassion" (Peacham).

Pseudomenos (pseu DO me nos; G. "liar").

An argument that puts the adversary in a position where he must tell a lie, whatever he says: ask a Cretan — proverbial liars — whether all Cretans are liars.

Pun (etymology uncertain).

A gourmet son, on seeing his father nearly set on fire by an over-chafed dish at a very authentic French restaurant, speaks of seeing finally an "authentic *père flambé*." In the same spirit, a journalistic wag describes the 35th anniversary issue of *Playboy* as a "journey down mammary lane." Or, unwittingly, an anthropologist writes of "The Eskimo screw as a culture-historical problem." Likewise President Kennedy, not knowing that "Berliner" nicknamed a local kind of breakfast roll, declared "Ich bin ein Berliner" and thereby proclaimed to the crowd, "I am a doughnut," thus playing a breakfast role he had not intended. Or Winston Churchill, ruminating on the life of a politician: "He is asked to stand, he wants to sit, and he is expected to lie."

Puns come in so many different forms that one scholar (Walter Redfern, *Puns*) confesses at the beginning of his book that he gave up trying to identify the separate species. I have tried to chronicle some — but by no means all — of the disputed subcategories in the entries cross-referenced below. The amplification which follows treats but a single *rhetorical*, as against *poetic*, function of the pun.

When President Kennedy stood before a tense multitude at the Berlin Wall and proclaimed himself a doughnut, he inadvertently threw the toggle switch that electrifies the pun. One pole of the switch yields the regular dependable language which tells us about the real world outside, the world where he too, like his listeners, was a Berliner. The other pole directs us into the chance-ridden, self-referential and self-pleasing world of language itself where, if we are not careful, we all turn into doughnuts. The pun is what the perception psychologists call a "bistable illusion," one of those pictures which looked at one way is a rabbit and another a duck. The eye, more consistent than the mind, cannot see both at the same time but instead puts our mind into a high-frequency oscillation between the two worlds. And the two worlds bear a high allegorical charge, the Berlin one being the world of the philosophers, a world where language is a translucent windowpane to a preexistent world beyond it, the doughnut one being the world of the rhetoricians, where the windowpane is an opaque painting of a constructed reality no longer "beyond" it. Thus we can say that the pun, at its heart, unites in its oscillation the two poles between which the whole scheme of Western education, the rhetorical paideia, has vibrated for two and a half millennia. That is why the bad reputation of the pun pretty well coincides with the repudiation of the rhetorical paideia in favor of Newtonian science, or what Marshall McLuhan, looking at the matter from the oral/literate technological perspective, called the "Gutenberg Galaxy."

To think of the pun in this way, as a bistable illusion, casts new light on how some other basic figures work in a rhetorical universe. **Irony**, for example, creates the same kind of bistable illusion but on a much larger scale. Think for a moment of that masterpiece of sustained irony, Erasmus's *Praise of Folly*. Erasmus creates for Folly a speech which can be read in two entirely different ways, one long speech sharing two diametrically opposed meanings. As we read, we continually oscillate between the poles of this bistable illusion. And the two poles between which we are drawn to and fro turn out to be just the two poles of the pun, the two worlds of rhetoric and philosophy. Folly is foolish if the world is philosophical, full of foundational realities and real motives. But if it is the playful and gamelike, the style-dominated world of rhetoric, Folly is Wisdom. And since our world is half and half, Wisdom and Folly are continually changing places. Irony as an argumentative technique is the preemption of both sides in a two-sided argument in just this way. Folly's speech preempts the whole argumentative ground, leaving us no place to stand which she does not already own. And since her ground allegorizes the basic disputational ground of Western thought, the quarrel between the Philosophers and the Rhetoricians over the nature of physical and social reality, Folly's speech becomes The Speech of Speeches, an irresistible centripetal force which draws us relentlessly into its own sphere. And is not such a Speech of Speeches the *fons et origo* of satire, whose reductive work depends on unmasking stylistic motive in the name of "real," or "sensible," or commonsense purposeful behavior?

Might we say that all rhetoric aspires to create a speech such as this? To preempt the whole ground for disagreement? Don't several of the argumentative figures work in this way? Surely **Chiasmus** aims to model both sides of a two-sided proposition and leave no further ground for debate, thus occupying an intermediate status in scale as a bistable illusion halfway between pun and irony. And when we ask ourselves questions and answer them through **Hypophora**, or in an **Asteismus** turn an opponent's words to our own purposes, isn't this an attenuated form of the same strategy? And what of allegory? Doesn't it depend on a toggle-switch of the punning sort, oscillating perpetually between a world of human motive driven by conceptual reasoning and a world driven by biogrammatical hungers? (See **Allegory** for a further discussion.)

Marshall McLuhan has written of "the pun that derails us from the smooth and uniform progress that is typographic order." Print forces us to choose one stage or the other of the bistable illusion's states. Electronic print allows the derailment to occur in real time. We can program the toggle, in various ways diagram or orchestrate the oscillation which traditional print tensions and suppresses. What will happen when such a force makes itself largely felt is anyone's guess; mine is that the experiments will start with the pun.

See also **Adnominatio; Antanaclasis; Paronomasia.**

Pysma (PYS ma; G. "question") — **Quaesitio.**

Asking many questions that require diverse answers. Peacham quotes Cicero's *Pro Roscio*:

In what place did he speak with them? With whom did he speak? How did he persuade them? Did he hire them? Whom did he hire? By whom did he hire them? To what end or how much did he give them?

Quaesitio (quae SI ti o; L. "seeking or searching after") — **Pysma**.

Qualifier. Puttenham's term for **Epitheton**.

Quarreller. Puttenham's term for **Antitheton**; *see* **Antithesis**.

Querimonia (que ri MO ni a; L. "complaint") — **Mempsis**.

Questioner. Puttenham's term for **Erotesis**.

Quick Conceite. Puttenham's term for **Synecdoche**.

Ratiocinatio (ra ti o ci NA ti o; L. "calm reasoning; reasoning by asking questions").
  Asking ourselves the reasons for our own statements.

> What's this, what's this? Is this her fault or mine?
> The tempter or the tempted, who sins most?
> (Measure for Measure, II, ii)

See also **Erotesis; Hypophora**.

Reason Rend. Puttenham's term for **Aetiologia**.

Rebounde. Puttenham's term for **Antanaclasis**.

Reciprocatio (re ci pro CA ti o; L. "alternation") — **Antanaclasis**.

Recompencer. Puttenham's term for **Antanagoge**.

Recordatio (re cor DA ti o; L. "recalling to mind") — **Anamnesis**.

Redditio (red DI ti o; L. "giving back; giving a reason") — **Prosapodosis**.

Redditio causae (CAU sae) — **Aetiologia**.

Redditio contraria (con TRA ri a) — **Antapodosis**.

Reditus ad propositum (RE di tus ad pro PO si tum).
  Returning to the proposition after a digression.

Redouble. Puttenham's term for **Anadiplosis**.

Reductio ad absurdum (re DUC ti o ad ab SUR dum; L. "reduction to absurdity").

To disprove a proposition, one validly deduces from it a conclusion self-contradictory or contradictory to acknowledged fact.

Reduplicatio (re du pli CA ti o) — **Anadiplosis**.

Refractio (re FRAC ti o; L. "breaking open") — **Antanaclasis; Antistasis**.

Refutation — **Confutation; Reprehensio**.

The fifth part of a six-part classical oration. This part answered the opponent's arguments. See **Arrangement: The parts of an oration** in chapter 2.

Regressio — **Epanodos (1)**.

Reinforcer. Puttenham's term for **Emphasis**; *see* **Significatio**.

Rejectio (re JEC ti o) — **Apodioxis**.

Relatio (re LA ti o; L. "bringing back, return") — **Anaphora**.

Remove. Puttenham's second term for **Metastasis**.

Repetitio (re pe TI ti o).
1. **Anaphora**.
2. **Epanalepsis**.

Replie. Puttenham's term for **Symploce**.

Report. Puttenham's term for **Anaphora**.

Reprehensio — **Refutation**.

Rerewarder. Puttenham's term for **Hypozeugma**.

Resemblance by Imagerie. Puttenham's term for **Icon**.

Resemblance Misticall. Puttenham's term for **Parable**.

Responce. Puttenham's term for **Anthypophora**; *see* **Hypophora**.

Restrictio (re STRIC ti o; L. "restriction, limitation").

Excepting part of a statement already made. "He is the most eloquent man in the field, myself excepted."

Reticentia (re ti CEN ti a; L. "keeping silent").
1. **Aposiopesis**.
2. Bidding someone hold his peace. Wilson calls it "A Whisht, or a warning to speak no more. . . , when we bid them hold their peace that have least cause to speak, and can do little good with their talking."

Retire. Puttenham's term for **Epanodos (1)**.

Reversio (re VER si o) — **Anastrophe**.

Rhetoric.
One of the seven liberal arts. Traditionally, rhetoric was invented in the early fifth century B.C. in Sicily, when the overthrow of the Syracusan tyrants created a great deal of litigation. A later tradition has the famous sophist Gorgias of Leontini bringing it whole to Athens in 427. But if we define rhetoric broadly as the "Art of Persuasion," its basic techniques must have been first tried out against Eve — as Milton dramatizes — not against the Syracusan tyrants. What Syracuse contributed, if the tradition is true, must have been a body of sophisticated theory. This body of theory formed the center of what we now call "liberal education" for most of the following two and a half millennia.

Rhetoric has always tended to outgrow its original concern with persuasive public speaking, or direct verbal communication, and to lend itself to written communication as well. And it has from earliest times vacillated between a concern with specific techniques only, available to the good and bad cause alike, and a larger ethical concern that continually tempts it to say that all persuasion is virtuous persuasion. Cato's definition of an orator as *vir bonus, dicendi peritus* (a good man, skilled in speaking) can stand for this second position as well as any, and would seem to bring almost all humane learning into the domain of rhetoric (as, indeed, Cicero sought to do in *De oratore*). Most theorists have taken as rhetoric's arena some ground measured between these two extremes. In Bacon's famous definition, for example ("The duty and office of rhetoric is to apply reason to imagination for the better moving of the will"), the ethical concern of rhetoric comes in almost as an assumption — "*duty* and office." Quintilian, on the other hand, though he emphasized the moral obligation of the orator, concluded his survey of definitions current in his day by defining the art of rhetoric as one whose "end and highest aim is to speak well" (*finis eius et summum est bene dicere* [II.xv.38]).

Cicero held that the orator had three "offices" or main functions: to teach, to please, to move. The area these three cover may indicate why rhetorical theory has so often in its history overlapped poetics. To draw the analogy between poetry and rhetoric on the one hand and pure and applied science on the other (poetry : pure science / rhetoric : applied science) may explain something about the domains of the two bodies of theory, but it by no means fully distinguishes them. Another categorization that may help is the one Kenneth Burke suggests (*A Rhetoric of Motives*, pp. 49–50) between persuasion to feel and persuasion to do, between attitude and act. An antislavery poem leads us to commiserate with slaves; an antislavery rhetoric leads us to free them. The difficulties of this distinction are clear, of course, the most obvious being that since the feeling must precede the act, poetry and rhetoric would become simply two stages or degrees of persuasion. A third criterion of differentiation between the two might be this: rhetoric aims to induce an emotion or state of mind which can be created in other ways as well (there are many ways to drive someone mad), while poetry aims to create an emotion in its audience which is (or aims to be) inseparable from the means used to create it (Lear's madness, and our response to it, are like no others). But this distinction hardly satisfies, either. In the area where the two bodies of theory overlap — the connotative, suggestive, metaphoric use of language — one must have recourse to whatever set of categories suits the present purpose.

As a parallel case of overlapping domains, one might adduce the (originally Platonic) conflict between rhetoric and philosophy. Plato argued (first in the *Gorgias*, then less harshly in the *Phaedrus*) that rhetoric was a sham art, really no art at all, because — concerned only with deception — it could have no true subject matter. Aristotle's counterargument, that rhetoric had to do with the *available means* of persuasion, and was thus as much a practical art as any other, should have settled the question, at least for all those who think that to know the truth is not always to follow it. To rhetoric Plato opposed dialectic, the means of searching out truth. This oversimplified distinction has lingered, so that "mere rhetoric" means artful, sometimes fanciful, lying. The persuasive form a truth comes dressed in is, in this conception, part of the truth itself. A final separation between rhetoric and philosophy seems as impossible as one between rhetoric and poetry. As Kennedy sums up the problem:

> The disagreement between Plato and the sophists over rhetoric was not simply an historical contingency, but reflects a fundamental cleavage between two irreconcilable ways of viewing the world. There have always been those, especially among philosophers and religious thinkers, who have emphasized goals and absolute standards and have

talked much about truth, while there have been as many others to whom these concepts seem shadowy or imaginary and who find the only certain reality in the process of life and the present moment. In general, rhetoricians and orators, with certain distinguished exceptions, have held the latter view, which is the logical, if unconscious, basis of their common view of art as a response to a rhetorical challenge unconstrained by external principles. The difference is not only that between Plato and Gorgias, but between Demosthenes and Isocrates, Virgil and Ovid, Dante and Petrarch, and perhaps Milton and Shakespeare.

(The Art of Persuasion in Greece, p. 15)

A third instance of conflicting areas of theory is the relation of logic (dialectic) to rhetoric. This relationship, in the Greek and Latin theorists, is extremely complex. The widest generalization might be that rhetoric was the theory of popular communication, and logic that of learned communication. Thus rhetoric was often compared to the open palm, available to all, logic to the closed fist. For the student of English rhetorical theory, the main conflict centered on the teachings of Peter Ramus (Pierre de la Ramée, 1515–1572). Howell has summarized them, as follows:

He ordained that logic should offer training in invention and arrangement, with no help whatever from rhetoric. He ordained that the topic of arrangement should take care of all speculations regarding the method of discourse, with no help whatever from invention. He ordained that rhetoric should offer training in style and delivery, and that style should be limited to the tropes and the schemes, with no help whatever from grammar, which was to be assigned only subject matter derived from considerations of etymology and syntax. The subject of memory, which we have seen to be a recognized part of traditional rhetoric since the youth of Cicero, was detached by Ramus from rhetoric, and was not made a special topic elsewhere in his scheme for the liberal arts, except so far as logic helped memory indirectly by providing the theoretical basis for strict organization of discourse.

(Logic and Rhetoric in England, p. 148)

Rhetoric thus becomes, for Ramus, as it has remained for us ever since, largely a matter of verbal ornament, of style. (This conception of rhetoric as a theory of verbal ornament is one of the three types of theorizing Howell finds in England in the Renaissance; the other two are *Ciceronian*, which adheres to the five-part traditional division of the art of rhetoric, and *formulary*, which teaches through a collection of examples. For a fuller discussion, see Howell, chapter 3.)

By an odd quirk which may reveal something of our naive national character, "rhetoric," in American education, has come to be synonymous with "prose composition." The underlying assumption of such a synonymity must be that the student, once she knows the arts of language, will use them to present clear meanings clearly, rather than to deceive. There is no reason not to use "rhetoric" in this way, but no one should mistake such a hopeful redefinition for the complex historical fact. In recent years, the movement in literary theory called Deconstruction has done its best to quash such naive hopefulness and restore rhetoric to its rightful throne as "*par excellence* the region of the Scramble, of insult and injury, bickering, squabbling, malice and the lie, cloaked malice and the subsidized lie" (Burke, *A Rhetoric of Motives*, p. 19). Just after this passage, though, Burke dwells on the irenic and socially integrative functions of rhetoric, and this aspect has attracted its "constructive" apologists as well. (See, for example, James Boyd White's essays on rhetoric and the law in *Heracles' Bow*.)

The constructive, integrative function of rhetoric derives, Eric Havelock has argued, from the Sophists: "Of course they taught rhetoric as a technique for the effective formulation of political ideas, but as ancillary to a bigger thing, a larger view of life and man altogether. If there is one quality which identifies them, and yet which is wholly incompatible with their traditional reputation, it is a sense of social and political responsibility" (*The Liberal Temper in Greek Politics*, p. 230). Ever since Aristotle, rhetoric has always supplied a theory of human motive. Thus G. R. Kerferd: "The superiority of one logos to another is not accidental, but depends on the presence of specific features. The study of these is the study of the art of rhetoric, and their successful development is the source of the power of logos over souls which is entitled *Psychagogia*. . . . Indeed Rhetoric, which is now an old fashioned term, is perhaps best understood as covering in antiquity the whole art of public relations and the presentation of images. It was the theory of this art that the sophists inaugurated" (*The Sophistic Movement*, p. 82).

Indeed, if we were to define rhetoric using a strictly contemporary terminology, we might call it the "science of human attention-structures." Such a definition, by restoring to rhetoric's domain in full force the last two of the traditional five parts, delivery and memory, would answer Plato's characterization of rhetoric as a pseudo-science having no subject matter. Memory, we are coming to see, is an active agency of creation not a passive curator of the past. Delivery, in its turn, would now include all that we think of as "non-verbal communication." And the manipulations of gesture and voice which defined delivery, we now know, are talents by no means restricted to *homo sapiens*, or indeed to primates. Allow this broad band of expressivity back into rhetoric's domain — and surely

it was there to begin with and we are to blame for attenuating it —
and rhetoric has a "scientific" subject matter which includes large
parts of, for example, sociology, social anthropology, and behavioral biology.

The twentieth century, and especially the last twenty years, have
in fact seen just such a revival of rhetorical thinking in many disciplines besides the university subject called "Rhetoric." I tried to
suggest the breadth and range of this revival in "Twenty Years After: Digital Decorum and Bistable Allusions."

Rhetorical Question — Erotesis.

Rhetorical Syllogism.
One in which the premises are only generally, not absolutely (scientifically proved) true. See **Enthymeme (3)**.

Rhodian Style.
The middle style between **Atticism** and **Asianism**.

Right Reasoner. Puttenham's term for **Dialogismus**.

Ringleader. Puttenham's term for **Prozeugma**.

Rogatio (ro GA ti o; L. "question") — **Hypophora**.

Sage Sayer. Puttenham's term for **Sententia**; *see* **Proverb**.

Sarcasmus (sar CAS mus; G. "mockery, sneering") — **Amara irrisio;**
Bitter Taunt; Exacerbatio.
A bitter gibe or taunt.

> However, General Joffre preserved his sangfroid amid these disastrous
> surprises to an extent which critics have declared almost indistinguish-
> able from insensibility.
>> (Churchill, *The World Crisis*, 4.24)

Sardismus — Soraismus.

Scesis onomaton (SCE sis   o NO ma ton; G. "relation of words").
1. A sentence constructed of substantives and adjectives only: "A
maid in conversation chaste, in speech mild, in countenance cheer-
ful, in behavior modest, in beauty singular, in heart humble and
meek, in honest mirth, merry with measure . . . " (Peacham).
2. Using a string of synonymous expressions: "We sinned; we
acted unjustly, we perpetrated evil."

Schematismus (sche ma TIS mus; G. "configuration").

Circuitous speech to conceal a meaning, either from fear or politeness, or just for fun. So Churchill, under the constraints of a wartime censorship too weak to censor his sense of fun, wrote to his wife about a future rail journey: "I mustn't mention how we are travelling; but we are coming by puff-puff" (Sir John Martin, in *Action This Day*, p. 143).

See also **Enigma; Noema; Significatio; Syllogismus.**

Scheme (G. "form, figure").
1. Any kind of figure or pattern of words.
2. A figure of arrangement of words in which the literal sense of the word is not affected by the arrangement.

See also **Colors; Difficult Ornament; Easy Ornament; Trope.**

Second Sophistic.
The Atticism, in imitation of the early Greek sophists, which became increasingly important in Rome from the second half of the first century A.D., and which tended to obscure both Latin rhetorical theory and practice.

Secundum quid (se CUN dum; L. "according to something").
A dicto simpliciter ad dictum secundum quid. Reasoning that because something is generally true, it is true in a highly specialized class: "To imprison a man is cruel; therefore, murderers should be allowed to run free."

See also **Fallacy (Logical).**

Securitas (se CU ri tas; L. "freedom from care") — **Asphalia.**

Sedulitas superflua (se DU li tas su PER flu a; L. "excessive zeal") — **Periergia.**

Selfe Saying. Puttenham's term for **Tautologia.**

Senecan Style.
The paratactic style of the Roman moralist Lucius Annaeus Seneca, which is usually contrasted with the Ciceronian **Period.** As a term in English studies, Senecan style usually means the anti-Ciceronian prose of the late sixteenth and early seventeenth centuries. The scholar who is still the authority in this field, the late Morris W. Croll, called this style *Attic*, harking back to the classical distinction between the *Asiatic*, or highly figured, and the Attic, or plainer style. Croll's description of this plainer style, as it was manifested in the seventeenth century, has been neatly summarized by Jonas Barish in "Baroque Prose in the Theater: Ben Jonson":

> The curt style, or, as it was sometimes called, the *stile coupé* or *stile serré*, owes its various names to its abruptness and jaggedness in contrast to Ciceronian "roundness"; and its characteristic device is the so-called "exploded period," composed of independent members set off from each other not by syntactic ligatures but by colons or semicolons (or, in the case of dramatic prose, often by commas). The members of such a period tend to brevity, as the name suggests, but also to irregularity of length, variation in form, and unpredictability of order, a set of traits which, as Croll observes, communicates the effect of live thinking rather than of logical premeditation. The "mere fact" or main idea of the period is liable to be exhausted in the first member; subsequent members explore the idea imaginatively, by means of metaphor, aphorism, or example, rather than through ordered analysis. (p. 185)

The seventeenth-century variation, or mutation, of the Ciceronian style (that is, the looser of the anti-Ciceronian styles), Barish summarizes this way:

> The loose style, Croll's other subcategory of the baroque, differs from the curt style in that it prefers to multiply connectives rather than to suppress them. It tends also to longer members and longer periods, but its character is determined by its habit of heaping up conjunctions and by the kind of conjunctions it chooses — simple coordinates such as *and* and *or*, which involve the least possible syntactic commitment to what has gone before, and even more typically, the stricter relative and subordinating conjunctions used as though they were mere coordinates. And all of this is done, as Croll urges, in order to free the period from formal restraints, to enable it to move with the utmost license from point to point, to follow nothing but the involutions of the thinking mind. For the enchaining suspensions of the Ciceronian period the loose style substitutes its own devices, the parenthesis and the absolute construction. (p. 189)

The uses of these two baroque, or, loosely, Senecan styles Barish then summarizes:

> If the curt style is peculiarly suited to expressions of quick wit, excitement, distraction, and the like, the loose style, by virtue of its greater floridity, lends itself well to purposes of formal declamation. (p. 192)

Scholars desiring more information should consult the Croll and Williamson volumes listed in *Works Cited*, as well as the two Barish articles.

Sentence — Period.

Croll pointed out that "sentence" was a grammatical, "period" a rhetorical, term, but this distinction has not been generally maintained.

Sententia (sen TEN ti a; L. "judgment, sentiment, opinion") — **Proverb**.

Sermocinatio (ser mo ci NA ti o; L. "conversation, discussion").
1. **Prosopopoeia**.
2. Peacham defines sermocinatio more narrowly, as when the speaker answers the remarks or questions of a pretended interlocutor.

> There will not be wanting those who will remind me that in this matter my opinion is not supported by age or experience. To such I shall reply that if what is written is false or foolish, neither age nor experience should fortify it; and if it is true, it needs no such support.
> (Churchill, *The Story of the Malakand Field Force*, chapter 18)

See also **Dialogismus; Ethopoeia (2); Hypophora**.

Sermo superfluus (SER mo su PER flu us) — **Macrologia**.

Sermo ubique sui similis (SER mo u BI que su i SI mi lis; L. "discourse everywhere like itself") — **Homiologia**.

Significatio (sig ni fi CA ti o; L. "sign; emphasis") — **Emphasis; Reinforcer**.

To imply more than is actually stated. You can do this by either a positive or a negative strategy, by the positive means of choosing an exceptionally strong word or descriptive phrase — our common-sense English meaning of "emphasis" as intensification — or by a reverse negative strategy, saying *less* than you mean, implying more than you say.

Positive strategy. Puttenham defines emphasis as "to enforce the sense of anything by a word of more than ordinary efficacy" (p. 184). So a fair lady is described as "O rare beauty, O grace and courtesy." Troilus says, "I am all patience" (*Troilus and Cressida*, V, ii). Here, the intensification is created by describing the person as a series of abstract qualities rather than personal attributes. Or intensification can come through **Hyperbole**, focusing on a single dramatic image. So the *Ad Herennium* gives the following example: "Out of so great a patrimony, in so short a time, this man has not laid by even an earthen pitcher wherewith to seek fire for himself."

Negative strategy. You can emphasize something by omitting it and requiring the audience to fill it in. The center of the negative strategy lies just here; as the *Ad Herennium* says, "it permits the hearer himself to guess what the speaker has not mentioned." You can issue this invitation by an ambiguity which invites complicitous completion. So Shakespeare's Venus says to Adonis, after she has trapped him down on the ground in a fierce hug:

"Fondling," she saith, "since I have hemm'd thee here
Within the circuit of this ivory pale,
I'll be a park, and thou shalt be my deer:
Feed where thou wilt, on mountain or in dale;
   Gaze on my lips, and if those hills be dry,
   Stray lower, where the pleasant fountains lie.

"Within this limit is relief enough,
Sweet bottom grass and high delightful plain,
Round rising hillocks, brakes obscure and rough,
To shelter thee from tempest and from rain:
   Then be my deer, since I am such a park,
   No dog shall rouse thee, though a thousand bark."
                     (*Venus and Adonis*, 229–240)

Or you can do it by ironical delicacy, as when, commenting on some Latin verses which would not scan, a later guest wrote in a Roman guestbook: "His feelings set quantity at abeyance." Or by any of the other figures which invite the hearer to complete a meaning or fill out a pattern.

Further discussion. A tricky term, since its two meanings, both pretty general, seem to go in opposite directions. I have sought in vain for a term describing such "two-directions-at-once" terms, words like *altitudo* or *bathos* which can mean opposites, *heighth* or *depth*. We might explore significatio a little further, however, as an example of the type.

Greek *emphasis* and Latin *significatio* are clear synonyms, but for what is less clear. Perhaps the *Ad Herennium*'s discussion of significatio provides the best starting point: "Emphasis is the figure which leaves more to be suspected than has been actually asserted. It is produced through Hyperbole, Ambiguity, Logical Consequence, Aposiopesis, and Analogy" (*Significatio est res quae plus in suspicione relinquit quam positum est in oratione. Ea fit per exsuperationem, ambiguum, consequentiam, abscisionem, similitudinem* [IV. liv.67]). Thus it is a general term which can apply to several figures and clusters of figures. Hyperbole leads directly to what I have called the positive strategy, the choice of a prepotent word or image. But when you call a fair lady "Beauty" or "Grace" you veer off strongly toward plain **Allegory**. And when you select a revelatory image to stand for a logical sequence (calling someone "lace-curtain Irish," for example, rather than offering a socio-economic equation), you are encroaching on the territory of **Syllogismus** (as indeed Quintilian does at VIII.iii.84). The negative strategy veers off toward the figures of deliberate, often playful indirection like **Schematismus**, to the figures of understatement like **Litotes**, and to the many patterns of ambiguity and **Irony**. Puttenham, for example, considers litotes right after he defines emphasis, and clearly is thinking of it as what I have called the negative strategy, to match the positive one which is his only definition for emphasis. Every time I, at least, try to press this term, I end up with another and seemingly more precise one.

Do the two meanings, the positive and the negative strategies, have any real common ground? It must lie in the idea of *interactivity*, of a metasignal multiplexed onto the plain utterance which invites the hearer to complete the meaning. The trouble with this interpretation is that, when you try to specify it, it expands toward the whole of speech and writing. Hence that fissionating pressure toward other figures which I have just described. Perhaps, though, this expansion is only to be expected. It does not seem too raffish to say that *significance* or *emphasis* both have interactivity at their center; we feel the need for a term which will describe those patterns which seek, one way or another, to make that interactivity noticed, self-conscious. And that self-conscious emphasis can be triggered in either of the two opposite directions of this bipolar term by adding to or subtracting from a norm.

Silence. Puttenham's term for **Aposiopesis.**

Simile (L. "like") — **Homoeosis; Similitude.**
One thing is likened to another, dissimilar thing by the use of *like, as,* etc.; distinguished from **Metaphor** in that the comparison is made explicit: "My love is like a red, red, rose."

Similitudo, in Latin rhetoric, was a general term for similitude of various kinds; types, according to Puttenham, are **Exemplum; Icon; Parable. Fable** is also sometimes reckoned part of this group. The modern reader may perhaps want to think of simile in the customary pairing with metaphor, and leave the other terms to form a loose and informal group clustering around illustrative anecdote.

Simile casibus (SI mi le   CA si bus; L. "alike in case") — **Homoioptoton.**

Simile determinatione (SI mi le   de ter mi na ti O ne; L. "alike in ending") — **Homoioteleuton.**

Similiter cadens (si MI li ter   CA dens; L. "closing or falling alike").
1. **Homoioptoton.**
2. Closing with the same **Cursus.**

Similiter desinens (DE si nens; L. "ending alike") — **Homoioteleuton.**

Similitude; alt. sp. **Similitudo — Simile.**

Single Supply. Puttenham's term for **Zeugma.**

Skesis (SKE sis) — **Paronomasia.**

Skotison (SKO ti son; G. "Darken it!").

In his discussion of clarity, Quintilian repeats from Livy an anecdote about a rhetoric teacher who taught his pupils to make all they said obscure: *Skotison!*, he would tell them, "Darken it!" "It was this same habit which gave rise to the famous words of praise from a rhetoric teacher, 'So much the better: even I could not understand you' " (VIII.ii.18). It is advice which has always found favor and we should have a name for it. How about *skotison*? A character in Mann's *Doctor Faustus* talks about "the eye of the guild" in referring to music containing hidden allusions and jokes which only the musicians, not the audience, can understand. At some periods in the history of Western discourse — perhaps today is one of them — this "eye of the guild" seems to sweep over the whole landscape of learned discourse. We need a word for this fondness for intentional obscurity. It is not, after all, an affair only of our time. Baldwin (*Medieval Rhetoric and Poetic*, p. 77) quotes a poem by Ausonius:

> Possem absolute dicere
> Sed dulcius circumloquar
> Diuque fando perfruar.
>
> ("I might tell thee outright; but for more pleasure I will talk in mazes and with speech drawn out get full enjoyment.")

And Samuel Johnson alludes to the same fondness when he talks of the "bugbear style" in the *Idler* No. 36:

> There is a mode of style for which I know not that the masters of oratory have yet found a name, a style by which the most evident truths are so obscured that they can no longer be perceived, and the most familiar propositions so disguised that they cannot be known. Every other kind of eloquence is the dress of sense, but this is the mask, by which a true master of his art will so effectually conceal it, that a man will as easily mistake his own positions if he meets them thus transformed, as he may pass in a masquerade his nearest acquaintance. This style may be called the "terrifick," for its chief intention is to terrify and amaze; it may be termed the "repulsive," for its natural effect is to drive away the reader; or it may be distinguished, in plain English, by the denomination of the "bugbear style," for it has more terror than danger, and will appear less formidable, as it is more nearly approached.

The anthropologist Clifford Geertz remarks of the stylized and self-conscious people he has studied so acutely: "The Balinese never do anything in a simple way that they can contrive to do in a complicated one." Neither, often, do we. A number of rhetorical figures — all the figures of brevity, ellipsis, and implication, for example, really draw from the same well, though perhaps with a more peaceable intention. Often the rhetorical figures act as self-interference rituals, little self-and-other mystifications we perform just for the formal pleasure of it. In a way, I suppose, we might profitably consider all rhetorical figuration under this rubric.

Discussions of obscurity in rhetoric are not so common as obscurity itself, but there is an interesting chapter on "The Concept of Obscurity in Greek Literature" in Kustas's *Studies in Byzantine Rhetoric*.

Slowe Returne. Puttenham's term for **Epanalepsis.**

Solecismus (so le CIS mus; G. "speaking incorrectly") — **Incongruitie.**

Ignorant misuse of cases, genders, and tenses. Said to be named from the bad Greek spoken by the Greek colonists at Soloi in Cilicia. Originally solecismus referred to words in combination, while **Barbarismus** was an error in a single word. (For those who wish to pursue the distinctions, Quintilian deals at great length with various definitions in I.v.34–54). An example from a Portuguese-English phrasebook:

> How is that gentilman who you did speak by and by?
> Is a German.
> I did think him Englishman.
> He is of the Saxony side.
> He speak the french very well.
> Tough he is German.
> He speak so much well italyan, french, spanish and english, that among the Italyans, they believe him Italyan, he speak the frenche as the Frenches himselves. The Spanishesmen believe him Spanishing, and the Englishes, Englisman.
> It is difficult to enjoy well so much several langages.

See also **Malapropism.**

Soother. Puttenham's term for **Euphemismus (2).**

Soraismus (so ra IS mus; G. "heaping up") — **Mingle Mangle; Sardismus.**

Mingling of languages ignorantly or affectedly.

> Most barbarous intimation! yet a kind of insinuation, as it were, in via, in way, of explication; facere, as it were, replication, or rather, ostentare, to show, as it were, his inclination, after his undressed, unpol-

ished, uneducated, unpruned, untrained, or rather, unlettered, or ratherest, unconfirmed fashion, to insert again my haud credo for a deer.

(*Love's Labor's Lost*, IV, ii)

In the same play, Rosaline needles Berowne about an ostentatious soraismus which comes at the end of his long speech vowing an end to ostentatious figuration:

Berowne. Figures pedantical . . . I do forswear them . . .
Henceforth my wooing mind shall be expressed
In russet yeas and honest kersey noes,
And to begin, wench — so God help me, law! —
My love to thee is sound, sans crack or flaw.
Rosaline. Sans "sans," I pray you.

(V, ii)

A note on the spelling. At book VIII.iii.59 of Quintilian, both the Loeb and the Oxford editions print *sardismos*. This represents an emendation of a ninth-century manuscript of Quintilian, which reads *soraismos*, on the basis of a reading *sardismos* in an eighth-century manuscript. Lausberg lists only sardismos, but the Renaissance authorities use variations on soraismus. Best to stick with soraismus, I think.

Sorites (so RI tes; G. "the fallacy of the heap").
A chain of **Categorical Syllogisms** abbreviated into an **Enthymeme**, which can have any number of premises. A fallacious chain of this sort ("the fallacy of the heap") is also sometimes called a sorites.

Speedie Dispatcher. Puttenham's term for **Expeditio**.

Sprezzatura (sprez za TU ra).
A coinage by Baldesare Castiglione in his *Il Libro del Cortegiano*, to describe the well-practiced naturalness, the rehearsed spontaneity, which lies at the center of convincing discourse of any sort, and which has been the always-sought but seldom well-described center of rhetorical "decorum," since Aristotle first tried to describe it.

Square of Opposition.
The diagram that shows the traditional ways in which propositions may oppose one another.

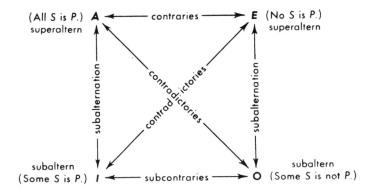

Stasis (STA sis; G. "placing, position") — **Issue**.

Status — **Issue**.

Stile coupé. *See* **Senecan Style**.

Stile serré. *See* **Senecan Style**.

Store. Puttenham's term for **Synonymia**.

Straggler. Puttenham's term for **Parecbasis**; *see* **Digression**.

Style (L. *elocutio*; G. *lexis; phrasis*).

The third of the five traditional parts of **Rhetoric**, that which included discussions of the **Figures** used to ornament discourse. Historically, the most talked-about, if not the most important, part of rhetorical theory. It was by the Ramist theorists maintained to be, with **Memory** and **Delivery**, the *only* part of Rhetoric, properly construed; **Invention** and **Arrangement** were thought part of **Logic**. Traditionally, those who have taken the narrower view of rhetoric as a collection of ornamental techniques have naturally emphasized style over the first two parts, and have tended to define the good style as the artificial one, the one as far as possible from everyday usage. See chapter 2.

Suasoria (sua SO ri a; L. "hortatory speech").

In Roman rhetorical training, a mock deliberative oration, often on an historical theme. A training in the techniques of argument, done by a young student before going on to the more advanced **Controversia**. The neophyte spoke in character, as an advisor to a famous historical or legendary figure.

See also **Declamatio**.

Subcontraries.
Two **Propositions** are subcontraries when they cannot both be false, though both may be true:

> Some rubies are valuable.
> Some rubies are not valuable.

Subjectio (sub JEC ti o; L. "placing under; annexing").
The questioner suggests the answer to his own question. For examples and further discussion see **Hypophora**.
See also **Prosapodosis**.

Subsannatio (sub san NA ti o; L. "mockery by gesture") — **Mycterismus**.

Substitute. Puttenham's term for **Hypozeuxis**.

Sufficient Cause.
A **Cause** in the presence of which a result must happen.

Sugchrisis; alt. sp. **Sygchrisis** — **Syncrisis**.

Superabundancia — **Pleonasmus**.

Superlatio — **Hyperbole**.

Surclose. Puttenham's second term for **Epiphonema**.

Surnamer. Puttenham's term for **Antonomasia**.

Swift Repeate. Puttenham's term for **Ploce**.

Sygchrisis (SYG chri sis; G. "comparison") — **Syncrisis**.

Syllepsis (syl LEP sis; G. "taking together") — **Double Supply**.
A verb lacks congruence with at least one subject that it governs: "The Nobles and the King was taken."
See also **Zeugma**.

Syllogism. *See* **Canonical Syllogism; Categorical Propositions; Disjunctive Syllogism; Hypothetical Syllogism**.

Syllogismus (G. "reasoning; inference").
Intimation; hinting at something. A syllogism even more abbreviated than an **Enthymeme**. Instead of a chain of reasoning with a

term missing or implied, we have a pregnant image that suggests the whole chain of reasoning. Peacham says Polyphemis used a pine tree as a staff — thus we "reason" to his gigantic size. Lear, instead of calling Kent a fool, says "Sirrah, you were best take my coxcomb." And Wellington Koo recounts that when he was growing up in China, if someone stood in your way, you said, "May I borrow your shadow?"

See also **Significatio.**

Symphoresis (sym pho RE sis; G. "bringing together") — **Congeries.**

Symploce (SYM plo ce; G. "intertwining") — **Complexio; Comprehensio; Conexum; Koinotes; Replie.**
Repetition of one word or phrase at the beginning, and of another at the end, of successive clauses, sentences, or passages; a combination of **Anaphora** and **Antistrophe (1)**. The following verses illustrate it with paradigmatic rigor:

> Most true that I must fair Fidessa love,
> Most true that fair Fidessa cannot love.
> Most true that I do feel the pains of love,
> Most true that I am captive unto love.
> Most true that I deluded am with love,
> Most true that I do find the sleights of love.
> Most true that nothing can procure her love,
> Most true that I must perish in my love.
> Most true that she contemns the god of love,
> Most true that he is snared with her love.
> Most true that she would have me cease to love,
> Most true that she herself alone is Love.
> Most true that though she hated I would love,
> Most true that dearest life shall end with love.
> (Bartholomew Griffin, *Fidessa*, 62)

See also **Conduplicatio.**

Synaeceosis — **Synoeciosis.**

Synaeresis (syn AE re sis; G. "drawing together, contraction").
Pronouncing as a diphthong two adjacent vowels that belong to different syllables within a single word: Pha_e_thon. The opposite of **Diaeresis (2).**

See also **Synalepha.**

Synalepha (syn a LE pha; G. "coalescing of two syllables into one"); alt. sp. **Synaloepha.**

A word ending with a vowel adjoins a word starting with a vowel, and the two vowels are fused into one: "I'll do't" for "I'll do it"; "t'attain" for "to attain." Quintilian (I.v.17) makes this synonymous with **Synaeresis**.

Synathroesmus (syn a THROES mus; G. "collection, union").
1. **Congeries**.
2. **Accumulatio**.

Synchisis (SYN chi sis; G. "mixture, confusion") — **Confusio**.
Confused word order in a sentence, as in this excerpt from the Preface to a curious Portuguese-English phrasebook: "We expect then, who the little book (for the care what we wrote him, and for her typographical correction) that may be worth the acceptation of the studious persons, and especialy of the Youth, at which we dedicate him particularly." (This example would seem to fit rather well Donatus's definition of this term: *hyperbaton ex omni parte confusum* [*Ars maior*, III, 6].)

Synchoresis (syn cho RE sis; G. "consent, agreement").
The speaker gives his questioner leave to judge him. So Falstaff, in the play-within-a-play in *1 Henry IV*, says to his tavern audience, "And here I stand: judge, my masters" (II, iv).
See also **Concessio**.

Syncope (SYN co pe; G. "cutting [short]").
Removing letter(s) or syllable(s) from the middle of a word: "ignomy" for "ignominy"; "heartly" for "heartily." We do it several times when we pronounce "Cholmondelay" as "Chumley," and P. G. Wodehouse parodies it when "Towcester Abbey" and its attendant Lord are pronounced "Toaster."

Syncrisis (SYN cri sis; G. "comparison, combination"); alt. sp. **Sugchrisis, Sygchrisis** — **Dissimilitude**.
Comparison and contrast in parallel clauses:

> The value of a life lies not in the length of days, but in the use we make of them. A man may live long, yet get little from life.
>
> (Montaigne)

> Cowards die many times before their deaths;
> The valiant never taste of death but once.
>
> (*Julius Caesar*, II, ii)

> They are not beautiful: they are only decorated. They are not clean: they are only shaved and starched. They are not dignified: they are only fashionably dressed. They are not educated: they are only college

passmen. They are not religious: they are only pewrenters. They are not moral: they are only conventional. They are not virtuous: they are only cowardly. They are not even vicious: they are only "frail."

(Shaw, *Man and Superman*)

A kind of **Antithesis.**

Synecdoche (syn EC do che; G. "understanding one thing with another") — **Intellectio; Quick Conceite.**

Substitution of part for whole, genus for species, or vice versa: "All hands on deck." Of this figure, Kenneth Burke has written: "The more I examine both the structure of poetry and the structure of human relations outside of poetry, the more I become convinced that this is the 'basic' figure of speech, and that it occurs in many modes besides that of the formal trope" (*The Philosophy of Literary Form*, p. 26). If this is so, at the center of figuration stands *scale-change*. To define *A*, equate it to a part of *B*, derived by magnification. Experience is described in terms of other experience, but at a different level of magnification. Scaling has certainly formed a central part of postmodern aesthetics, and of the aesthetics of computer-generated electronic text as well. And similarity of part to whole, self-similarity as it is called, is a central characteristic of the fractal geometry introduced into modern thinking by chaos theory. The putative centrality of synecdoche is receiving at least a fair trial in the current sensorium.

See also **Antonomasia; Metonymy.**

Syngnome (SYN gno me; G. "fellow-feeling, forbearance").
Forgiveness of injuries:

> To whome ye forgive any thing, I forgive also: for if I forgave any thing, to whom I forgave it, for your sakes forgave I it in the person of Christ; lest Satan should get an advantage of us: for we are not ignorant of his devices.
>
> (2 Cor. 2:10)

Synoeciosis (syn oe ci O sis; G. "binding together"); alt. sp. **Synaeceosis, Syneciosis** — **Crosse-Couple.**
An expanded **Oxymoron**; a **Paradox.**

> She dwells with Beauty — Beauty that must die;
>   And Joy, whose hand is ever at his lips
> Bidding adieu; and aching Pleasure nigh,
>   Turning to Poison while the bee-mouth sips:
> Ay, in the very temple of Delight
>   Veil'd Melancholy has her sovran shrine.
>
> (Keats, *Ode on Melancholy*)

Synonymia (syn o NY mi a) — **Communio; Interpretatio; Store.**

Amplification by synonym:

> What is become of that beautiful face,
> Those lovely looks, that favor amiable,
> Those sweet features, and visage full of grace,
> That countenance which is alonly able
> To kill and cure?
>
> (Puttenham, p. 214)

Synthesis. *See* **Composition.**

Synzeugmenon (syn ZEUG me non; G. "yoked together") — **Zeugma.**

Systole (SYS to le; G. "drawing together, contracting") — **Contractio.**
Shortening a naturally long vowel or syllable; opposite of **Diastole.**

Systrophe (SYS tro phe; G. "collection") — **Conglobatio.**
Heaping up of descriptions of a thing without defining it:

> Man is an example of imbecility, the spoil of time, an image of unconstancy, a captive of calamity, a prisoner to pains, a servant to covetousness, finally, a food for worms.
>
> (Peacham, p. 137)

(For an extensive discussion, see Salomon Hegnauer, "The Rhetorical Figure of Systrophe," in Vickers, *Rhetoric Revalued.*)

See also **Congeries.**

Tapinosis (ta pi NO sis; G. "reduction; humiliation") — **Abbaser; Humiliatio.**
Undignified language that debases a person or thing: "rhymester" for "poet," "verses" for "poetry." Generally considered a vice, not a self-conscious technique.

See also **Meiosis.**

Tautologia (tau to LO gi a; G. "saying the same things") — **Selfe Saying.**
Repetition of the same idea in different words:

> *Lepidus.* What manner o'thing is your crocodile?
> *Antony.* It is shap'd, sir, like itself, and it is as broad as it has breadth. It is just so high as it is, and moves with its own organs. It lives by that which nourisheth it, and the elements once out of it, it transmigrates.
> *Lepidus.* What colour is it of?
> *Antony.* Of its own colour too.

> *Lepidus.* 'Tis a strange serpent.
> *Antony.* 'Tis so. And the tears of it are wet.
> (*Antony and Cleopatra*, II, vii)

See also **Macrologia.**

Taxis (TAX is; G. "**Arrangement,** order") — **Arrangement.**
Peacham makes it a figure: "Distributes to every subject his most proper and natural adjunct." Touchstone says:

> As the ox hath his bow, sir, the horse his curb, and the falcon her bells, so man hath his desires; and as pigeons bill, so wedlock would be nibbling.
> (*As You Like It*, III, iii)

Tell Cause. Puttenham's term for **Aetiologia.**

Testamentum (tes ta MEN tum; L. "will; something acknowledged before witnesses").
When not used literally, may mean **Diatyposis (2).**

Testatio (tes TA ti o; L. "a bearing witness") — **Martyria.**

Thaumasmus (thau MAS mus; G. "marveling") — **Admiratio.**
Exclamation of wonder:

> O, wonder!
> How many goodly creatures are there here!
> How beauteous mankind is! O brave new world,
> That has such people in't!
> (*The Tempest*, V, i)

Thesis.
One of the two categories into which the Greek rhetorician Hermagoras of Temnos divided the subject of rhetoric. The thesis was an *indefinite* question, pursued without reference to specific time and place: "Are mothers-in-law offensive?" The opposite category was **Hypothesis**, a *definite* question tied to time and place: "Is *my* mother-in-law offensive?" The one could easily shade into the other. Thus the terms referred to the common pivot we all need when elevating a personal vexation to a matter of principle or demoting it from one.

The traditional centrality, and difficulty, of this term, and the associated term **Issue**, perhaps justify an amplification. First, the multiple terminology. In Latin, theses are called *quaestiones*, either *infinitae* or *universales*, as against hypotheses, which are *quaestiones finitae* or *speciales* or just *causae*. (Mixing the paired terms, as Wilson does in the *Arte of Rhetorique* [p. 23], when he uses *infinite* rather than *indefinite*, has misled at least one compiler of terms.) Cicero also used *propositum* and *consultatio* as synonyms for thesis. The Greek word was not Latinized into *thesis* until Seneca, according to Bonner's discussion in *Roman Declamation* (pp. 2ff.). Thus in English, *theses* are *questions* and *hypotheses* are *causes*. To further confuse the issue, a mock oration based on a *hypothesis* was itself called a hypothesis, and later by the Romans a **Suasoria** and **Controversia**.

Larger conceptual structures have been built on the distinction as well. Bonner discusses the term as one of the earliest Greek rhetorical exercises in what later became Roman **Declamatio**, and gives as typical kinds of theses "the universe and its problems," "law and government," "man and his social duties," and similar bags of chestnuts. Theses, since they dealt with such large questions, were often thought to be special philosophical territory, especially by the philosophers; rhetoric should stick to the hypotheses, which included all the questions of fact needed for the legal or political debate orators pursued. The Athenian rhetorical school of Hermagoras incurred the wrath of the philosophers, and of Cicero, for just such a transgression. It is hard, though, to think of any argument which does not at some point oscillate between general and particular without regard to such scholarly turf disputes. Richard McKeon argues more widely that the central difference between philosophy and rhetoric turns on this distinction, and on the definition of an *issue*: "The complex and changing relations between philosophy and rhetoric, and the effects of the transmutation of philosophy into rhetoric, are shadowed forth in the history of the schematisms and distinctions used to differentiate issues or questions" (*Rhetoric: Essays in Invention and Discovery*, pp. 60–61; see also p. 127). In fact, this cluster of terms provides an acute introduction to McKeon's very important, and very condensed, argument that the essence of rhetoric's history, and its relation to philosophy, lies in the *changes in meaning* of its basic terms. Kenneth Burke, in a suggestive discussion in *A Rhetoric of Motives*, identifies thesis with poetic *idea*, hypothesis with poetic *image* (p. 85).

Students wishing to venture further into this tangled wood might start with Quintilian's discussion in II.iv.22ff. and III.v.4ff., and with Bonner's excellent modern one in *Roman Declamation*. (For another path into the forest, see **Issue**.)

Threnos (THRE nos; G. "dirge"); alt. sp. **Threnody** — **Lamentatio**.

A lamentation, Shakespeare's *The Phoenix and the Turtle*, for example.

See also **Commiseratio**.

Tmesis ([t]ME sis; G. "a cutting").

Originally "the artificial separation of a preposition from its verb in poetry after Homer, especially by the interposition of enclitics and particles" (Goodwin and Gulick, *Greek Grammar*). Then, interposition of a word or phrase between the parts of a compound word; thus a synonym for **Diacope (2)**. Now, by a further extension, sometimes **Diacope (1)**.

Tolerantia (to le RAN ti a; L. "endurance") — **Apocarteresis**.

Too Full Speech. Puttenham's term for **Pleonasmus**.

Topics (G. *topoi*).
The topics were for Aristotle, as they have been for rhetoricians since, both the stuff of which arguments are made and the form of those arguments. Neither Aristotle nor those theorists following him always made it clear with which aspect they were concerned. The twenty-eight valid and ten fallacious topics of **Invention** listed in chapter 2 are formal, rather than material; they are the traditional topics. Aristotle distinguished them, general topics applicable to all subjects alike, from those that could be applied only to a specific subject or question. The long list of topics is often shortened to basic types: genus and species, nature, authority, consequence, time and place, word, etc. Later, more general usage has confused the topics with the *loci communes* or commonplace observations or literary situations; both are part of that planned spontaneity, that **Sprezzatura**, which was an orator's principal means of dazzling his audience. (See **Invention: The commonplaces**, in chapter 2.)

Father Ong has discussed the topics and their connection with the dynamics of an oral culture in *The Presence of the Word*:

> The doctrine of the commonplaces picks up and codifies the drives in oral cultures to group knowledge of all sorts around human behavior and particularly around virtue and vice. In one sense of the term, a commonplace or *locus communis* was what we would think of as a "heading," but, instead of being so conceptualized, it was thought of as some kind of "place" (*locus* in Latin; *topos* in Greek, whence our word "topic") in which were stored arguments to prove one or another point. Whether this place was taken to be in the mind or in one's notes or elsewhere remained always quite vague and unsettled. In his *Topica* (ii) Cicero defines a *locus* as the "seat of an argument," a definition which Quintilian follows in his *Institutio oratoria* (v.10.20). In any event, such headings or places were "common" when they could be used for all subjects, not merely for certain specific ones. . . . Commonplaces thus understood we might style here the analytic commonplaces, since they in effect analyze a subject in terms of various headings.
>
> Another type of commonplace or *locus communis* met with in both

Greek and Latin antiquity had also been noted by Quintilian in his same work (x.5.12; cf. i.11.12). In this second sense a commonplace was a prefabricated passage for an oration or other composition. (pp. 80–81)

What one finds in the doctrine and use of the commonplaces are thus the essential tendencies which an oral culture, as described by Lord and Havelock, develops because of its information storage problem: a tendency to operate verbally in formulas and formulaic modes of expression combined with a tendency to group material for memory and recall around action in the human life-world, thus around interactions between persons and around questions of virtue and vice, plus a tendency, which combines the two foregoing tendencies, to make individuals themselves into types, thereby shaping them to formulaic treatment. (pp. 84–85)

Topographia (top o GRA phi a) — **Counterfait Place**.
Description of a place. A type of **Enargia**.

> From a hill-top near by, where the wood had been recently cut off, there was a pleasing vista southward across the pond, through a wide indentation in the hills which form the shore there, where their opposite sides sloping toward each other suggested a stream flowing out in that direction through a wooded valley, but stream there was none.
>
> (Thoreau, *Walden*)

Topos — **Topics**.

Topothesia (top o THE si a; G. "description of a place") — **Loci positio**.
Description of imaginary, nonexistent places. A type of **Topographia**.

Traductio (tra DUC ti o; L. "leading along; a transferring or metonymy; repetition of a word") — **Translacer**.
A general term in the *Ad Herennium* (IV.xiv.20) for repetitive word play with an interval between words; see **Ploce; Polyptoton**.

Traiectio in alium (tra IEC ti o in A li um; L. "pushing onto another").
Shifting of responsibility. Henry V to the Archbishop of Canterbury:

> For God doth know how many now in health
> Shall drop their blood in approbation
> Of what your reverence shall incite us to.
>
> (*Henry V*, I, ii)

Transcensio (trans CEN si o; L. "climbing over") — **Hyperbaton**.

Transgressio (trans GRES si o; L. "going across") — **Hyperbaton**.

Transiectio (trans IEC ti o; L. "passing over") — **Hyperbaton**.

Transitio (trans I ti o; L. "going across") — **Metabasis**.

Translacer. Puttenham's term for **Traductio**.

Translatio — **Metaphor**.

Transmotio (trans MO ti o; L. "transposing") — **Metastasis**.

Transmutation — **Metonymy**.

Transnominatio (trans no mi NA ti o) — **Metonymy**.

Transplacement — **Antanaclasis**.

Transport. Puttenham's term for **Metaphor**.

Transposition — **Antisthecon; Metathesis**.

Transumptio (tran SUMP ti o; L. "assuming one thing for another") — **Metalepsis**.

Trespasser. Puttenham's term for **Hyperbaton**.

Tricolon (TRI co lon; G. "having three members").
The three-unit pattern common in many prose styles.

> His father was one of those somewhat obscure sages whom early America produced: mystics of independent mind, hermits in the desert of business, and heretics in the churches. They were intense individualists, full of veneration for the free souls of their children, and convinced that everyone should paddle his own canoe, especially on the high seas.
>
> (George Santayana, "William James," *Character and Opinion in the United States*)

The first sentence exemplifies tricolon, the second a popular subtype, tricolon *crescens*.

Trope (G. "a turn") — **Turn**.
Theorists have differed in defining this term, and any single definition would be prescriptive. Such consensus as there is wants trope to mean a **Figure** that changes the meaning of a word or

words, rather than simply arranging them in a pattern of some sort. (Thus the distinction would roughly correspond to that between true and false wit in the time of Pope.) That the placing of a word in a highly artificial pattern — a **Scheme** — usually involves some change of its meaning is a point theorists have more often ignored than quarreled over.

Some theorists would like trope to be used for changes in meaning of one word only; for more than one word, figure. Quintilian, on the other hand, points out that change in meaning occurs on a larger scale than in single words, and that change in signification is the crucial issue. Donatus (followed by Bede) agrees, defining trope as a change from its normal significance of any utterance (*dictio*). For Quintilian, a figure is a form or pattern of speech or writing which differs from the ordinary. So, we might say that, for him, a trope is a change in meaning, a figure is a change in form. In book I.viii.16, he divides the figures (*schemata*) into figures of speech (*lexis*) and figures of thought (*dianoia*). His use of these terms in books VIII and IX is by no means clear to me, especially in VIII.vi.40, where the whole distinction seems to collapse. The student who wishes to press Quintilian on the matter might well begin with the opening discussion of book IX. Still another set of categories is presented in Fortunatianus's *Ars rhetorica* (Halm, p. 126.24ff.). He divides figures into three types: (1) λέξεως, of one word; (2) λόγου, of more than one word; (3) διανοίας, of thought, in whatever form. The central problem — when does a change in meaning become a change in thought? — obscures his further distinction of figures into figures of thought (διανοίας) and figures of words (λέξεως). Disagreement among the authorities is summarized by Lausberg, section 600ff., a good place to begin for further inquiry.

Two fundamental distinctions wander through the considerable theoretical disagreement: (1) changes in form and changes in meaning; (2) the size or scope of the change. (For the origin of [1] and the development of [2], see *Ad Herennium*, IV.xii.18, and Harry Caplan's note "c" thereto, pp. 274–275.) Scholars have used this cluster of terms with a confidence that is belied by the primary disagreement about them.

The issues involved seem complex enough to preclude an adequate distinction. The body of opinion which makes trope a truly metaphorical change in a word's use, a change in meaning, and scheme a superficial or merely decorative change, really took hold in modern theorizing — so far as I can trace it — with the work of the late Morris W. Croll. Croll used all his terms with authority, but his use of them might trouble modern students more than it does. Jonas

Barish ("The Prose Style of John Lyly") has pointed out the problems a rigid trope-scheme distinction creates:

> On the whole, a contemporary reader is likely to be disturbed by the earnestness with which Croll propounds the Renaissance distinction between "figures of thought" (tropes) and "figures of sound" (schemes). This distinction, which drives a wedge between style and content, and treats them as though they enjoyed separate and independent existence, if it interferes even with objective descriptions of style, interferes still more with any effort to get at the heart of a writer's artistic universe, where style and meaning interpenetrate. (pp. 15–16)

And at more than one point in *The Senecan Amble*, Williamson shows how the same figure is (metaphorical) trope in one writer and (ornamental) scheme in another. Or we might adduce a shape poem as a pattern both trope and scheme at the same time.

It is easy enough, once you have a list of ornaments clearly divided between easy and difficult, sound and thought, trope and scheme, to characterize, or castigate, an author for using the easy figures, or the schemes, rather than the difficult figures, or the tropes. But it is by no means clear that such a predetermined division will do justice to any particular text, especially to a literary one. Take a simple example. **Hyperbaton**, a generic term for departure from ordinary word order, is a trope. Yet under it we must group several of the figures of words (**Anaphora, Conduplicatio, Isocolon, Ploce**), since they clearly depend on an "unnatural" word order, the kind Lyly favored and was reproached for. The distinction immediately breaks down, of course, because "natural" is impossible to define. What is "natural" for *Euphues* or Sidney's *Arcadia* is hardly the word order of everyday speech. The point to be taken is that the trope-scheme distinction contains a hidden premise of "naturalness" which may be unacceptable to a literary critic.

Take a more complex example. Euphues, at the beginning of *Euphues*, is answering a Polonius-like warning about the evils that may befall him, by playing elaborately on the word "nature":

> Now whereas you seem to love my nature, & loathe my nurture, you bewray your own weakness, in thinking that nature may anyways be altered by education, & as you have ensamples to confirm your pretence, so I have most evident and infallible arguments to serve for my purpose: It is natural for the vine to spread. It is proper. . . .

These are schemes, easy ornaments (**Ploce** and **Polyptoton** and withal a **Paronomasia** on "nurture"). Yet the whole passage (of which I have quoted only the beginning) is radically metaphorical, aims to redefine both "nature" and "nurture." Further, both redefinitions are argumentative techniques, and the kind of persuasion they are meant to effect (their "naturalness," their rhetorical **Decorum**) will depend on a full understanding of the dramatic context. Such an understanding here yields the conclusion that the real subject of the passage is neither "nature" nor "nurture" but wit. Euphues' real argument is that his wit is deep enough to avoid the dangers so fully foreseen for him. The passage must then finally be described as a hyperbolic periphrasis that builds a complex and ironical metaphor for wit. **Hyperbole, Periphrasis,** and **Metaphor** are all tropes, of course.

The historian of rhetoric will want to preserve all the distinctions that have been made. But it seems a doubtful wisdom for the literary critic to restrict himself to categories inadequate to describe all but the simplest literary texts.

Tropological Level. *See* **Allegory.**

Turn.
The English term for **Trope**; it was widely used in the seventeenth and eighteenth centuries for a broad range of syntactical figures of speech.

Turne Tale. Puttenham's term for **Apostrophe.**

Turpis locutio (TUR pis lo CU ti o) — **Cacemphaton.**

Twinnes. Puttenham's term for **Hendiadys.**

Uncouthe. Puttenham's term for **Acyrologia.**

Underlay. Puttenham's second term for **Epizeuxis.**

Undistributed Term (of a **Syllogism**).
Refers to only a part of class designated by term.

Urbanitas (ur BA ni tas; L. "refinement, elegance") — **Asteismus.**

Utis (OO tis; G. "no one"); alt. sp. **Outis.**
The Nobody Argument: "The Nobody argument is an argument whose major premise consists of an indefinite and a definite clause, followed by a minor premise and conclusion; for example, 'If anyone is here, he is not in Rhodes; but there is someone here, therefore there is not anyone in Rhodes'" (Diogenes Laertius, "Zeno," VIII.82).

Vices of Language.
"I do fear colourable colors," says Holofernes. And which of us does not? Perhaps it is the counsel of depraved relativism that every

vice was once, until o'ercolored, a virtue, but it is clearly the counsel of rhetoricians: therefore no **Figure** is always a vice except those that deliberately say so — and even they may be redeemed. Conversely, any virtue can be viciously used. To divide figures, outside any context, into *vices* and *virtues* seems less foolish than impossible.

There is, however, one easy and universally accepted way to tell them apart. If you notice a verbal pattern, it is a vice. If not, a virtue. Practically everyone agrees that this is so, and true of behavior as much as of verbal style. Abraham Fraunce, in the *Arcadian Rhetoric*, is almost the only authority I know who thinks the road of excess leads to the palace of wisdom: "thus much of elocution in tropes and figures, in all which observe this one lesson, the more the better." Yet the difficulties posed for rhetoric itself by this basic prohibition of verbal self-consciousness ought to have been noticed by *someone*.

The whole of rhetorical training aims at making us aware of the figures and thus ready, willing, and able to notice them. The better your rhetorical education, then, the more vice you are likely to see. The premise of rhetoric is an audience ignorant of its practices, an audience which rhetoric does its best to abolish. Furthermore, there is persistent evidence from classical antiquity onward that audiences were not ignorant but, by modern standards certainly, extremely knowledgeable. They relished speeches as entertainments. To do this, you must name the figures as they flourish and multiply. In fact, how can figures work their will upon us unless we *do* notice them, at least to some degree? How, for the matter of that, can any **Metaphor** work unless we notice it as such?

What must really be at issue, if all of this built-in self-contradiction is to make any sense, is some kind of tacit and yet partly self-conscious agreement *not to notice* certain things which we still know are going on. The Virtue-Vice distinction, that is, finally bases itself on the same tacit "Let's Pretend" agreement that undergirds Western **Decorum** of all sorts. We base our social reality on a self-acknowledged tacit agreement about what to notice and what not to, and when, and then agree to think this temporary accommodation reality itself. Rhetorical theorists have not come clean — have intentionally deceived themselves — about the Virtue-Vice distinction for reasons that reach down to the grounding of Western social reality.

The world of digital computing suggests a useful analogy here. The revolution computers have brought to our lives comes from converting information into a digital form — a series of simple Off/On decisions. Language works differently, by analogy, metaphorically, most of us would now agree. And the figures work by analogy, as well, whether the analogy be of sound, sight, or meaning. But riding on top of these analogies, like a multiplexed signal as it were, is a *digital* channel, which dictates a simple on/off decision: do we look self-consciously *at* the verbal surface or unselfconsciously *through* it? The digital channel and the analogue one continually interact when the figures go into action in human communication. We've not noticed — we've trained ourselves *not* to notice — this fundamental digital decision.

Thus before a modern reader decides that an earlier writer has laid his rhetorical ornament on with a trowel, she might look with profit at how much troweling the context requires. No one thinks that Holofernes, in *Love's Labor's Lost*, speaks for Shakespeare, but analogous confusions often pass current where the dramatic context is less immediately clear. In fact, it might be argued that a writer cannot possibly go haywire to the degree that the moralizing way of thinking (which gives us the phrase "vices of language") maintains. If the flowers of rhetoric are so dense as to obscure any kind of denotative meaning, we can only assume that the "meaning" intended is the floral display itself. Surely an age that cut its teeth on symbolist poetry need not be troubled by a presentation of words for their own sake. One step beyond such display puts us, of course, into the treatise or rhetorical diploma-piece category, and again the thing justifies itself.

The only test for the arts of rhetoric is effectiveness, not virtue: when a rhetorical pitch calls attention to itself as rhetorical, it does not, *pace* Aristotle (*Rhetoric*, III, 1404b), or Longinus (*On the Sublime*, XVIII), necessarily lose its effectiveness. It simply moves over into another, more self-conscious kind of appeal, one where the rules of the game are different.

See also **Euphuism.**

Votum (VO tum; L. "vow") — **Euche (1).**

Wondrer. Puttenham's term for **Paradox.**

Zeugma (ZEUG ma; G. "yoking") — **Adnexio; Epezeugmenon; Junctio; Single Supply; Synzeugmenon.**

A kind of **Ellipsis** in which one word, usually a verb, governs several congruent words or clauses. Puttenham calls zeugma the *single supply*, "because by one word we serve many clauses of one congruity, and may be likened to the man that serves many masters at once, but all of one country." He distinguishes three kinds and offers these examples, each of which uses a *verb* as the single governing word:

Prozeugma:

> Her beauty *pierced* mine eye, her speech mine woeful heart,
> Her presence all the powers of my discourse.

Mesozeugma:

> Fair maids' beauty (alack) with years it *wears away*,
> And with weather and sickness, and sorrow as they say.

Hypozeugma:

> My mates that wont to keep me company,
> And my neighbors, who dwelt next to my wall . . .
> In my quarrel they *are fled* from me all.

> (pp. 164–165)

W. K. Wimsatt, using a definition of zeugma in which the single governing word need not be a verb, has fitted a line from Pope to each:

> *Who* could not win the mistress, wooed the maid.
> And now a bubble *burst*, and now a world.
> Where nature moves, and rapture warms the *mind*.

> (*The Verbal Icon*, p. 177)

Further discussion. There is some confusion in the commentary which perhaps should be ventilated. First, since L. *verbum* can mean either "verb" or "word," some have said that zeugma must mean that the word which governs several elements must be a *verb*, as in the Puttenham examples above. Quintilian (whom perhaps Puttenham followed) seems to mean this, judging by his examples, in IX.iii.62ff. Others (see Wimsatt's examples above) do not require that the governing word always be a verb, and certainly Pope's frequent uses of zeugma, from which Wimsatt departs, do not always work this way.

Second, zeugma has in usage overlapped with **Syllepsis.** To me it makes sense to restrict syllepsis to its narrow sense — one verb lacking congruence with at least one subject that it governs — and to use zeugma for the less strict instances of double governance, as when Pope's nymph "stains her honor or her new brocade."

Third, **Adjunctio** has been used as synonym for zeugma, with *prejunctio, medio junctio,* and *postjunctio* used as Latin parallels for prozeugma, mesozeugma, and hypozeugma (see Sonnino, p. 22). The evidence for this synonymity is shaky and it just confuses things. Better to restrict adjunctio, **Conjunctio,** and **Disjunctio** to the meanings they have in *Ad Herennium* IV.xxvii.37–38:

> *Adjunctio:* "when the verb holding the sentence together is placed not in the middle, but at the beginning or the end. At the beginning as follows: 'Fades physical beauty with disease or age.' At the end, as follows: 'Either with disease or age physical beauty fades.'"

Conjunctio: "when both the previous and the succeeding phrases are held together by placing the verb between them, as follows: 'Either with disease physical beauty fades, or with age.'"

Disjunctio: "when each of two or more clauses ends with a special verb, as follows: 'By the Roman people Numantia was destroyed, Carthage razed, Corinth demolished, Fregellae overthrown.'"

These three terms are *not*, it should be noted, parallel to prozeugma, mesozeugma, and hypozeugma. In pondering the differences, it is helpful to distinguish between *position* — beginning, middle, and end — and whether the governing word is a *verb* or just a *verbum*.

Fourth, zeugma is sometimes used as synonymous with **Hypozeuxis** (e.g. Bede, *De schematibus* [Halm, p. 608], and later theorists). Better to leave hypozeuxis to its own special meaning as a kind of contrary zeugma, where each clause has its own verb.

Fifth, zeugma sometimes overlaps with **Symploce**, repetition of one word or phrase at the beginning, and another at the end, of successive clauses. Again, it will make things simpler if we discriminate between the two.

Sixth, synzeugmenon and (following Quintilian, I suppose) epezeugmenon are sometimes used for zeugma. Why not stick to the short form?

Seventh, zeugma is clearly a kind of ellipsis, but a special kind which we do well to keep separate.

And now that all this is clear, how should we classify this line from *The Goon Show*? "Here, take this pencil and draw the blinds!"

2 / The Divisions of Rhetoric

RHETORIC

The three branches

Deliberative (legislative; to exhort or dissuade; L. *genus delibera-tivum*; G. *genos symbouleutikon*).
Judicial (forensic; to accuse or defend; L. *genus iudiciale*; G. *genos dikanikon*).
Epideictic or **Panegyric** (ceremonial; to commemorate or blame; L. *genus demonstrativum*; G. *genos epideiktikon* or *panegyrikon*).

Aristotle explains the basis of this division thus:

> Rhetoric falls into three divisions, determined by the three classes of listeners to speeches. For of the three elements in speech-making — speaker, subject, and person addressed — it is the last one, the hearer, that determines the speech's end and object. The hearer must be either a judge, with a decision to make about things past or future, or an observer. A member of the assembly decides about future events, a juryman about past events: while those who merely decide on the orator's skill are observers. From this it follows that there are three divisions of oratory — (1) political, (2) forensic, and (3) the ceremonial oratory of display.
>
> *(Rhetoric, I, 1358a)*

Epideictic rhetoric, the rhetoric of "praise or blame," has always seemed to me to cause a classificatory problem. The kind of display rhetoric often called "epideictic" was, for a start, frequently found in the forum and the lawcourt. And isn't "praising" a category different in kind from "legal" and "judicial," which have to do with particular arenas and social purposes? To correspond to them, it ought to be "domestic," or "private," but those don't fit either. Perhaps we might better follow Aristotle in calling it "ceremonial." That term, at least, would correspond to "judicial" and "deliberative." Might we also say that deliberative and judicial rhetoric are fundamentally purposive in motive, epideictic fundamentally playful? That the self-pleasing aspects of rhetorical performance have tended to cluster in this third category? Perelman and Olbrechts-Tyteca suggest this possibility when they point out that epideictic oratory "seemed to have more connection with literature than with argumentation." The first two kinds of rhetoric, they continue, judicial and deliberative, were appropriated by philosophy, and epideictic became a part of literary prose (*The New Rhetoric*, pp. 48–49).

Aristotle argues that from these three kinds of oratory follow different kinds of time, of purpose, and of argument:

Time:

> These three kinds of rhetoric refer to three different kinds of time. The political orator is concerned with the future. . . . The party in a case at law is concerned with the past. . . . The ceremonial orator is . . . concerned with the present, since all men praise or blame in view of the state of things existing at the time.
>
> Rhetoric, I, 1358b)

(Aristotle seems to feel the sponginess of this distinction himself, for he adds that ceremonial orators "often find it useful also to recall the past and to make guesses at the future.")

Purpose:

> Rhetoric has three distinct ends in view, one for each of its three kinds. The political orator aims at establishing the expediency or the harmfulness of a proposed course of action. . . . Parties in a law-case aim at establishing the justice or injustice of some action. . . . Those who praise or attack a man aim at proving him worthy of honour or the reverse. . . .
>
> Rhetoric, I, 1358b)

Argument:

> . . . in political oratory there is less inducement to talk about non-essentials. Political oratory is less given to unscrupulous practices than forensic, because it treats of wider issues. . . . There is no need, therefore, to prove anything except that the facts are what the supporter of a measure maintains they are. In forensic oratory this is not enough; to conciliate the listener is what pays here.
>
> Rhetoric, I, 1354b)

(The oratory of praise would, on this model, seem to be all conciliation.)

The three branches of oratory have sometimes, by a kind of triadic magnetism, been confused or conflated with the other big triadic division, that of the three levels of style and the occasions appropriate for their use. For this other distinction, see **Style: The three types**, below. The whole dispute about the branches of oratory or rhetoric in classical times is handily summarized by Quintilian, III.iv.

The five parts

Invention	(L. *inventio*)	(G. *heuresis*)
Arrangement	(L. *dispositio*)	(G. *taxis*)
Style	(L. *elocutio*)	(G. *lexis*)
Memory	(L. *memoria*)	(G. *mneme*)
Delivery	(L. *actio*)	(G. *hypocrisis*)

> . . . since all the activity and ability of an orator falls into five divisions, . . . he must first hit upon what to say; then manage and marshal his

discoveries, not merely in orderly fashion, but with a discriminating eye for the exact weight as it were of each argument; next go on to array them in the adornments of style; after that keep them guarded in his memory; and in the end deliver them with effect and charm.

(Cicero, *De oratore*, I.xxxi.142–143)

The Ramists (see **Rhetoric** in chapter 1) would reduce these five parts to two, style and delivery, giving invention and arrangement to logic, and leaving out memory altogether, as a subsidiary classification. Father Ong remarks that the five parts "had originally been not 'parts' of an 'art' but more or less successive activities involved in ancient Greek liberal education" (*Rhetoric, Romance, and Technology*, pp. 56–57). They were the activities any orator must pursue.

INVENTION

Two kinds of proof
(after Aristotle's *Rhetoric*)

1. **Inartificial proof**: All that today would be called "evidence" — sworn testimony, documents, scientific analyses, laws.
2. **Artificial proof**: Three main types.
   a. Establishing the persuader's good character and hence credibility. This is called **Ethos**.
   b. Putting the audience in an appropriate mood, by playing on its feelings. This is called **Pathos**.
   c. Proving, or seeming to prove, the case. The plainest term for this is rational argument or, to use a word which carries many meanings, **Logos** (*logic*).

Two types of logical proof

1. **Deductive**
   a. If the premises are scientifically demonstrated, the term for the argument is **Syllogism.**
   b. If the premises are only probably true, the term for the argument is **Enthymeme**. (Enthymemes are either demonstrative or refutative.) This is the more common form in rhetoric.
2. **Inductive**
   a. If all instances of the phenomenon are accounted for, the induction is scientific.
   b. If only selected instances are cited, the argument is from example. This is the more common form in rhetoric.

Two kinds of topics (*topoi*)
(after Aristotle's *Rhetoric*)

1. Topics useful in a special area of knowledge only (*idioi topoi*).
2. Topics useful in arguments of all kinds (*koinoi topoi*). Four main ones are given:
   a. What can and cannot happen
   b. What has and has not happened
   c. What will or will not happen
   d. Size

At another point in the *Rhetoric*, Aristotle introduces twenty-eight valid and ten invalid topics useful in devising enthymemes. They follow.

Twenty-eight valid topics
(after Aristotle's *Rhetoric*)

1. Restate your contention in an opposite way: e.g., instead of "Excess is bad," say "Moderation is good." If the opposite statement holds, so will the original one.
2. Redefine a key term slightly to support your contention, or suggest a synonym that seems better to support it.
3. Use a correlative idea. You want to prove *B* justly punished, so prove *A* just in punishing him.
4. Argue *a fortiori*. Prove *A* has acted in a cruel way at one time by showing that at another he acted still more cruelly.
5. Argue from circumstances of past time. What has been promised at one time must be performed at another, even though times and circumstances may have changed.
6. Turn an accusation against the accuser. The implied moral superiority of the accuser is thus attacked. The topic will not work if the accusation is obviously just, since if you do something, you cannot effectively reproach others for doing the same thing.
7. Define your terms so as to place the argument in a favorable light.
8. Play upon various senses of a word.
9. Divide your argument into its logical parts.
10. Argue from plain induction (parallel cases).
11. Argue from authority or previous verdict.
12. Argue your contention part by part.
13. Argue from consequences, good or bad.
14. When an action may have good or bad consequences, invert your opponent's arguments. Aristotle's example: Don't take up

oratory. If you say truth, men will hate you; if you lie, the gods will hate you. Take up oratory. If you lie, men will love you; if you say the truth, the gods will love you. (Variation of 13.)

15. Oppose an argument by seeming to allow it and then maintaining that things are not what they seem. If the opponent maintains thus, argue things are what they seem.
16. Argue from logical consequences. If a man is old enough to fight for his country, he is old enough to vote. Are we then to say that those too sick to fight should not vote?
17. Argue that if two results are the same, their causes must be the same.
18. Apply an opponent's earlier decision to a later case, to his disadvantage.
19. Take the possible motive for the one actually prevailing.
20. In arguing individual motive, point to general motives or prohibitions (for or against, depending on which side you have taken).
21. Make people believe an improbability by pointing to an even greater one that is yet true.
22. Catch your opponent out on inaccuracies and self-contradictions.
23. Refute slander by showing that it was evoked by a mistaken view of the facts.
24. Prove effect by showing the presence of its cause, or vice versa.
25. Show that a client or a cause had a better argument and failed to use it. Only trustful innocence would make such a mistake.
26. Disprove an action by showing it inconsistent with previous actions.
27. Use previous mistakes as a defense (or explanation) for present ones.
28. Support an argument by playing upon the meaning of names. ("Mr. Stern is a harsh man.")

For the purposes of prose exposition, these topics are often presented in reductive form as the arguments from time, analogy, cause and effect, class, comparison and contrast, etc. A version of these can be found in Cicero's *Topica*, II.6ff. and *De oratore*, II.39ff.

Ten invalid topics or fallacies of arguments
(after Aristotle's *Rhetoric*)

1. Conclude an argument, as if at the end of a reasoning process, without having gone through the process.
2. Play on illogical, fortuitous similarity of words. ("A sauce pan must be noble, for so was the great god Pan.")

3. Make a statement about the whole that is true only of individual parts, or vice versa.
4. Use indignant language.
5. Use a single, unrepresentative example.
6. Take the accidental as essential.
7. Argue from consequence.
8. Argue *post hoc, ergo propter hoc.*
9. Ignore crucial circumstances.
10. Suggest, from fraudulent confusion of general and particular, that the improbable is probable, and vice versa.

The commonplaces

(L. *loci communes*; G. *koinoi topoi*)

The term is a vague one, and the category so large as to prohibit enumeration. A commonplace was a general argument, observation, or description a speaker could memorize for use on any number of possible occasions. So an American statesman who knows he will be asked to speak extempore on the Fourth of July might commit to memory reflections on the bravery of the Founding Fathers, tags from the Declaration of Independence, praise of famous American victories, etc. A few scattered traditional *loci*: death is common to all; time flies; the contemplative vs. the active life; the soldier's career vs. the scholar's; praise of a place as paradisiacal; the uses of the past; a short, celebrated life vs. a long, obscure one. The commonplace is the general term for, or at least overlaps, the device Aristotle defined more narrowly, and placed specifically in the definition of invention, in the lists above. Thus *loci*, properly speaking, has two overlapping meanings: commonplace observations, and common *sources* of arguments. Collections of rhetorical commonplaces, of whatever sort, have always been surveys, as Kenneth Burke writes in blending the two meanings, "of the things that people generally consider persuasive, and of methods that have persuasive effects" (*A Rhetoric of Motives*, p. 56). Another distinction frequently made from antiquity onward has been the difference between general commonplaces, suitable for any subject, and particular or special ones, restricted to a single subject.

Pope humorously described this confusing body of doctrine in the *Peri Bathous*: "I therefore propose that there be contrived with all convenient dispatch, at the public expense, a *Rhetorical Chest of Drawers*, consisting of three Stories, the highest for the *Deliberative*, the middle for the *Demonstrative*, and the lowest for the *Judicial*. These shall be divided into *Loci*, or *Places*, being repositories for Matter and Argument in the several kinds of oration or writing" (chapter xiii, "A

Project for the Advancement of the Bathos"). Pope's satiric stance here draws attention to a characteristic oscillation, in such discussions, between places in the mind and places in the world. The commonplaces are always the places where we are "on familiar ground." Thus the complicated doctrine of the commonplaces veers off, in one direction, toward smaller-scale figures like **Epitheton** and **Proverb**, and in another direction, toward the larger-scale design of a full memory theater. The fondness for the collage and the ironized cliché in contemporary art would seem to constitute a visual analogue to a generalized cultural memory theater, indicating perhaps that in a period of secondary orality some of the old primary oral habits such as the commonplace are reasserting themselves.

Modern persuasive techniques have tended to make much less use of the commonplaces than did earlier periods, largely, as Howell makes clear (*Logic and Rhetoric in England*, pp. 23–24, and elsewhere), because we no longer trust traditional wisdom, are far more interested in investigating the world anew. For an oral culture, of course, commonplaces, like all formulas for thought, were where thought and utterance began, not just where they were conveniently parked. Thus in addition to a spectrum of meaning defined by argument at one end and ornament at the other, we can construct a spectrum with creation at one extreme and amplification at the other.

An interesting parallel to the classical verbal commonplaces has arisen recently in the world of electronic, computer-based text, where large libraries of images and icons — visual commonplaces — have been made available cheaply to anyone needing them.

For an illuminating discussion of literary use of commonplaces, see Rosemond Tuve, *Elizabethan and Metaphysical Imagery*, pp. 284 ff. See also Ong's discussion in *The Presence of the Word*, pp. 31ff., 81ff., and elsewhere. Sister Joan Marie Lechner's *Renaissance Concepts of the Commonplaces* begins with a thorough survey of previous doctrines. *See also* **Proof** in chapter 1.

The main points at issue

Stasis is the Greek term for the main point at issue in a legal argument (the Latin term is *constitutio* or *status*): who has done what, when, and how. Some theorists further narrow the definition to the starting point of a case — the circumstances that give rise to it — or to the first point raised by an opponent in a legal case. (For fuller discussion see **Issue** in chapter 1).

Thesis and hypothesis

Hermagoras divided political questions into two types:

1. **Thesis**: a general argument, one that does not deal with particular cases (L. *quaestio*).
2. **Hypothesis**: argument about a particular case (L. *causa*). Its two subdivisions:
   a. Question of fact or justice
   b. Question of law

   Its seven elements:
   a. Actor
   b. Action
   c. Time
   d. Place
   e. Cause
   f. Manner
   g. Starting point

ARRANGEMENT: THE PARTS OF AN ORATION

From the Greeks onward, the various parts of an oration have borne a body of theorizing so dense and extensive as almost to defy summary. Various theorists argue for various numbers of parts, from two up to seven (e.g. Wilson, pp. 209ff.) or even more when one further subdivides. Some theorists think four the norm, others five or six. To avoid the unnecessary confusion of overlapping classifications, I reproduce here the basic six parts according to the well-known discussion in *Rhetorica ad Herennium* (I.iii.4), adding only a few common equivalent terms. For a comparative table of the parts according to various other authorities, see Lausberg, vol. 1, pp. 148–149.

1. **Exordium** (G. *prooimion*; L. *exordium*) — catches the audience's attention.
2. **Narration** (G. *prothesis*; L. *narratio*) — sets forth the facts.
3. **Division** (L. *divisio* or *propositio* or *partitio*) — sets forth points stipulated (agreed upon by both sides) and points to be contested.
4. **Proof** (G. *pistis*; L. *confirmatio* or *probatio*) — sets forth the arguments that support one's case.
5. **Refutation** (L. *confutatio* or *reprehensio*) — refutes opponent's arguments.
6. **Peroration** (G. *epilogus*; L. *conclusio* or *peroratio*) — sums up arguments and stirs audience.

Aristotle saw two essential elements, the statement of the issue (πρόθεσις) or what is usually called the narration, and the arguments for and against it (πίστις) or proof. At most, he thought, an introduction and conclusion framing the two essential parts would make a total of four. "A speech has two parts. You must state your case, and you must prove it. . . . It follows, then, that the only necessary parts of a speech are the Statement and the Argument. These are the essential features of a speech; and it cannot in any case have more than Introduction, Statement, Argument, and Epilogue" (προοίμιον, πρόθεσις, πίστις, ἐπίλογος, Rhetoric, III, 1414a–b). This might be thought of as a common-sense four-part core organization in which argument is enveloped by emotion: (1) ingratiating introduction; (2) state your case; (3) prove your case; (4) sum up in an ingratiating way.

Aristotle goes on to comment in exasperation on the needless additional parts being specified by other writers. His exasperation did not prevail and additional parts kept multiplying. Quintilian argues for five parts instead of four: *prooemium, narratio, probatio, refutatio, peroratio* (III.ix.1ff.). The author of *Rhetorica ad Herennium* adds a sixth, *divisio*, between *narratio* and *confirmatio*. And later a *digressio* was added after the *narratio*. There are also discussions of the various parts in book I of *De inventione*, and in numerous later rhetorical treatises.

The only principles which might be said to govern the number of divisions used were the nature of the speech (whether it was deliberative, judicial, or epideictic), and the circumstances of presentation. Different occasions called, not so surprisingly, for different arrangements. The only consistent practice followed in the expansions beyond the Aristotelian four parts was to subdivide the central statement-and-proof section in various ways, leaving the exordium and peroration as constants.

If there is any characteristic form to be found among the various schemes for the parts, it would seem to be a strategy of alternating emotional and evidential appeals, first cultivating the good will of the hearers (judge, jury, or legislators) and then setting forth the facts of the case.

> *Simplest structure*: State your case and prove it.
>
> *First complication*: Encapsulate this statement with emotional appeals fore and aft.
>
> *Second complication*: Interrupt the factual statement with one or more emotional appeals.
>
> *Third complication*: Divide your argumentation into subsections.
>
> *Da capo*: More interpolated emotional appeals and argumentative subdivisions.

Quintilian, for example, argues that emotional appeals are appropriate in the "statement of facts" — why not conciliate the judge there, too? (IV.ii.111). Ever since Aristotle argued that emotional appeals have no place whatsoever in a proper argument (*Rhetoric*, III, 1414 a), entering only because of our weak and fallen nature, it has been taken for granted that emotional appeals are a necessary evil only; a needful trick but still a trick. We might reason, though, if we can put aside this persistent Platonism for a moment, that "facts" do not occur in an emotional vacuum, and that there might be something to be said for recreating the emotional atmosphere in which the "facts" occurred. That, too, is part of a full human truth. That atmosphere can be distorted and manipulated, of course; but so can the "facts." Perhaps, then, the alternating structure of the oration, however many parts either argument or emotional appeal contained, has worked — almost against its own advice, and certainly unawares — to create a complex and fully social "factuality."

How easily such a basic expansive technique can generate subsections can be seen from a short statement about the peroration in the *Rhetorica ad Herennium*: "Conclusions, among the Greeks called *epilogoi*, are tripartite, consisting of the Summing Up, Amplification, and Appeal to Pity. We can in four places use a Conclusion: in the Direct Opening, after the Statement of Facts, after the strongest argument, and in the Conclusion of the speech" (II.xxx.47). Thus the final section should not only sum up the argument but sum up the emotional appeal as well. "Amplification" here means using a series of commonplaces to intensify the emotional appeal to the audience. And so, presumably, it would generate its own subcycles of argument and emotion!

How easily the proliferating terminology can become confused when moving from Greek to Latin to English can be seen by looking at the Rhys Roberts translation of the passage in *Rhetoric* 1414a cited above. As translated, after asserting that there are only two essential parts to a speech, stating your case and proving it, Aristotle goes on to ridicule "narration" as *not* an essential part. Aristotle's term for "statement of the case" is πρόθεσις and his word for "proof" is πίστις (τούτων δὲ τὸ μὲν πρόθεσις ἐστι τὸ δὲ πίστις). For everyone else following, πρόθεσις is "narratio." And yet the word Aristotle uses when he is repudiating "narration" as an essential term is διήγεσις, which may indeed mean "narration."

Although extensively discussed in its component details, the form of the oration has not received the scholarly attention it deserves, as the form not only of formal speeches but of much writing and speaking not specifically rhetorical. Its structure has influenced the way we think and argue for intellectual positions of every sort. Thus we always try to establish a specific controllable relation to an audience, always *seem* to take our opponent's arguments into account (paraphrase his weak ones, distort his strong ones), always dilate on our own good reasons, always offer a loaded summary before we stop. The ingredients of the form, then, vary considerably, but the form itself is used, albeit unknowingly, by an enormous number of people. As Father Ong remarks, apropos the parts of the oration: "A glance at the texts in use, whether classical or medieval or . . . Tudor, for all coexisted, reveals an extraordinarily strict discipline in composition. It reveals also the degree to which the oration as such tyrannized over ideas of what expression as such — literary or other — was" (*Rhetoric, Romance, and Technology*, p. 53). The opposite way of thinking to the linear development of the formal oration is the associative pattern, which, at its worst, gives us Mistress Quickly's rambling monologues, and at its best, *Tristram Shandy*. The best example today of this nonlinear way of argumentation surely must be electronic hypertext.

Beyond its rhetorical use, the basic oration structure often can be detected, writ large, where the formal argumentative element is secondary. We tend to take the basic oration structure as an inevitable pattern of dialectic thought. In fact, there seems no more reason to regard such a structure as an inevitable form for an argument than there does to regard beginning-middle-end as the only form for a narrative. The oration's primary assumption, for example, is that all arguments are or can be polar opposites (the *dialectic* assumption, odd as this seems), and such an assumption does violence to any issue that falls into the "both-and" rather than the "either-or" category. The classical oration structure, that is, can offer a form for argument but not for compromise. How many compromises, it is then reasonable to ask, have been hindered by the *form*? *See* **Dissoi logoi**.

STYLE

The three types

1. The low or plain style (*genus humile* or *extenuatum*)
2. The middle style (*genus medium* or *modicum* or *mediocre* or *temperatum*)
3. The grand style (*genus grande* or *grave*)

An analogous, but not identical, set of categories is often found:

1. The Attic, or unornamented, brief style
2. The Asiatic, or ornamented, full style
3. The Rhodian, somewhere between (1) and (2)

The Greek critic Demetrius, in *On Style*, offers a fourfold division:

1. Plain

2. Grand
3. Elegant
4. Forceful

One modern scholar of rhetoric has maintained that two fundamental styles existed in Greece from the earliest times. If so, this two-part division provided the first categorization of style in Western Europe. The three-part division has been by far the most common, however, probably because it is so vague. This division has been made on the basis of one or more of the following: (a) subject (generally, the more important the topic, the higher the style); (b) diction (presence or absence of figurative language); (c) effect on the audience (the grand style had the greatest emotional effect); (d) syntax or composition (the grand style was made up of balanced elements in intricate arrangements; the plain style used shorter periods, followed more closely the processes of discursive thought). The three-part division represents a most useful tacit bargaining pattern: the high style will represent a maximum of the entity measured; the low a minimum; the middle, somewhere in between. The high, middle, and low styles each had defective counterparts, of course: the swollen, the loose (*dissolutum*), and the meager.

Kenneth Burke, paraphrasing Cicero, suggests the following rationale for the three levels of style:

> In his *Orator* . . . Cicero distinguishes three styles (*genera dicendi, genera scribendi*): the grandiloquent, plain, and tempered. And he names as the three "offices" of the orator: (1) to teach, inform, instruct (*docere*); (2) to please (*delectare*); (3) to move or "bend" (*movere, flectere*).
>
> He also refers to styles in a more personal or individual sense, when observing that orators are next of kin to poets, and that each poet has his own way of writing (and in a critical digression he gives a catalogue of formulas for succinctly characterizing and savoring the distinctive qualities in the personal style of various writers well known to antiquity). However, the three over-all styles of oratory are not thought of thus, as personal expression, but as a means for carrying out the three "offices." That is, the plain style is best for teaching, the tempered style for pleasing, and the ornate (grandiloquent) style for moving. Though human weakness makes an orator more able in one or another of these styles, the ideal orator should be master of all three, since an oration aims at all three functions.
>
> (*A Rhetoric of Motives*, pp. 73–74)

The original Ciceronian discussion is in *Orator*, sections 69 and 100–101; Augustine takes up and elaborates this distinction in *On Christian Doctrine*, IV.34–35.

It might also be possible to use as metaphor not "level" but "spectrum." We might, for example, place styles on a spectrum of opacity. At one extreme would be a style like Lyly's in *Euphues*, an extremely opaque style that we are meant to notice as stylistic surface. We do not, that is, condemn it for hiding a clear prose meaning — a plain narrative — behind it, because there is none behind it. Such meaning as it creates comes from the stylistic surface. To galvanize a modern critical cliché, the style is the meaning. At the other end of such a spectrum, the aim would be translucence, the purely denotative style which mandates "one word, one thing." Such an ideal has operated strongly in the English-speaking world ever since the rise of science in the seventeenth century. At this extreme, the style would be pure means to describe event. At the opposite end, style would be itself the event. A way of bending the spectrum into a circle might be found by trying to place a prose like Hemingway's on it. Such a style, which continually calls attention to itself by its mannerisms but whose mannerisms all aim to create the effect of an extremely denotative, translucent prose — nothing but the facts — partakes of both ends of the spectrum. In other words, such a style suggests that the degree of ornament of a style and the self-consciousness of a style are not the same thing. Two further categories would then seem to be possible: the style (plain or ornate) which acknowledges that it is a style, a rhetoric, an effort at persuasion, and the style (plain or ornate) which does not. The final conclusion that this train of reasoning suggests is this: as an addition to the classical categories of style — based on the degree of ornament, largely — we might categorize on the basis of the degree of self-consciousness with which the style presents itself.

G. M. A. Grube has called the whole distinction between levels of style into question:

> The formula of three styles is even less likely to have originated with [Cicero]. It occurs in the first century only in Roman writers where each style has its own diction *and* word arrangement; even then every writer or speaker is expected to use all three styles at different times, so that the notion of three equally acceptable styles, plain, grand, and intermediate, is largely a myth. . . . The main evidence here is alleged to be a passage of Dionysius of Halicarnassus which quotes Theophrastus as saying that Thrasymachus of Chalcedon originated a τρίτη λέξις, between the poetic and the simple.
>
> (*The Greek and Roman Critics*, pp. 107–108)

One can be sure, however, that so handy a distinction will endure, mythical though it be.

The three, four, or twenty virtues

As an alternative to *levels*, we can think of style in terms of *types* or *virtues*. Theophrastus, in his lost *On Style*, isolated four virtues, which Cicero used in the *De oratore* as the basis for his discussion of style:

1. Purity (correctness)
2. Clarity
3. Decorum (G. *to prepon* — that which is fitting to time, place, etc.)
4. Ornament

The *Rhetorica ad Herennium* offers three categories:

1. *Elegantia*
   a. *Latinitas* (correctness, good Latin)
   b. *Explanatio* (clarity)
2. *Compositio* (avoiding harsh sound clashes and excessively figured language; making the style uniformly polished)
3. *Dignitas* (embellishment by a variety of figures tastefully used)

Quintilian offers a slightly different threefold division: "Style has three kinds of excellence, correctness, lucidity, and elegance (for many include the all-important quality of appropriateness under the heading of elegance)."

The most complex traditional division into types, however, has been that of Hermogenes, a second-century A.D. theorist who distinguished no fewer than twenty types and subtypes of style. The basic types were *Clarity, Grandeur, Beauty, Rapidity, Character,* and *Sincerity.* Taken together, these created the stylistic ideal for Hermogenes, *Force* or *Awesomeness.* From *Clarity* depended two subtypes, *Purity* and *Distinctness. Grandeur* was subdivided into *Solemnity, Asperity, Vehemence, Brilliance, Florescence, Abundance.* From *Character* subdepended *Simplicity, Sweetness, Subtlety,* and *Modesty,* and from *Sincerity* the subtype *Indignation.* (I've followed here the diagram contained in Cecil W. Wooten's excellent introduction to his recent translation, *Hermogenes' "On Types of Style".*)

Of the relation of Hermogenes's system to the simpler three-level distinction, a modern scholar has written:

> In contrast to the Latin stylistic system of the three *genera dicendi* which unimaginatively classified all styles as high, middle, or low, the Hermogenean forms offered a technique by which one could create or judge a precise set of physical, moral, and emotional qualities. Hermogenes . . . reconstructed the basis of each form by analyzing it into its notional contents, figures of thought, diction, figures of diction, kola, periodization, and rhythms. The Hermogenean forms are the descendants of earlier "virtues of speech" found in Aristotle, Isocrates, Dionysius of Halicarnassus, and others. The culminating Hermogenean form, awesomeness (δεινότης), which was the utilization of all the forms in a manner perfectly suited to the occasion, clearly reflects the traditional stylistic virtue of τὸ πρέπον, or *decorum* in Latin.
>
> (Monfasani, *George of Trebizond,* pp. 252–253)

The figures

The term *figure* in its most general meaning refers to any device or pattern of language in which meaning is enhanced or changed. The term has two subcategories:

1. Figure of words
    a. **Trope**: use of a word to mean something other than its ordinary meaning — a **Metaphor**, for example.
    b. **Scheme**: a figure in which words preserve their literal meaning, but are placed in a significant arrangement of some kind.
2. Figure of thought: a large-scale trope or scheme, or a combination of both — **Allegory**, for example.

This categorization is prescriptive (see **Trope** in chapter 1). All these terms have been used interchangeably at one time or another to refer to the numerous devices of language which were classified first by the Greek rhetorical theorists and later, in increasing numbers, by the Latin rhetoricians. Sometimes the same verbal pattern was given two different names, depending upon whether it was thought to be a trope or a scheme. J. W. H. Atkins's *English Literary Criticism: The Medieval Phase* gives in an Appendix (pp. 200ff.) a list of the figures categorized as above. For readers wishing further charts breaking down in different ways the figures as between trope and scheme, and kinds of both, Sonnino (pp. 244ff.) gives charts based on Quintilian, Trapezuntius, Scaliger, Fraunce, and Melancthon, and Murphy (*Rhetoric in the Middle Ages*, pp. 36–37) compares those in the *Ad Herennium* to those in Donatus's *Barbarismus*. Sister Miriam Joseph offers a chart which gives a numerical breakdown of the different types of figures in three classical and many Renaissance theorists. In the Renaissance, Peacham offered various kinds of diagrammatic breakdowns in *The Garden of Eloquence*.

In trying to control the vertigo such lists often induce, I have sometimes found useful G. N. Leech's suggestion that difficult ornaments may be called "difficult" because they create "a disruption, at one particular level, of the normal patterns of linguistic organization," whereas easy ornaments are "easy" because they include "a *superfluity* of meanings among which we must choose" (p. 153). For a discussion of the trope and scheme in the world of Ramist rhetoric, see Ong, *Ramus, Method, and the Decay of Dialogue*, pp. 274ff.

MEMORY

The classical doctrine of memory as one of the five parts of rhetoric distinguished two kinds of memory: natural and artificial. Natural memory is self-explanatory. Artificial memory is trained using one of the "memory-theater" mnemonic methods common since classical Greece; these exploit the power of the visual cortex by associating a particular pattern of argument with a particular visual scene. Such scenes comprise two elements, backgrounds and images (i.e., foreground figures in background scenes). Usually a familiar building, room, or public place served as the visual model.

> The first step was to imprint on the memory a series of *loci* or places. The commonest, though not the only, type of mnemonic place system used was the architectural type. . . . We have to think of the ancient orator as moving in imagination through his memory building *whilst* he is making his speech, drawing from the memorised places the images he has placed on them. The method ensures that the points are remembered in the right order, since the order is fixed by the sequence of places in the building.
>
> (Yates, *The Art of Memory*, p. 3)

And since, as we now know, the experiences which move the limbic system most deeply are the best remembered, both background and foreground information should be as dramatic as possible. It is as well to remember, too, that a memory theater, for a culture still partly oral, was a machine for spontaneous invention of a speech; for us in a wholly literate culture, it is much more likely to be simply a device to memorize a speech already written down, a device of replication.

Perhaps the memory-system most familiar to us now is the icon-based "desktop" introduced as a user interface for personal computers. The spread of electronic text, the accompanying growth of animation, and the resultant radical change in the icon/alphabet ratio for ordinary communication, will surely revive the classic mnemonic techniques. It is also interesting to reflect on the classic doctrine in light of current thinking about memory; see, for example, Israel Rosenfield's *The Invention of Memory: A New View of the Brain*. For discussions of the classic doctrine, see *Rhetorica ad Herennium*, III.xvi–xxiv, and Quintilian, XI.ii.

DELIVERY

Delivery, as one of the five basic parts of rhetoric, was itself divided into two parts — voice and gesture — and these were variously and greatly subdivided. Voice training of a very basic sort was obviously needed in an unamplified and very long-winded age, just to condition the lungs. And following that, a doctrine of appropriate voices for various occasions was developed. For gesture, an elaborate catalogue of body poses and hand positions was to be mastered;

the stage was sometimes held up as an appropriate model for such mastery. The doctrines of delivery lasted well into the nineteenth century and were, for most of Western history, centrally important.

B. L. Joseph's *Elizabethan Acting* contains illustrations of typical histrionic poses. Plates of hand gestures are included in John Bulwer's *Chirologia: or the Natural Language of the Hand* (1644) and Gilbert Austin's *Chironomia* (1806). A good short introduction to the subject is John Mason's *Essay on Elocution and Pronunciation* (1748). Henry Siddons's *Practical Illustrations of Rhetorical Gesture and Action; Adapted to the English Drama* (1822) does what the title says and is illustrated with fascinating plates. A delightfully comic, though little-known, nineteenth-century treatise is Andrea de Jorio's discussion of classical gestures as they survived on the streets of Naples, *La mimica degli antichi, investigata nel gestire napoletano* (1832). There was also in the Middle Ages an elaborate system for counting by hand gestures, and Guido of Arezzo used a map of the hand to indicate notes on the musical scale. The whole signifying baggage carried by formalized gesture is splendidly parodied by Rabelais in the debate between Panurge and Thaumaste (*Gargantua & Pantagruel*, II.xix).

Delivery has been much studied in our own time, but not by students of rhetoric. The behavioral biologists and psychologists call it "nonverbal communication" and have added immeasurably to our knowledge of this kind of human expressivity. See, for example, *Non-Verbal Communication*, edited by Robert A. Hinde. Silent films offer a less academic catalogue of the basic gestures of emotional reenactment. And another area where students of rhetoric seldom look, cartoon animation, offers much for a student of gesture. See, as a striking example, *Disney Animation: The Illusion of Life*, by Frank Thomas and Ollie Johnston. As the use of animation continues to grow in electronic communication, and as the icon/alphabet ratio in everyday communication continues to tilt from word to image, Delivery may find itself returned to its traditional eminence.

For discussions of the classic doctrine, see *Rhetorica ad Herennium*, III.xi.15, and Quintilian, XI.iii.

3 / The Terms by Type

These lists aim to help a student move from a text to the term that describes it. No accurate, dependable, airtight division into discrete categories exists, to my knowledge, even for the figures alone. (It is hard to see how one could make such a division, so fundamentally and dynamically do the categories mix and match. For a brief example of how difficult categorization can be, see the discussion of the trope-scheme division under **Trope**.) This categorization hopes for nothing beyond easy reference to the alphabetical list.

Addition, subtraction, and substitution: Letters and syllables

antistoecon: substituting one letter or sound for another within a word.

aphaeresis: omitting a syllable from the beginning of a word.

apocope: omitting the last syllable or letter of a word.

diaeresis: dividing one syllable into two.

diastole: lengthening a syllable or vowel that is usually short.

epenthesis: addition of a letter, sound, or syllable to the middle of a word.

metaplasm: moving from their natural place letters or syllables of a word; generic term that includes most of the words in this section.

metathesis: transposition of letters out of normal order in a word.

paragoge: adding a letter or syllable to the end of a word.

prothesis: adding a letter or syllable to the beginning of a word.

synaeresis: pronouncing as a diphthong two adjacent vowels that belong to different syllables within a word.

synalepha: eliding two adjacent vowels at the end of one word and the beginning of the next.

syncope: removing letters or syllables from the middle of a word.

systole: shortening a naturally long vowel or syllable.

Addition, subtraction, and substitution: Words, phrases, and clauses

anantapodoton: omission of a correlative clause from a sentence.

anthimeria: functional shift, using one part of speech for another.

antiptosis: substitution of one case for another.

asyndeton: omission of conjunctions between words, phrases, clauses.

brachylogia: omission of conjunctions between single words.

diacope: separation of the elements of a compound word by another word or words.

ellipsis: omission of a word easily supplied.

enallage: substitution of one case, person, gender, number, tense, mood, part of speech, for another.

parelcon: addition of superfluous words.

zeugma: use of one word to govern several congruent words or clauses.

Amplification

accumulatio: heaping up praise or accusation to emphasize or summarize points or inferences already made.

aetiologia: giving a cause or reason.

apophasis: pretending to deny what is really affirmed.

apoplanesis: evading the issue by digressing.

asianism: a style full of figures and words.

auxesis: words or clauses placed in climactic order.

bomphiologia: bombastic speech.

cohortatio: amplification that moves the hearer's indignation.

congeries: word heaps.

diaeresis: dividing genus into species in order to amplify.

diallage: bringing several arguments to establish a single point.

digestion: an orderly enumeration of points to be discussed.

dinumeratio: (1) amplifying a general fact or idea by giving all of its details; (2) a summary or recapitulation.

dirimens copulatio: a series of not-only/but-also comparisons.

distinctio: explicit reference to various meanings of a word.

distribution: dividing the whole into its parts.

divisio: dividing into kinds or classes.

epanodos: expanding a statement by discussing it part by part.

epexegesis: adding words or phrases to clarify or specify further.

epicrisis: the speaker quotes a passage and comments on it.

epimone: frequent repetition of a phrase or question, in order to dwell on a point.

epitheton: qualifying a subject with an appropriate adjective.

expeditio: rejecting all but one of various alternatives.

macrologia: long-winded speech; using more words than necessary.

megaloprepeia: elevation and gravity of style.

metanoia: qualifying a statement by recalling it and expressing it in a better way.

palilogia: repetition for vehemence or fullness.

paradiegesis: a narrative digression used to introduce one's argument.

parenthesis: a word, phrase, or sentence inserted as an aside.

periergia: superfluous elaboration.

periphrasis: circumlocution.

peristasis: amplifying by describing attendant circumstances.

synonymia: amplification by synonym.

systrophe: heaping up descriptions of a thing without defining it.

Balance, antithesis, and paradox

antanagoge: balancing an unfavorable aspect with a favorable one.

anticategoria: mutual accusation or recrimination.

antimetabole: inverting the order of repeated words.

antinomy: comparing one law, or a part of a law, to another.

antiphrasis: irony of one word — calling a "dwarf" a "giant."

antisagoge: (1) assuring a reward to those who possess a virtue, or a punishment to those who hold it in contempt; (2) stating first one side of a proposition, then the other, with equal vigor.

antithesis: conjoining contrasting ideas.

ceratinae: the "horns" of a dilemma.

chiasmus: inverting the order of repeated words or phrases.

climax: mounting by degrees through linked words or phrases, usually of increasing weight and in parallel construction.

conjunctio: clauses or phrases expressing similar ideas are held together by placing the verb between them.

contrarium: one of two opposite statements is used to prove the other.

crocodilinae: a kind of dilemma.

dialysis: (1) arguing from a series of disjunctive propositions; (2) a statement of a problem followed by particularization of the alternatives.

dilemma: argument that offers an opponent unacceptable choices.

dirimens copulatio: a series of not-only/but-also comparisons.

disjunctio: use of different verbs to express similar ideas in successive clauses.

enigma: a riddle.

euphuism: an elaborate prose style that emphasizes balance and antithesis.

horismus: a brief definition, often antithetical.

hypophora: asking questions and answering them.

hypozeuxis: every clause in a sentence has its own subject and verb.

isocolon: phrases of equal length and (usually) corresponding structure.

litotes: denial of the contrary.

oxymoron: a condensed paradox.

paradox: a seemingly self-contradictory statement which yet is shown to be true.

paromoiosis: a parallelism of sounds between words of two clauses of approximately equal length.

polysyndeton: using a conjunction between each clause.

progressio: building a point around a series of comparisons.

prosapodosis: supporting each alternative with a reason.

sermocinatio: the speaker answers the remarks or questions of a pretended interlocutor.

syncrisis: comparing contrary elements in contrasting clauses.

synoeciosis: an expanded paradox.

taxis: distributing to every subject its proper adjunct.

Brevity

brachylogia: brevity of diction.

brevitas: concise expression.

epiphonema: a striking epigram used for summary.

epitrochasmus: a swift movement from one statement to another.

fable: a short, allegorical story.

oxymoron: a condensed paradox.

proverb: a short, pithy statement of a general truth. Category includes adage, aphorism, apothegm, gnome, maxim, sententia.

zeugma: use of one word to govern several congruent words or clauses.

Description

anatomy: the analysis of an issue into its constituent parts.

anemographia: description of the wind.

astrothesia: description of a star.

characterismus: description of body or mind.

chorographia: description of a nation.

chronographia: description of time.

dendrographia: description of a tree.

ecphrasis: a self-contained description, often of a commonplace subject, which can be inserted at a fitting place in a discourse.

effictio: a head-to-toe itemized description of a person.

enargia: clear, lucid, vivid description; also, generic term for various types of description.

ethopoeia: (1) description of natural propensities, manners, affections; (2) putting oneself in the place of another, so as to both understand and express the other person's feelings more vividly.

geographia: description of the earth.

hydrographia: description of water.

icon: painting resemblance by imagery.

mimesis: imitation of gesture, pronunciation, utterance.

onomatopoeia: use or invention of words that sound like their meaning.

pragmatographia: vivid description of an action or event.

prosopographia: (1) description of imaginary persons or bodies; (2) lively description of a person.

topographia: description of a place.

topothesia: description of imaginary, nonexistent places.

Emotional appeals

amphidiorthosis: to hedge or qualify a charge made in anger.

anacoenosis: asking the opinion of one's readers or hearers.

anticategoria: mutual accusation or recrimination.

antirrhesis: rejecting an argument because of its insignificance, error, or wickedness.

apaetesis: a matter put aside in anger is resumed later.

apocarteresis: giving up one hope and turning to another.

apodioxis: rejecting an argument indignantly as impertinent or absurdly false.

aporia: true or feigned doubt or deliberation about an issue.

aposiopesis: stopping suddenly in midcourse, leaving a statement unfinished.

apostrophe: breaking off a discourse to address some person or personified thing either present or absent.

ara: curse or imprecation.

asphalia: one offers oneself as surety for a bond.

argumentum ad misericordiam: appeal to the mercy of the hearers.

augendi causa: raising the voice for emphasis.

bathos: the emotional appeal that, intentionally or not, evokes laughter rather than transport, which sinks rather than soars.

bdelygma: expression of hatred or abhorrence.

cataplexis: threatening punishment, misfortune, or disaster.

categoria: reproaching a person with his wickedness to his face.

cohortatio: amplification that moves the hearer's indignation.

commiseratio: evoking pity in the audience.

comprobatio: complimenting one's judges or hearers.

consolatio: consoling one who grieves.

deesis: vehement supplication of gods or men.

diasyrmus: disparagement of opponent's arguments.

dicaeologia: excusing by necessity.

ecphonesis: an exclamation expressing emotion.

emphasis: implying more than is actually stated.

encomium: praise of a person or thing by extolling inherent qualities.

epiplexis: asking a question in order to reproach.

ethos: the emotions or character which a speaker re-enacts in order to affect an audience.

eucharistia: giving thanks.

euche: (1) vow or oath to keep a promise; (2) prayer for evil; curse.

eulogia: commending or blessing a person or thing.

euphemismus: (1) prognostication of good; (2) circumlocution to palliate something unpleasant.

eustathia: pledge of constancy.

exuscitatio: emotional utterance that seeks to move hearers to like feelings.

indignatio: arousing the audience's scorn and indignation.

insultatio: derisive, ironical abuse of a person to his face.

mempsis: complaining against injuries and pleading for help.

mycterismus: mockery of an opponent, accompanied by gestures.

ominatio: a prophecy of evil.

onedismus: reproaching someone as ungrateful or impious.

optatio: a wish exclaimed.

orcos: an oath.

paeanismus: an exclamation of joy.

paraenesis: warning of impending evil.

pathopoeia: a general term for arousing passion or emotion.

pathos: term variably used: techniques of stirring emotions, the emotions themselves, the emotion a speaker feels, the emotions a speaker tries to evoke in others.

philophronesis: attempt to mitigate anger by gentle speech and humble submission.

protrope: exhorting hearers to action by threats and promises.

sarcasmus: a bitter gibe or taunt.

syngnome: forgiveness of injuries.

tapinosis: undignified language that debases a person or thing.
thaumasmus: exclamation of wonder.
threnos: lamentation.

Example, allusion, and citation of authority

aenos: quoting wise sayings from fables.
analogy: reasoning or arguing from parallel cases.
anamnesis: recalling ideas, events, or persons of the past.
antinomy: a comparison of one law, or part of a law, to another.
apodixis: referring to generally accepted principles or experience for confirmation.
apomnemonysis: quotation of an approved authority from memory.
chreia: (1) a short exposition of a deed or saying of a person whose name is mentioned; (2) a short rhetorical exercise that develops and varies a moral observation.
diatyposis: recommending useful precepts to someone else.
epicrisis: quoting a passage and commenting on it.
exemplum: an example cited, either true or feigned; illustrative anecdote.
fable: a short, allegorical story.
martyria: confirming something by one's own experience.
oraculum: "quoting" God's words or commandments.
parable: teaching a moral by means of an extended metaphor.
paradiegesis: a narrative digression used to introduce one's argument.
proverb: a short, pithy statement of a general truth. Category includes adage, aphorism, apothegm, gnome, maxim, sententia.
simile: explicit comparison.

Metaphorical substitutions and puns

adianoeta: an expression that has an obvious meaning and an unsuspected secret one beneath.
allegory: an extended metaphor.
antanaclasis: homonymic pun.
antapodosis: a simile in which the objects compared correspond in several respects.
antistasis: repetition of a word in a different or contrary sense.

antonomasia: descriptive phrase for proper name or proper name for quality associated with it.

asteismus: facetious or mocking answer that plays on a word.

cacemphaton: scurrilous jest; lewd allusion or double entendre.

catachresis: implied metaphor; extravagant, farfetched metaphor.

euphemismus: circumlocution to palliate something unpleasant.

fable: a short allegorical story that points a lesson or moral.

hyperbole: exaggerated or extravagant terms used for emphasis and not to be taken literally.

icon: painting resemblance by imagery.

irony: implying a meaning opposite to the literal meaning.

meiosis: belittling, often through a trope of one word.

metalepsis: present effect attributed to a remote cause.

metaphor: changing a word from its literal meaning to one not properly applicable but analogous to it; assertion of identity rather than, as with simile, likeness.

metonymy: substitution of cause for effect, effect for cause, proper name for one of its qualities, or vice versa.

parable: teaching a moral by means of an extended metaphor.

paronomasia: punning; playing on sound or meaning of words.

schematismus: circuitous speech to conceal a meaning.

simile: explicit comparison.

synecdoche: substitution of part for whole, genus for species, or vice versa.

tapinosis: undignified language that debases a person or thing.

Repetition: Letters, syllables, and sounds

alliteration: recurrence of an initial consonant sound, and sometimes of a vowel sound.

assonance: resemblance of internal vowel sounds in neighboring words.

consonance: resemblance of stressed consonant sounds where the associated vowels differ.

homoioptoton: using various words with similar case endings in a sentence or verse.

homoioteleuton: using various uninflected words with similar endings in a sentence or verse.

paroemion: a resolute alliteration in which every word in a sentence or phrase begins with the same letter.

paromoiosis: a parallelism of sounds between words of two clauses of approximately equal length.

Repetition: Words

adnominatio: repetition of a word with change in letter or sound.

anadiplosis: repetition of the last word of one line or clause to begin the next.

anaphora: repetition of the same word at the beginning of successive clauses or verses.

antistasis: repetition of a word in a different or contrary sense.

antistrophe: repetition of a closing word or words at the end of several successive clauses, sentences, or verses.

conduplicatio: repetition of a word or words in succeeding clauses.

diacope: repetition of a word with one or a few words in between.

diaphora: repetition of a common word rather than a proper name to signify qualities of the person as well as naming him.

epanalepsis: repetition at the end of a clause or sentence of the word or phrase with which it began.

epizeuxis: repetition of a word with no other words in between.

palilogia: repetition for vehemence or fullness.

ploce: repetition of a word with a new signification after the intervention of another word or words.

polyptoton: repetition of words from the same root but with different endings.

polysyndeton: use of a conjunction between each clause.

symploce: repetition of one word or phrase at the beginning, and of another at the end, of successive clauses, sentences, or passages; a combination of anaphora and antistrophe.

Repetition: Clauses, phrases, and ideas

antistrophe: repetition of a word or phrase at the end of several clauses, sentences, or verses.

commoratio: emphasizing a strong point by repeating it several times in different words.

disjunctio: use of different verbs to express similar ideas in successive clauses.

epanodos: a general statement is expanded part by part, the terms used in the summary being repeated in the fuller discussion.

epimone: refrain; frequent repetition of a phrase or question.

exergasia: repeating the same thought in many figures.

homiologia: tedious, redundant style.

hypozeuxis: every clause in a sentence has its own subject and verb.

isocolon: phrases of equal length and (usually) corresponding structure.

palilogia: repetition for vehemence or fullness.

pleonasmus: needless repetition.

scesis onomaton: using a string of synonymous expressions.

synonymia: amplification by synonym.

tautologia: repetition of the same idea in different words.

Techniques of argument

adynata: a stringing together of impossibilities; sometimes, a confession that words fail us.

aetiologia: giving a cause or reason.

alloiosis: breaking down a subject into alternatives.

amphidiorthosis: to hedge a charge made in anger by qualification.

anacoenosis: asking the opinion of one's hearers or readers.

analogy: reasoning or arguing from parallel cases.

antanagoge: balancing an unfavorable aspect with a favorable one.

antirrhesis: rejecting an argument because of its insignificance, error, or wickedness.

antistrephon: an argument that turns one's opponent's argument or proofs to one's own purpose.

apaetesis: a matter put aside in anger is resumed later.

apodioxis: rejecting an argument indignantly as impertinent or absurdly false.

apodixis: confirming a statement by reference to generally accepted principles.

apomnemonysis: quotation of an approved authority.

apophasis: pretending to deny what is really affirmed.

apoplanesis: evading the issue by digressing; irrelevant answer to distract attention.

aporia: true or feigned doubt or deliberation about an issue.

aposiopesis: stopping suddenly in midcourse, leaving a statement unfinished.

argumentum ad baculum: appealing to force to settle the question.

argumentum ad hominem: (1) abuse of your opponent's character; (2) basing your argument on what you know of your opponent's character.

argumentum ad ignorantiam: a proposition is true if it has not been proved false.

argumentum ad misericordiam: appealing to the mercy of the hearers.

argumentum ad populum: appealing to the crowd.

argumentum ad verecundiam: appealing to reverence for authority, to accepted traditional values.

argumentum ex concessis: reasoning from the premises of one's opponent.

cacosistaton: an argument that can serve as well on either side of a question.

ceratin: an argument so couched that, seemingly, all possibilities equally prove it true (or false).

chleuasmos: a sarcastic reply that mocks an opponent and leaves him no answer.

cohortatio: amplification that moves the hearer's indignation.

comprobatio: complimenting one's judges or hearers.

concessio: conceding a point either to hurt an adversary or to prepare for a more important argument.

contrarium: one of two opposite statements is used to prove the other.

correctio: (1) correcting a word or phrase used previously; (2) preparing the audience to hear something unpleasant.

dehortatio: dissuasion; advice to the contrary.

deliberatio: evaluating possible courses of action; weighing arguments.

diaeresis: dividing genus into species in order to amplify.

diallage: bringing several arguments to establish a single point.

dialogismus: speaking in another person's character.

dialysis: arguing from a series of disjunctive propositions.

diasyrmus: disparagement of opponent's arguments.

diatyposis: recommending useful precepts to someone else.

dicaeologia: defending oneself by pleading necessity or reasonable excuse.

digestion: an orderly enumeration of points to be discussed.

digression: an interpolated anecdote, especially one prepared in advance for insertion at the appropriate time.

dilemma: argument that offers an opponent only unacceptable choices.

dinumeratio: a recapitulation or summary.

distinctio: explicit reference to various meanings of a word, thereby removing ambiguities.

eidolopoeia: presenting a dead person as speaking, or the speech thus assigned.

elenchus: aggressive argumentative exchange and cross-examination.

enthymeme: (1) maintaining the truth of a proposition from the assumed truth of its contrary; (2) logic: abridged syllogism, one of the terms being omitted as understood; (3) rhetoric: a "syllogism" in which the premises are only generally true, a rhetorical syllogism.

epagoge: an inductive argument.

epilogue: inferring what will follow from what has been spoken or done before.

epitrochasmus: a swift movement from one statement to another.

epitrope: conceding agreement or permission to an opponent, often ironically.

erotesis: a "rhetorical question" implying but not giving an answer.

ethopoeia: putting oneself in the place of another, so as to understand and express that person's feelings more vividly.

euphemismus: (1) prognostication of good; (2) circumlocution to palliate something unpleasant.

exemplum: an example cited, either true or mythical; an illustrative story or anecdote.

expeditio: rejection of all but one of various alternatives.

exuscitatio: emotional utterance that seeks to move hearers to a like feeling.

fable: a short allegorical story that points a lesson or moral.

fictio: attributing rational actions and speech to nonrational creatures.

hypophora: asking questions and immediately answering them.

indignatio: arousing the audience's scorn and indignation.

insinuatio: the "subtle approach," one kind of opening or introduction.

insultatio: derisive, ironical abuse of a person to his face.

koinonia: consulting with one's opponents or with the judges.

leptologia: subtle speaking, quibbling.

meiosis: to belittle, often through a trope of one word.

metanoia: qualifying a statement by recalling it and expressing it in a different way.

metastasis: (1) passing over an issue quickly; (2) turning back an insult or objection against the person who made it.

noema: deliberately obscure, subtle speech.

occultatio: emphasizing something by pointedly seeming to pass over it.

onedismus: reproaching someone as ungrateful or impious.

oraculum: the "quoting" of God's words or commandments.

ordo artificialis: beginning *in medias res,* in the middle of things.

ordo naturalis: beginning *ab ovo,* "from the egg," i.e. from the beginning.

parable: teaching a moral by means of an extended metaphor.

paradiegesis: a narrative digression used to introduce one's argument.

pareuresis: (1) offering an excuse of such weight that it overcomes all objections; (2) inventing a false pretext.

paromologia: conceding a point either from conviction or to strengthen one's own argument.

parrhesia: (1) candid speech; (2) begging pardon in advance for necessary candor.

periphrasis: circumlocution.

peristrophe: converting an opponent's argument to one's own use.

philophronesis: trying to mitigate anger by gentle speech and humble submission.

praemunitio: defending oneself in anticipation of an attack.

praeparatio: preparing an audience before telling them about something one has done.

proecthesis: (1) defending one's acts or statements, by giving reasons and circumstances; (2) pointing out what ought to have been done, and then what was done.

progressio: advancing by steps of comparison.

prolepsis: foreseeing and forestalling objections in various ways.

prooemium: the "direct approach," one kind of opening or introduction.

prosapodosis: supporting each alternative with a reason.

protrope: exhorting hearers to act by threats or promises.

pseudomenos: an argument that forces one's adversary to lie.

pysma: asking many questions that require diverse answers.

ratiocinatio: asking ourselves the reasons for our own statements.

reditus ad propositum: returning to the subject after a digression.

reductio ad absurdum: to disprove a proposition, one validly deduces from it a conclusion self-contradictory or contradictory to acknowledged fact.

restrictio: excepting part of a statement already made.

secundum quid: reasoning that because something is generally true, it is true in a highly specialized class.

sermocinatio: the speaker answers the remarks or questions of a pretended interlocutor.

significatio: to imply more than one says.

skotison: deliberately obscure speech.

subjectio: the questioner suggests the answer to his own question.

syllogismus: intimation; hinting at something.

synchoresis: the speaker gives his questioners leave to judge him.

utis: the "nobody argument."

Ungrammatical, illogical, or unusual uses of language

acyrologia: use of an inexact or illogical word; malapropism.

alleotheta: substitution of one case, gender, number, tense, or mood for another.

amphibologia: ambivalence of grammatical structure, usually by mispunctuation; ambiguity, either intended or inadvertent.

anacoluthon: ending a sentence with a different structure from that with which it began.

anastrophe: unusual arrangement of words or clauses within a sentence, often for poetic effect.

anoiconometon: improper arrangement of words.

anthimeria: functional shift, using one part of speech for another.

anthypallage: change of grammatical case for emphasis.

antiptosis: substituting one case for another.

aschematiston: unskillful use of figures.

barbarismus: unnatural word-coinage or mispronunciation.

cacemphaton: sounds combined for harsh effect.

cacosyntheton: awkward transposition of the parts of a sentence.

cacozelia: affected diction made up of adaptation of Latin words; inkhorn terms.

catachresis: farfetched metaphor.

enallage: substitution of one case, person, gender, number, tense, mood, part of speech, for another.

graecismus: use of Greek idiom.

hebraism: use of Hebrew idiom.

hendiadys: expression of an idea by two nouns connected by "and" instead of a noun and its qualifier.

hypallage: awkward or humorous changing of agreement or application of words.

hyperbaton: a generic term for various forms of departure from ordinary word order.

hysterologia: a phrase is interposed between a preposition and its object.

hysteron proteron: syntax or sense out of normal logical or temporal order.

ignoratio elenchi: irrelevant conclusion.

malapropism: a form of cacozelia; vulgar error through an attempt to seem learned.

metaplasm: moving letters or syllables of a word from their place; a generic term.

metathesis: type of metaplasm; transposition of letters out of normal order in a word.

non sequitur: a statement that bears no relationship to the context preceding.

petitio principii: the premise and conclusion say the same thing in different words, or the premise needs proof as much as the conclusion.

poicilogia: overly ornate speech.

post hoc ergo propter hoc: assigning the wrong cause, by mistaking a temporal for a causal relationship.

secundum quid: reasoning that because something is generally true, it is true in a highly specialized class.

solecismus: ignorant misuse of cases, genders, and tenses.

soraismus: mingling of languages ignorantly or affectedly.

syllepsis: one verb lacking congruence with at least one subject that it governs.

synchisis: the word order of a sentence is confused.

4 / Some Important Dates

ca. **483–376 B.C.**	Gorgias
436–338	Isocrates
ca. **370 (?)**	Plato, *Phaedrus*
ca. **357**	Plato, *Gorgias*
ca. **330**	Aristotle, *Rhetoric*
fl. ca. **150**	Hermagoras
86–82	[Cicero], *Rhetorica ad Herennium*
84	Cicero, *De inventione*
55	Cicero, *De oratore*
46	Cicero, *Orator* and *Brutus*
44	Cicero, *Topica*
fl. **late 1st c. B.C.**	Dionysius of Halicarnassus, *On Composition; On the Ancient Orators*
ca. **1st c. A.D.**	[Demetrius], *On Style*
A.D. 95	Quintilian, *Institutio oratoria*
1st *or* **3rd c.**	[Longinus], *On the Sublime*
late 2nd c.	Hermogenes, *On Types of Style*
mid-4th c.	Donatus, *Ars grammatica*
396–427	Augustine, *De doctrina Christiana*
ca. **410–439**	Martianus Capella, *De nuptiis Philologiae et Mercurii*
early 6th c.	Priscian, *Institutiones grammaticae*
ca. **700**	Bede, *Liber de schematibus et tropis*
ca. **1200**	Geoffrey of Vinsauf, *Poetria nova; Summa de coloribus rhetoricis*
1512	Erasmus, *De copia*
1530 (?)	Leonard Cox, *The Arte or Crafte of Rhetoryke*

1540	Joannes Susenbrotus, *Epitome troporum ac schematum et grammaticorum et rhetoricorum*
1544	Audomarus Talaeus, *Institutiones oratoriae*
1550	Richard Sherry, *A Treatise of Schemes and Tropes*
1553	Thomas Wilson, *The Arte of Rhetorique*
1555	Richard Sherry, *A Treatise of the figures of Grammar and Rhetorike*
1555	Peter Ramus, *Dialectique*
1563	Richard Rainolde, *A Booke Called the Foundacion of Rhetorike*
1576	John Sturm, *De universa ratione elocutionis rhetoricae*
1577	Henry Peacham, *The Garden of Eloquence* (revised and enlarged edition, 1593)
1584	Dudley Fenner, *The Arts of Logike and Rhetorike*
1586	Angel Day, *The English Secretorie*
1588	Abraham Fraunce, *The Arcadian Rhetorike*
1589	George Puttenham, *The Arte of English Poesie*
1598	Charles Butler, *Rhetoricae Libri Duo*
ca. **1599**	John Hoskyns, *Direccions for Speech and Style*
1637	Thomas Hobbes, *A Brief of the Art of Rhetorique*
1657	John Smith, *The Mysterie of Rhetorique Unvail'd*
1727	Alexander Pope, *Peri Bathous*
1776	George Campbell, *The Philosophy of Rhetoric*
1828	Richard Whateley, *Elements of Rhetoric*
1866	Alexander Bain, *English Composition and Rhetoric* (revised and enlarged edition, 1887)
1950	Kenneth Burke, *A Rhetoric of Motives*
1958	Chaim Perelman and L. Olbrechts-Tyteca, *The New Rhetoric: A Treatise on Argumentation*

5 / Works Cited

Classical Treatises

(LCL = Loeb Classical Library)

Aristotle. *Ars rhetorica*. Edited by W. D. Ross. Oxford: Oxford University Press, 1959.

―――. *Rhetorica*. Translated by W. Rhys Roberts. In *The Works of Aristotle Translated into English*, ed. W. D. Ross, vol. 11. Oxford: Clarendon Press, 1924.

Cicero. *Brutus*. Translated by G. L. Hendrickson. *Orator*. Translated by H. M. Hubbell. LCL, 1939.

―――. *De inventione* and *Topica*. Translated by H. M. Hubbell. LCL, 1949.

―――. *De oratore*. Translated by E. W. Sutton and H. Rackham. 2 vols. LCL, 1942.

―――. *Philippics*. Edited and translated by D. R. Shackleton Bailey. Chapel Hill: University of North Carolina Press, 1986.

[Cicero]. *Ad C. Herennium: De ratione dicendi (Rhetorica ad Herennium)*. Translated by Harry Caplan. LCL, 1954.

[Demetrius]. *On Style*. Translated by W. Rhys Roberts. Rev. ed. LCL, 1932.

Diogenes Laertius. *Lives of Eminent Philosophers*. Translated by R. D. Hicks. 2 vols. LCL, 1925.

Dionysius of Halicarnassus. *The Critical Essays*. Translated by Stephen Usher. 2 vols. LCL, 1974–85.

Donatus. *Ars grammatica (maior)*. In *Grammatici latini*, ed. Heinrich Keil, 4.355–402. Leipzig: Teubner, 1864.

Halm, Karl, ed. *Rhetores Latini Minores*. Leipzig: Teubner, 1863.

Hermogenes. *On Types of Style*. Translated by Cecil W. Wooten. Chapel Hill: University of North Carolina Press, 1987.

Quintilian. *Institutio oratoria*. Translated by H. E. Butler. 4 vols. LCL, 1920–22.

Medieval and Renaissance Treatises

Augustine. *On Christian Doctrine*. Translated by D. W. Robertson, Jr. Indianapolis: Bobbs-Merrill, The Library of Liberal Arts, 1958.

Bulwer, John. *Chirologia: or the Natural Language of the Hand* [1644]. Edited by James W. Cleary. Carbondale: Southern Illinois University Press, 1974.

Day, Angel. *The English Secretorie* [1586]. Facsimile reproduction of 1599 edition, with introduction by Robert O. Evans. Gainesville, Fla.: Scholars' Facsimiles and Reprints, 1967.

Erasmus, Desiderius. *Collected Works of Erasmus*, vols. 23–24: *Literary and Educational Writings*, 1–2. Edited by Craig R. Thompson. Vol. 23, *Antibarbari*, trans. Margaret Mann Phillips, and *Parabolae*, trans. R. A. B. Mynors. Vol. 24, *De copia*, trans. Betty I. Knott, and *De ratione studii*, trans. Brian McGregor. Toronto: University of Toronto Press, 1978.

Faral, Edmond, ed. *Les arts poétiques du XIIe et du XIIIe siècle*. Paris: Edouard Champion, 1924.

Fenner, Dudley. *The Artes of Logike and Rhetorike* [1584]. Facsimile reproduction in *Four Tudor Books on Education*, ed. Robert D. Pepper. Gainesville, Fla.: Scholars' Facsimiles and Reprints, 1966.

Fraunce, Abraham. *The Arcadian Rhetorike* [1588]. Edited by Ethel Seaton. Oxford: Basil Blackwell, 1950.

Hoskyns, John. "Direccions for Speech and Style" [ca. 1599]. In *Life, Letters, and Writings of John Hoskyns, 1566–1638*, ed. Louise Brown Osborn, 103–166. Yale Studies in English, 87. New Haven: Yale University Press, 1937.

Peacham, Henry. *The Garden of Eloquence* [1577]. Facsimile reproduction. Menston, England: Scolar Press, 1971.

———. *The Garden of Eloquence* [1593]. Facsimile reproduction, with introduction by William G. Crane. Gainesville, Fla.: Scholars' Facsimiles and Reprints, 1954.

Puttenham, George. *The Arte of English Poesie* [1589]. Edited by Gladys Doidge Willcock and Alice Walker. Cambridge: Cambridge University Press, 1936.

Rainolde, Richard. *A Booke Called the Foundacion of Rhetorike* [1563]. Facsimile reproduction. Menston, England: Scolar Press, 1972.

Sherry, Richard. *A Treatise of Schemes and Tropes* [1550]. Facsimile reproduction, with introduction and index by Herbert W. Hildebrandt. Gainesville, Fla.: Scholars' Facsimiles and Reprints, 1961.

———. *A Treatise of the Figures of Grammar and Rhetorike*. London, 1555.

Smith, John. *The Mysterie of Rhetorique Unvail'd* [1657]. Facsimile reproduction. Menston, England: Scolar Press, 1969.

Susenbrotus, Joannes. *Epitome troporum ac schematum et grammatico-rum et rhetoricorum* [Zurich, 1540]. London, 1567.

George of Trebizond [Georgius Trapezuntius]. *Rhetoricorum Libri V.* Paris, 1532.

Wilson, Thomas. *The Arte of Rhetorique* [1553]. Edited by Thomas J. Derrick. New York and London: Garland, 1982.

Modern Treatises and Discussions

Atkins, J. W. H. *English Literary Criticism: The Medieval Phase.* New York: Macmillan, 1943.

Auerbach, Erich. *Literary Language and Its Public in Late Latin Antiquity and in the Middle Ages.* Translated by Ralph Manheim. London: Routledge and Kegan Paul, 1965.

Austin, Gilbert. *Chironomia* [1806]. Edited by Mary Margaret Robb and Lester Thonssen. Carbondale: Southern Illinois University Press, 1966.

Bain, Alexander. *English Composition and Rhetoric.* 2nd ed. New York: American Book Co., 1887.

Baldwin, Charles Sears. *Medieval Rhetoric and Poetic (to 1400).* New York: Macmillan, 1928; Gloucester, Mass.: Peter Smith, 1959.

Barish, Jonas A. "The Prose Style of John Lyly." *ELH* 23 (1956), 14–35.

———. "Baroque Prose in the Theater: Ben Jonson." *PMLA* 73 no. 3 (1958), 184–195.

Baxandall, Michael. *Giotto and the Orators: Humanist Observers of Painting in Italy and the Discovery of Pictorial Composition, 1350–1450.* Oxford: Clarendon Press, 1971.

Bonner, S. F. *Education in Ancient Rome.* Berkeley and Los Angeles: University of California Press, 1977.

———. *Roman Declamation in the Late Republic and Early Empire.* Liverpool: Liverpool University Press, 1949; reprint, 1969.

Brooke-Rose, Christine. *A Grammar of Metaphor.* London: Secker and Warburg, 1958.

Brown, Richard Harvey. "Reason as Rhetorical: On Relations among Epistemology, Discourse, and Practice." In *The Rhetoric of the Human Sciences*, ed. Nelson et al. (see below), 184–197.

Burke, Kenneth. *A Grammar of Motives* [1945]. Berkeley and Los Angeles: University of California Press, 1969.

———. *Permanence and Change: An Anatomy of Purpose.* 3rd ed. Berkeley, Los Angeles, and London: University of California Press, 1984.

———. *The Philosophy of Literary Form: Studies in Symbolic Action.* 2nd ed. Baton Rouge: Louisiana State University Press, 1967.

——. *A Rhetoric of Motives* [1950]. Berkeley and Los Angeles: University of California Press, 1969.

Campbell, Jeremy. *The Improbable Machine.* New York: Simon and Schuster, 1989.

Carroll, William C. *The Great Feast of Language in "Love's Labour's Lost."* Princeton: Princeton University Press, 1976.

Constable, Giles. *Letters and Letter-Collections.* Typologie des sources du moyen âge occidental, 17. Turnhout: Brepols, 1976.

Copi, Irving M. *Introduction to Logic.* 7th ed. New York: Macmillan, 1986.

Croll, Morris J. *Style, Rhetoric, and Rhythm.* Edited by J. Max Patrick et al. Princeton: Princeton University Press, 1966.

Curtius, Ernst Robert. *European Literature and the Latin Middle Ages.* Translated by Willard R. Trask. Bollingen Series, 36. New York: Pantheon, 1953.

D'Alton, J. F. *Roman Literary Theory and Criticism* [1931]. York: Russell and Russell, 1962.

Dupriez, Bernard. *Gradus: Les procédés littéraires.* Paris: Union générale d'éditions, 1980.

Espy, Willard R. *The Garden of Eloquence: A Rhetorical Bestiary.* New York: E. P. Dutton, 1983.

Evans, Bergen and Cornelia. *A Dictionary of Contemporary American Usage.* New York: Random House, 1957.

Fletcher, Angus. *Allegory: The Theory of a Symbolic Mode.* Ithaca: Cornell University Press, 1964.

Fontanier, Pierre. *Les figures du discours.* Introduction by Gérard Genette. Paris: Flammarion, 1977.

Fowler, H. W. *A Dictionary of Modern English Usage* [1926]. Corrected reprint, Oxford: Clarendon Press, 1937.

Frye, Northrop. *Anatomy of Criticism: Four Essays.* Princeton: Princeton University Press, 1957.

——. *The Great Code: The Bible and Literature.* New York: Harcourt Brace Jovanovich, A Harvest/HBJ Book, 1982.

——. *The Well-Tempered Critic.* Bloomington: Indiana University Press, 1963.

Gellrich, Jesse M. *The Idea of the Book in the Middle Ages: Language Theory, Mythology, and Fiction.* Ithaca: Cornell University Press, 1985.

Goodwin, William W. *Greek Grammar.* Revised by Charles B. Gulick. Waltham, Mass.: Blaisdell, 1958.

Grube, G. M. A. *The Greek and Roman Critics.* London: Methuen, 1965.

Havelock, Eric A. *The Liberal Temper in Greek Politics.* New Haven: Yale University Press, 1957.

Hegnauer, Salomon. "The Rhetorical Figure of Systrophe." In *Rhetoric Revalued*, ed. Brian Vickers, 179–186. Medieval and Renaissance Texts and Studies, 19. Binghamton, N.Y.: Center for Medieval and Early Renaissance Studies, 1982.

Hinde, R[obert] A., ed. *Non-Verbal Communication*. Cambridge: Cambridge University Press, 1972.

Hock, Ronald F., and Edward N. O'Neil. *The Chreia in Ancient Rhetoric*. Vol. 1, *The Progymnasmata*. Atlanta: Scholars Press, 1986.

Hough, Graham. *A Preface to "The Faerie Queene."* New York: W. W. Norton, 1962.

Howell, Wilbur Samuel. *Logic and Rhetoric in England, 1500–1700*. New York: Russell and Russell, 1961.

Hunter, G. K. *John Lyly: The Humanist as Courtier*. London: Routledge and Kegan Paul, 1962.

Jorio, Andrea de. *La mimica degli antichi, investigata nel gestire napoletano*. Naples, 1832.

Joseph, B. L. *Elizabethan Acting*. 2nd ed. London: Oxford University Press, 1964.

Joseph, Sister Miriam. *Shakespeare's Use of the Arts of Language*. New York: Hafner, 1947.

Kelly, H. A. "*Occupatio* as Negative Narration: A Mistake for *Occultatio/Praeteritio*." *Journal of Modern Philology* 74 (1976–77), 311–315.

Kennedy, George. *The Art of Persuasion in Greece*. Princeton: Princeton University Press, 1963.

Kerferd, G. B. *The Sophistic Movement*. Cambridge: Cambridge University Press, 1981.

Kustas, George L. *Studies in Byzantine Rhetoric*. Analecta Vlatadon, 17. Thessaloniki: Patriarchal Institute for Patristic Studies, 1973.

Lanham, Richard A. "The Extraordinary Convergence: Democracy, Technology, Theory, and the University Curriculum." *South Atlantic Quarterly* 89 (1990), 27–50.

———. "The 'Q' Question." *South Atlantic Quarterly* 87 (1988), 653–700.

———. "Twenty Years After: Digital Decorum and Bistable Allusions." *Texte* 8/9: *La Rhétorique du Texte* (1989), 63–98.

Lausberg, Heinrich. *Handbuch der literarischen Rhetorik*. 2nd ed. 2 vols. Munich: Max Hueber Verlag, 1973.

Lechner, Sister Joan Marie. *Renaissance Concepts of the Commonplaces*. New York: Pageant Press, 1962.

Leech, G. N. "Linguistics and the Figures of Rhetoric." In *Essays on Style and Language*, ed. Roger Fowler, 135–156. London: Routledge and Kegan Paul, 1966.

Mason, John. *An Essay on Elocution, or, Pronunciation* [1748]. Facsimile reproduction. Menston, England: Scolar Press, 1968.

McKeon, Richard. *Rhetoric: Essays in Invention and Discovery.* Edited with an introduction by Mark Backman. Woodbridge, Conn.: Ox Bow Press, 1987.

Mellinkoff, David. *The Conscience of a Lawyer.* St. Paul, Minn.: West Publishing Co., 1973.

Monfasani, John. *George of Trebizond: A Biography and A Study of His Rhetoric and Logic.* Leiden: E. J. Brill, 1976.

Murphy, James J. *Rhetoric in the Middle Ages: A History of Rhetorical Theory from St. Augustine to the Renaissance.* Berkeley, Los Angeles, and London: University of California Press, 1974.

Nelson, John S., Allan Megill, and Donald N. McCloskey, eds. *The Rhetoric of the Human Sciences: Language and Argument in Scholarship and Public Affairs.* Madison: University of Wisconsin Press, 1987.

Ogden, C. K., and I. A. Richards. *The Meaning of Meaning.* 8th ed. 1946. New York: Harcourt, Brace and World, A Harvest Book, n.d.

Ong, Walter J. *The Presence of the Word: Some Prolegomena for Cultural and Religious History.* New Haven: Yale University Press, 1967; paperback ed., Minneapolis: University of Minnesota Press, 1981.

————. *Ramus, Method, and the Decay of Dialogue: From the Art of Discourse to the Art of Reason* [1958]. Paperback ed., Cambridge, Mass., and London: Harvard University Press, 1983.

————. *Rhetoric, Romance, and Technology: Studies in the Interaction of Expression and Culture.* Ithaca: Cornell University Press, 1971.

Peckham, Morse. *Man's Rage for Chaos: Biology, Behavior, and the Arts.* Philadelphia: Chilton Books, 1965.

Perelman, Ch[aim], and L. Olbrechts-Tyteca. *The New Rhetoric: A Treatise on Argumentation.* Translated by John Wilkinson and Purcell Weaver. Notre Dame, Ind.: University of Notre Dame Press, 1969.

Polheim, Karl. *Die lateinische Reimprosa.* Berlin: Weidmannsche Buchhandlung, 1925.

Pope, Alexander. *Selected Poetry and Prose.* Edited by William K. Wimsatt, Jr. New York: Rinehart, 1952.

Princeton Encyclopedia of Poetry and Poetics. Enlarged Edition. Edited by Alex Preminger, Frank J. Warnke, and O. B. Hardison, Jr. Princeton: Princeton University Press, 1974.

Quinn, Arthur. *Figures of Speech: 60 Ways to Turn a Phrase.* Salt Lake City: Gibbs M. Smith, Inc., 1982.

Redfern, Walter. *Puns.* Oxford: Basil Blackwell/André Deutsch, 1984.

Richards, I. A. *The Philosophy of Rhetoric* [1936]. Paperback ed., New York: Oxford University Press, 1965.

Rix, Herbert David. *Rhetoric in Spenser's Poetry.* Pennsylvania State College Studies, 7. State College, Pa., 1940.

Rosenfield, Israel. *The Invention of Memory: A New View of the Brain.* New York: Basic Books, 1988.

Rubel, Veré L. *Poetic Diction in the English Renaissance: From Skelton through Spenser.* New York: Modern Language Association of America, 1941.

Siddons, Henry. *Practical Illustrations of Rhetorical Gesture and Action; Adapted to the English Drama* [1822]. New York: Benjamin Blom, Inc., 1968.

Smyth, Herbert Weir. *Greek Grammar.* Revised by Gordon M. Messing. Cambridge, Mass.: Harvard University Press, 1956.

Sonnino, Lee A. *A Handbook to Sixteenth-Century Rhetoric.* London: Routledge and Kegan Paul, 1968.

Taylor, Warren. *Tudor Figures of Rhetoric.* Chicago, 1937. Distributed by the University of Chicago libraries.

Thomas, Frank, and Ollie Johnston. *Disney Animation: The Illusion of Life.* New York: Abbeville Press, 1984.

Tuve, Rosemond. *Elizabethan and Metaphysical Imagery: Renaissance Poetic and Twentieth-Century Critics.* Chicago: University of Chicago Press, 1947.

Vickers, Brian. *In Defence of Rhetoric.* Oxford: Clarendon Press, 1988.

White, James Boyd. *Heracles' Bow: Essays on the Rhetoric and Poetics of the Law.* Madison: University of Wisconsin Press, 1985.

Williamson, George. *The Senecan Amble: A Study in Prose Form from Bacon to Collier.* London: Faber and Faber, 1951; Chicago: University of Chicago Press, 1966.

Wilson, Edward O. *Biophilia.* Cambridge, Mass., and London: Harvard University Press, 1984.

Yates, Frances A. *The Art of Memory.* Chicago: University of Chicago Press, 1966.